Balancing Privacy and Free S

In an age of smartphones, Facebook, and YouTube, privacy may seem to be a norm of the past. This book addresses ethical and legal questions that arise when media technologies are used to give individuals unwanted attention. Drawing from a broad range of cases within the U.S., U.K., Australia, Europe, and elsewhere, Mark Tunick asks whether privacy interests can ever be weightier than society's interest in free speech and access to information.

Taking a comparative and interdisciplinary approach, and drawing on the work of political theorist Jeremy Waldron concerning toleration, the book argues that we can still have a legitimate interest in controlling the extent to which information about us is disseminated. The book begins by exploring why privacy and free speech are valuable, before developing a framework for weighing these conflicting values. By taking up key cases in the U.S. and Europe, and the debate about a "right to be forgotten," Tunick discusses the potential costs of limiting free speech, and points to legal remedies and other ways to develop new social attitudes to privacy in an age of instant information sharing.

This book will be of great interest to students of privacy law, legal ethics, internet governance, and media law in general.

Mark Tunick is Professor of Political Science at the Wilkes Honors College, Florida Atlantic University, where he teaches political theory and constitutional law. He has B.S. degrees in Political Science and Management from MIT and his Ph.D. in Political Science from the University of California, Berkeley.

Routledge Research in Information Technology and E-Commerce Law

Balancing Privacy and Free Speech

Unwanted attention in the age of social media

Mark Tunick

Routledge
Taylor & Francis Group
LONDON AND NEW YORK

First published 2015
by Routledge
2 Park Square, Milton Park, Abingdon, Oxon, OX14 4RN

and by Routledge
711 Third Avenue, New York, NY 10017

Routledge is an imprint of the Taylor & Francis Group, an informa business

First issued in paperback 2016

British Library Cataloguing in Publication Data
A catalogue record for this book is available from the British Library

Library of Congress Cataloging-in-Publication Data
Tunick, Mark, author.
Balancing privacy and free speech : unwanted attention in the age of social media / Mark Tunick.
pages cm. — (Routledge research in information technology and e-commerce law)
Includes bibliographical references and index.
ISBN 978-1-138-79105-3 (hbk : alk. paper) — ISBN 978-1-315-76313-2 (ebk : alk. paper) 1. Social media—Law and legislation. 2. Privacy, Right of. 3. Freedom of expression. I. Title.
K564.C6T86 2014
323.44'8—dc23
2014011165

ISBN13: 978-1-138-79105-3 (hbk)
ISBN13: 978-1-138-68975-6 (pbk)

DOI: 10.4324/9781315763132

To Daniel, Marilyn, Rachel, and Ralph, and the memory of Amy.

Contents

Table of cases

Acknowledgments

My interest in unwanted attention solidified while preparing a paper about Dateline NBC's "To Catch a Predator" program, in which men are lured by a decoy posing as an underage teen to what they believe is her house, and then are exposed on national television as "sexual predators." One man could not bear this attention and fatally shot himself. This convinced me that privacy interests can sometimes be more substantial than the interest the media has in reporting information it claims to be newsworthy. I first learned about this program from a student, and in many ways this book is a result of countless exchanges with students, colleagues, and a variety of audiences ranging from international baccalaureate students to life-long learners with whom I have led discussions on the topic of privacy in the age of YouTube. I would like to acknowledge just a few of these individuals here: Jory Canfield, Rachel Corr, Seth Donahoe, Julie Earles, Andrew Faris, Jaclyn Goldstein, Lauren Gomez, Alan Gray, Alex Lange, Kevin Lanning, Claudel Louis, Rachel Luria, Maxwell MacEachern, Wesley Mathieu, Mumbi Ngugi, Alexa Robinson, Celine Rodriguez, Rachel Tunick, Meridith Wailes, and Daniel White. I am fortunate to teach at FAU's Wilkes Honors College, where not only can I can interact with bright and engaging students and team-teach with an anthropologist, historian, or an organic chemist, but I am supported by a Dean and staff that has eased the burden of juggling research and writing with teaching and administrative duties.

As a political theorist I have always tried to bring the work of philosophers such as Hegel, Locke, and Mill to bear on issues of current relevance relating to topics such as punishment, privacy, and property rights. To adequately address such issues one must reach beyond the confines of a single discipline, and my work tends to draw on law, anthropology, economics, psychology, film, literature, and philosophy as well as political theory. This book is no exception. I would therefore like to acknowledge a few former teachers who impressed upon me the value of interdisciplinary scholarship: Suzanne Berger, Robert Bellah, Norman Jacobson, and Hanna Pitkin. I also want to acknowledge a few other former teachers who were sources of inspiration: Joshua Cohen, Louis Menand III, and Jeremy Waldron; and express my appreciation to the anonymous reviewers for Routledge for suggestions that proved invaluable.

1   Introduction

Unwanted attention

In between pitches during a major league baseball game, Fox Sports Network television cameras focused in on a portly man, one of about 15,000 fans in the stadium, showing him intently eating a salad as one of the Fox announcers remarked, with a chuckle, "Salad won't be enough for this guy!"

The fan may never have learned that he was on television; if he had, he might not have cared. Yet a case might be made that Fox Sports Network acted badly: that it invaded his privacy—his right to be left alone and not be thrust into the public eye and publicly humiliated—by giving him attention that one might assume was unwelcome. On the other hand, can anyone reasonably expect privacy while attending a public sporting event in plain view of thousands? Did the baseball fan not consent to the possibility that he would appear on television simply by being in a public place in plain view of others?

This is one of an exploding number of examples of potentially unwelcome attention in which the interest in gathering and disseminating information, protected in the United States by the First Amendment rights of free speech and a free press, and in the European Union by the right of freedom of expression laid out in Article 10 of the European Convention on Human Rights (ECHR), may conflict with an interest in privacy. Unlike the baseball fan, those receiving unwanted attention in some of these cases clearly suffer severe consequences:

Rutgers college student Tyler Clementi did not welcome the attention when his roommate secretly captured video of Tyler kissing another man in their dormitory room and shared the video with others. Soon after, Tyler committed suicide by jumping off a bridge.[1]

Texas assistant district attorney Louis Conradt did not welcome the attention when a SWAT team entered his home in the company of camera crews from NBC's program "To Catch a Predator." Conradt had apparently

---

1   John Schwartz, "Bullying, Suicide, Punishment," *New York Times*, October 2, 2010.

DOI: 10.4324/9781315763132-1

engaged in sexually explicit online chat with a decoy posing as an under-age teen. He had turned down the decoy's offer to meet her in person, so instead NBC came to him. Unable to face the public shame of being accused of being a child predator before a national television audience, he shot and killed himself.[2]

Marvin Briscoe did not welcome the attention when *Reader's Digest* published a story about hijacking that disclosed his name and the fact that he committed a crime twelve years before, a crime for which he had already received his punishment and which he had tried to put behind him. Because of the article, Briscoe's daughter and friends found out about his past crime, which he had kept a secret, and abandoned him.[3]

Police have not welcomed the attention when citizens secretly recorded them making traffic stops or arrests. Some of these citizens were subsequently charged with violating anti-wiretap laws or interfering with police business.[4] Nor did a married man welcome the attention when CBS filmed him walking down a street hand in hand with a female co-worker who was not his wife as part of a story about romance in New York City.[5]

In each of these cases, there is a conflict between those who want to gather and disseminate information and those who do not welcome the attention. While each of these cases is from the United States, unwanted attention is a global phenomenon. In Kenya, for example, viewers of a show entitled "Road Hog" that is part of a primetime news program on CitizenTV are encouraged to submit videos of bad drivers. The producers air the video, zoom in on the vehicle's license plate number, and broadcast the name of the owner as a chorus shouts "Ahhhh … Shame on You!"[6]

The democratization of the media

Some of the above examples involve traditional media, which include newspapers, magazines, and television. But over the last several years the likelihood of receiving unwanted attention has risen dramatically because of the proliferation of new technologies such as smartphones and the widespread use of Internet video-hosting services and social media such as social networking sites and weblogs. As a result, information that the traditional media exposed in an original broadcast or publication—information that in the past might have been soon forgotten— can now be archived and readily accessible years later. Episodes of "To Catch a Predator" that were

---

2   See Mark Tunick, "Reality TV and the Entrapment of Predators," in Robson and Silbey, eds., *Law and Justice on the Small Screen* (Oxford: Hart Publishing, 2012).
3   *Briscoe v. Readers Digest Assn.*, 4 Cal.3d 529 (1971).
4   See *Commonwealth v. Hyde*, 434 Mass. 594 (2001); *Commonwealth v. Manzelli*, 864 N.E.2d 566 (2007); and Dana Mishra, "Undermining Excessive Privacy for Police: Citizen Tape Recording," *Yale Law Journal* 117:1549–1558 (2008).
5   *DeGregorio v. CBS*, 473 N.Y.S.2d 922 (1984).
6   I thank Mumbi Ngugi for making me aware of this program.

first broadcast in the early 2000s are available on NBC's website, and video clips from "Road Hog" are available on YouTube.[7] But another, distinct feature of the age of social media is that anyone and not just the news and entertainment media can now broadly disseminate information. Individuals use the Internet and social media to accuse people of a wide range of uncivil behavior and in some cases to seek out and punish them.[8] Disgruntled clients used one U.K. website to name and shame solicitors with whom they were dissatisfied, until a court ordered that the website, called "Solicitors from Hell," be taken down.[9] Some websites display mugshots of individuals who have been convicted of a sexual offense, or of driving under the influence, or who were merely arrested but not yet convicted.[10] Sometimes information is shared with an intent to be punitive, as when individuals use "revenge porn" websites or Twitter to share naked pictures of people they once dated.[11] But sometimes it may be shared with the best of intentions, as when a catechist in a Swedish parish set up a website to share information with parishioners, and revealed that a colleague had a foot injury—information that the court in Sweden regarded as protected personal data.[12] In one case that received considerable press, a Korean woman refused to pick up the mess that her dog left in the middle of a subway car, and someone shared a photo of the incident through social media. Some individuals who viewed the photo identified and shared details about her and as a result she received threats, was publicly humiliated, and reportedly left her university.[13] To anyone who looks at her with Google Glass with face recognition she will be known as "Dog Poop Girl." (Google Glass enables one to access information about objects in one's sight;[14] it is a technology with significant implications for privacy that I will discuss in later chapters.)

Unlike in any previous period in human history, virtually any individual can now cast unwanted attention on someone by making their image or

---

7   See www.nbcnews.com/id/10912603/; www.YouTube.com/watch?v=K9HvhmKWc8Y. "Road Hog" also has its own Twitter page: https://twitter.com/CitizenRoadHog.

8   See Daniel Solove, *The Future of Reputation* (New Haven: Yale University Press, 2007), Chapter 4; and Tom Downey, "China's Cyberposse," *New York Times Magazine*, March 3, 2010 (on "human flesh search").

9   *The Law Society v. Kordowski* [2011] EWHC 3185.

10 See, e.g., www.mugshotsonline.com; www.azduimugshots.com; http://offender.fdle. state.fl.us.

11 See www.myex.com/ ; and www.womenagainstrevengeporn.com/ (both accessed February 27, 2014). Cf. Oren Yaniv, "Judge Dismisses Case against Brooklyn Man Who Shared Nude Photos of [Ex-] girlfriend on his Twitter Account," *New York Daily News*, February 19, 2014.

12 *Criminal Proceedings against Bodil Linqvist*, Case C-101/01 (Sweden, 2002); online at http://eur-lex.europa.eu/LexUriServ/LexUriServ.do?uri=CELEX:62001J0101:EN:HTML.

13 Jonathan Krim, "Subway Fracas Escalates Into Test of the Internet's Power to Shame," *Washington Post*, July 7, 2005. Cf. Solove, *The Future of Reputation*, pp. 1–4.

14 See www.google.com/glass/start/, accessed December 21, 2013.

information about them readily accessible to millions of people. Over 2.4 billion people around the world use the Internet on any given day;[15] and by one estimate 1 billion people will have smart phones by 2016 and therefore the ability to easily capture images and share them on the Internet.[16] YouTube reports that there have been over 1 trillion playbacks of user-uploaded videos from its website as of 2012 and that 100 hours of video is uploaded to its site every minute, which is nearly three times the number of hours of video uploaded per minute that it reported in 2011.[17] The boundaries that distinguish journalists from ordinary people are becoming blurred, with some self-proclaimed citizen watchdogs taking on the role of "citizen journalist."[18]

We might refer to this phenomenon as the democratization of the media. Prior to the age of social media, it took considerable resources to convey information to a broad audience beyond the circle of one's friends, family, and coworkers, and the obstacles to publishing served as a check on those who might otherwise act impulsively. But today's technology makes it possible for anyone to share information widely with a click of a button and little incentive to think about the implications. The unintended consequences of sharing information through social media have included the downfall of politicians, as when New York Representative Anthony Weiner used Facebook and Twitter to send promiscuous text messages and risqué photos of himself to women not his wife. This material got into the hands of a conservative web blogger and quickly went viral, creating national headlines and possibly ruining his political career.[19] Online postings similarly led to the downfall of a German state legislator and a Chinese official.[20]

The democratization of the media has been associated with profound social changes. Some suggest that the new social media dulls us by having us communicate in short snippets with the result that our attention span is shortened and we form snap judgments that distort the truth.[21] Others point to its benefits. Some have suggested that the use of Facebook and Twitter

---

15   Internetworldstats.com, accessed January 10, 2013. The figure is for internet usage on June 30, 2012.

16   Zack Whittaker, "One Billion Smartphones by 2016, says Forrester," zdnet.com, February 13, 2013.

17   www.YouTube.com/t/press_statistics, accessed January 7, 2013, December 24, 2013, and June 7, 2011.

18   See Anderson, "The Mythical Right to Obscurity," *I/S* 7:544-602 (2012), p. 552, citing Krim, "Subway Fracas Escalates."

19   Raymond Hernandez, "Weiner Resigns in Chaotic Final Scene," *New York Times*, June 17, 2011. The threat to his career might have arisen also from his originally lying by denying what he did; see Michael Barbaro and David Chen, "Weiner Faces Calls to Resign and Tries to Make Amends," *New York Times*, June 7, 2011. Weiner unsuccessfully reentered the race for mayor of New York in the summer of 2013.

20   Nicholas Kulish, "Affair with Teenage Girl and Facebook Postings Sink German Politician," *New York Times*, August 18, 2011; and Andrew Jacobs, "Web Tell-All on an Affair Brings Down a Chinese Official," *New York Times*, January 19, 2013.

21   Bill Keller, "The Twitter Trap," *New York Times*, May 18, 2011.

to organize political protests contributed to the resignation of Egypt's President Mubarak in 2011.[22] Non-journalists have captured images of the police beat down of Rodney King in 1991, the devastating Asian tsunami of 2004, and abuses at the Abu Ghraib prison facility in Iraq.[23] A Craigslist ad and Facebook postings reportedly helped lead to the capture of a suspect in an attempted car bombing in New York City's Times Square.[24]

The benefits of ready public access to so much information are hard to exaggerate. At the same time, the democratization of the media poses an unprecedented threat to individuals' privacy. To be sure, threats to privacy are not new. Concerns about being exposed by amateur photographers emerged with the invention of the instamatic camera.[25] In 1936, a woman sued Pathé News because one of the newsreels it showed to theater audiences displayed her and other overweight women using new gym equipment. Pathé News claimed that this was a matter of legitimate public interest and newsworthy; the woman felt violated.[26] What is new is the ease with which anyone can now generate publicity and do harm.

The question of whether we should protect free speech and access to information even if it intrudes upon individuals' privacy is particularly difficult because each value is so important. When we limit access to information by building walls, locking doors, shading windows, or restricting speech, we make it harder to expose crimes, perversities, deception, and fraud. Distributing a video of police using excessive force during a traffic stop might call attention to and deter police misconduct.[27] Passing out leaflets with photos and descriptions of youths who are terrorizing a neighborhood in the London Borough of Brent could reassure the public that the police are aware of the problem and encourage citizens to provide information that leads to their arrests.[28] After ABC broadcast secretly taken video of unsafe food handling practices at Food Lion stores, the public was outraged by the supermarket chain's misconduct and Food Lion suffered enormous financial losses.[29] On the other hand, disseminating information

22 Jennifer Preston, "Movement Began with Outrage and a Facebook Page That Gave It an Outlet," *New York Times*, February 5, 2011; cf. Emily Parker, *Now I know Who My Comrades Are* (New York: Farrar, Straus and Giroux, 2014), pp. 1–5. For a contrary view, see Evgeny Morozov, *The Net Delusion* (New York: Public Affairs, 2012).

23 Seth Kreimer, "Pervasive Image Capture and the First Amendment: Memory, Discourse, and the Right to Record," *University of Pennsylvania Law Review* 159(2):335–409 (2011), pp. 347–50. See also "Visibility Before All," *Economist*, January 14–20, 2012, pp. 58–59.

24 See Bianca Bosker, "Faisal Shahzad Arrested," *Huffington Post*, May 4, 2010.

25 Kreimer, p. 351; and Samuel Warren and Louis Brandeis, "The Right to Privacy," *Harvard Law Review* 4:193–220 (1890).

26 *Sweenek v. Pathe News*, 16 F.Supp. 746 (1936).

27 See Ian Lovett, "Fatal Encounter with Police is Caught on Video, but Kept from the Public," *New York Times*, May 15, 2013.

28 *R v. Metropolitan Police Commissioner* [2004] EWHC 2229 (allowing distribution of the leaflets despite privacy concerns).

29 *Food Lion v. ABC*, 194 F.3d 505 (1999).

that someone wants to keep private can be deeply troubling, as is apparent when the unwanted attention they received led Clementi and Conradt to take their own lives.

Courts in the United States have long dealt with conflicts between privacy and free speech typically by deferring to the free press and its acknowledged role as a servant for the public good. But their decisions may not be the right guides today in a world in which embarrassing information can spread more widely than ever before and be permanently accessible. Numerous courts outside the U.S., unwilling simply to defer to free speech interests, adopt a proportionality test to weigh the relative importance of privacy and free speech interests; but there is considerable disagreement among these courts about which interest should prevail when they conflict. Courts in one member state of the European Union may take quite a different approach than that taken by courts in another member state;[30] and as we will see, judges within the same member state often disagree about how to reconcile the ECHR's Article 10 right to freedom of expression and Article 8 right to respect for private and family life.

This book addresses the question of how we are to balance privacy and free speech in the age of social media. My discussion will emphasize legal developments in the United States, where there is perhaps the greatest need to reassess the relative importance of free speech and privacy. But as unwanted attention in the age of social media is a global phenomenon, I will draw extensively on examples and/or case law from the U.K. and elsewhere, including Australia, Canada, China, Estonia, Finland, Germany, Israel, Italy, New Zealand, Spain, and Sweden.

The argument is now commonly made that since so many people carry digital cameras and share what they see on sites like Facebook and YouTube, we simply can no longer expect privacy when we go out in public—privacy is a norm of the past.[31] This sort of argument is not new, either. As early as 1902, a judge in the U.S. rejected the view "that a man has the right to pass through this world [w]ithout having his picture published [o]r his eccentricities commented upon either in handbills, circulars, catalogues, periodicals or newspapers";[32] and Judge Horridge of the King's Bench in England declared in 1916 that "no one possesses a right of preventing another person photographing him any more than he has a right of preventing another person giving a description of him, provided the

---

30   See David Erdos, Oxford Privacy Information Law and Society Conference: "The 'Right to be Forgotten' and Beyond," June 12, 2012. Online at www.csls.ox.ac.uk/conferences/oxpilsconference2012.

31   Bobbie Johnson, "Privacy No Longer a Social Norm, says Facebook founder," guardian.co.uk, January 10, 2010.

32   *Roberson v. Rochester Folding Box Co.*, 171 N.Y. 538, 544 (1902) (denying relief to plaintiffs whose photograph was used in an advertisement for flour without their consent).

description is not libelous or otherwise wrongful."[33] But the claim that one has a right to avoid attention may seem particularly quaint and unrealistic in the age of smartphones and YouTube.

I argue instead that even if we cannot expect people to avert their eyes when we are in a public place, or to keep secret the fact that we once committed a crime, we still can have a legitimate interest in controlling the extent to which information about us is disseminated. In deciding whether to limit access to information for the sake of privacy we must take into account the potential costs of restricting free speech. But a society need not unthinkingly accede to unlimited use of new technologies of information sharing merely because they are readily available and have powerful and attractive applications. A thoughtful and tolerant society will critically evaluate the potential uses of these technologies and develop norms and laws that let us realize their benefits while protecting against their abuses.

Permissible and impermissible speech

Most of us would agree that there should be some restrictions on the information that is widely shared. Though courts in the United States have frequently been sympathetic to the free speech claims of the media, even they have occasionally imposed restrictions on speech. In one case, a publisher was sued for publishing a book entitled *Hit Man*. The book, written by a professional killer, showed, step by step, how to murder someone without getting caught, and promoted the lifestyle of the hit man. One reader followed the advice given in the book and committed a murder, and the murder victim's family asked the court to hold the publisher, Paladin Enterprise, liable for wrongful death.[34] The First Amendment prohibits Congress and, by its incorporation into the Fourteenth Amendment, states, from "abridging the freedom of speech, or of the press." Paladin argued that if the state were to impose legal sanctions against it for publishing the book, the state would unconstitutionally be restricting its First Amendment rights. Paladin lost. Nor did the First Amendment shield a person who made a videotape of a rape which they then delivered to a network for broadcast on national television.[35] Nor did it shield those who published information about a woman's sexual proclivities in a newspaper's gossip column and on various websites.[36] A court in New Zealand held that the right to free

---

33 *Sports and General Press Agency, Ltd v. "Our Dogs" Publishing Co., Ltd* [1916] 2 KB 880 (rejecting plaintiff's plea for an injunction to keep the defendant from publishing a photo taken at a dog show although the defendant was not authorized to take photos of the show).
34 *Rice v. The Paladin Enterprises, Inc.*, 128 F.3d 233 (4th Cir. 1997).
35 *Doe v. Luster*, 2007 Cal. App. Unpub. Lexis 6042 (2007).
36 *Benz v. Washington Newspaper Publishing Co. and Bisney*, 34 Media L. Rep. 2368 (2006) (allowing defamation and public disclosure of private facts claims to proceed against the publisher of the *Washington Examiner*).

expression does not give a magazine publisher the right to print a photo of a naked woman who consented to being photographed but not to having the photo published in a magazine;[37] and courts in England have held that it does not give newspapers the right to publish a photo of a well-known entertainer having sex in a brothel;[38] or to report the identity of the two boys who were convicted of murdering 2-year-old James Bulger.[39]

But it is just as clear that in some cases free speech should prevail over privacy or security concerns. It should be permissible for a person who witnesses the police beating down a suspect on a public street to document the event; and one should not be arrested for photographing the exterior of a federal building, even in light of security concerns after the September 11, 2001 attacks.[40] But there are less clear cut cases where it may be difficult to draw a line between permissible and impermissible speech, and hard to decide which is more important: privacy, or living in a society in which information is freely exchanged and people can express themselves without fear.

If we agree that some speech should be limited for the sake of privacy, a further question remains: what means should we use to restrict that speech? Should those who give someone unwanted attention be imprisoned? Should courts issue injunctions to prevent publication of potentially abusive material so that people never need suffer the abuse, or should we instead rely on post-publication legal remedies that provide compensation and punitive damages based on actual harm caused—and if no harm is caused, as might be the case when someone uploads an embarrassing video of someone to YouTube that no one ever views, there would be no case for damages? Or instead of using the law to blame and deter overzealous citizen-journalists, should we rely rather on ethical codes of conduct and moral reproaches? Or should regulations be put into place affecting what technology is available to the public, or the structure of the Internet, to make it more difficult for certain information to be gathered or conveyed?[41] To decide what limits if any should be placed on free speech for the sake of privacy, we need to assess the value of these competing interests and ask where a reasonable balance between privacy and free speech lies. But we also eventually need to address how we might implement policies that achieve that balance.

---

37 *L v. G* [2002] DCR 234.

38 *Theakston v. MGN Ltd* [2002] EWHC 137 (QB).

39 *Venables v. News Group Newspapers Ltd* [2001] 1 All ER 908.

40 Kreimer, pp. 363–366 (discussing arrests of landscape photographers and others for taking pictures of a federal courthouse or a train).

41 Cf. Lawrence Lessig, *Code and other Laws of Cyberspace* (New York: Basic Books, 1999) (discussing four sorts of constraints: law, norms, market, and architecture).

Goals

Other theorists have already called attention to the risks to privacy posed by the Internet; some have persuasively argued that privacy needs to be taken more seriously. Two works that I want to single out are Daniel Solove's *The Future of Reputation* and Adam Moore's *Privacy Rights*.[42] Both defend privacy while recognizing the need to balance competing values, and provide a wealth of examples of unwanted attention, several of which I draw on in developing my argument. Solove emphasizes how exposure on the Internet is pernicious because information there can become permanent and seen by so broad an audience. Both recognize the need for a nuanced approach that avoids seeing information in a binary way as either public or private. Moore, for example, emphasizes how granting access to information is not to yield control over its use, or to authorize you to broadcast this information. Both are attentive to the legal issues at stake and offer specific reforms;[43] and Moore, taking a philosophical approach to privacy, identifies several considerations that can help us weigh the competing interests of privacy and free speech. I have benefited from and draw on their work as well as the work of numerous other theorists who discuss privacy more generally, such as Anita Allen, Stanley Benn, Charles Fried, Annabelle Lever, Helen Nissenbaum, Julian Petley, Priscilla Regan, Jeffrey Rosen, Beate Rössler, and Raymond Wacks; in addition, Jeffrey Reiman, Elizabeth Paton-Simpson and Joseph Siprut all have written especially clear and thoughtful articles concerning privacy in public places that I draw on to formulate parts of my argument. In the rest of this introductory chapter I lay out some of the distinct goals I set in this book to advance existing defenses of privacy.

Building a framework for addressing conflicts between privacy and free speech

One of my objectives is to develop a distinct framework to help us think about cases of unwanted attention. "Framework" is a metaphor; as I will discuss in later chapters, in using it I do not mean to propose a pat formula for resolving conflicts. By framework I refer rather to a set of questions we can ask to order our thoughts, and principles we can formulate to test our intuitions.

---

42   Solove, *The Future of Reputation* (2007); Adam Moore, *Privacy Rights: Moral and Legal Foundations* (University Park, Pennsylvania: Pennsylvania State University Press, 2010).
43   Solove's work is especially helpful in proposing reforms to U.S. law: he recommends broadening the appropriation tort, recognizing legal duties of confidentiality, permitting plaintiffs to keep their names confidential, and promoting informal attempts to resolve privacy disputes while relying on lawsuits as a credible threat and last resort for egregious cases; Moore recommends tort reforms, and for egregious video voyeurism even criminal punishment (pp. 127–132).

The approach I take assumes that there are good reasons to value privacy but also good reasons to value the ability of people to collect, distribute, and access information, and that some weighing is necessary when these values conflict. When faced with an apparent conflict, we first need to ask whether privacy is truly at stake. People may desire privacy but their desire may be misplaced. What they believe to be an interest in privacy may not be a legitimate interest. For example, I might not want anyone at work to know I am applying for another job; but if I tell too many friends and one of them knows someone at work, or if I forget to pick up a copy of my application's cover letter that I sent to a shared printer where I currently work, and word gets out as a result, this may become a "public fact" in which I cannot reasonably expect privacy.

Suppose you do have a legitimate privacy interest in certain information, such as what you did or said, or in some fact about you such as that you were once arrested. That privacy interest may be less important than competing interests. To assess the relative weight of privacy and free speech interests we will need to draw on accounts of why privacy and free speech are valuable and determine which if any of those accounts provide convincing reasons in the case at hand. One reason privacy is valuable is that it lets us preserve our dignity. If you photograph me taking a shower at a gym without my knowledge and upload it to the Internet, you affront my dignity, and my dignity interest outweighs your interest in free expression. But in other cases where one is exposed, dignity is not at stake, as when someone shares a video of an employee in a backroom stealing office supplies.[44] When we examine the reasons to value free speech we will find that not all speech is of equal value. Some information which we might regard as "private facts" that clearly implicate privacy may not be newsworthy; other private facts may be newsworthy to some, but that might not justify sharing them with the general public. On the other hand, some facts, private or public, may be so newsworthy that they ought to be shared with the public even if doing so intrudes upon someone's privacy.

We must also take into account the scope of rights to free expression provided by laws such as the First Amendment that appear to offer special protections to journalists or the "press." Should these protections extend to weblogs of citizen-journalists? To reality television programs such as NBC's "To Catch a Predator"? To tabloid reports on a supermodel's drug addiction or the marital infidelities of a soccer star?[45] If we regard such works as news

---

44   Cf. *Köpke v. Germany* [2010] ECHR 1725 (upholding a supermarket's use of covert video surveillance to catch an employee stealing money from the tills).

45   See *Campbell v. MGN Ltd* [2004] UKHL 22 (allowing publication of the fact that supermodel Naomi Campbell has a drug addiction but ruling, 3-2, that *The Mirror* should not have published details about the treatment or publish a photo of her leaving a rehabilitation clinic); and *A v. B plc* [2002] EWCA Civ 337, and *Rio Ferdinand v. MGN Ltd* [2011] EWHC 2454 (QB) (refusing to prevent a newspaper from publishing information about a soccer player's extramarital infidelity, based on Article 10 of the ECHR).

journalism, they might be shielded from privacy tort or similar claims on the ground that society's interest in having a free press outweighs interests in privacy. But if we do not think they contribute to serious discussion of issues of public importance and rather provide mere entertainment, we might not want to lend them the shield provided to the traditional news media; we might think the interest in having access to titillating details about someone's private life does not outweigh that person's privacy interests.[46]

A distinct problem arises when we try to weigh privacy and free speech because people vary widely in the extent to which they seem to care about privacy. Suppose only a small minority of individuals in a society have a significant preference for privacy. Why should a majority who care little for privacy appease that minority by bearing the burden of pro-privacy policies that may mean that more crime will go undetected and free speech will be restricted? Why accommodate an individual whom the majority regard as supersensitive? One of the central goals of this book is to address this question, which I do in part by turning to an important paper by the political theorist Jeremy Waldron that focuses on the value of toleration in a liberal society. I argue that in a liberal society we should be sensitive to the needs of even a small minority for whom privacy is important when doing so does not keep us from adequately pursuing our own aims. Priscilla Regan argues that pro-privacy legislation is less likely to be enacted in the U.S. when privacy is viewed narrowly in terms of individual utility or as an individual right, as opposed to something of value to society: "arguments for privacy have not successfully transcended self-interest."[47] An argument for privacy based on toleration might be understood to transcend self-interest. Even someone with no preference for privacy might acknowledge that others can have an interest in privacy, and recognize the value of living in a society in which we are sensitive to their needs.

The title of this book refers to conflicts between "Privacy" and "Free Speech" but in some cases the conflict may not seem really to be between these two values. For one, rights to free speech are not always at stake. For example, several states have enacted statutes known as "Megan's laws" that require the members of a community to be notified if a registered sex offender moves to their neighborhood. These laws have been challenged by sex offenders not only because of the intrusion upon their privacy of having their past crimes and current address and photograph available online, but also because the unwanted attention has led to violent attacks

46   Cf. Raymond Wacks, *Privacy and Media Freedom* (Oxford: Oxford University Press, 2013), p. 36: "It is not unreasonable to enquire whether the media are acting out of a genuine desire to serve the public interest, or whether publication of the story is in pursuit of profit, prurience, or even rancor."

47   Priscilla Regan, *Legislating Privacy* (Chapel Hill: University of North Carolina Press, 1995), p. 182; cf. pp. xiv–v, 3–4, 17, 178, 212.

against them.[48] In this situation, there arguably is no First Amendment free speech claim: the government and not the media or ordinary citizens displays the information and in doing so it is exercising not free speech but simply its police powers.[49] In the U.K., challenges have been made to the official retention of past criminal records or other "relevant information" of one's past misdeeds that could be disclosed for a number of reasons including the assessment of one's suitability for admission to certain professions.[50] Such conflicts are not between privacy and free speech narrowly construed, but between privacy and access to information. Nevertheless, a similar weighing of values is required: we need to assess the potential costs involved in keeping information private, and in disclosing it.

In a few of the cases I shall discuss, some might question whether privacy really is at stake. The aspect of the case of the portly baseball fan that may be most troubling is that a snide comment was made about him to a broad audience; merely televising him eating salad without any comment would not have raised concerns in most people even though some might find the publicity unwelcome. Some might argue that if Fox Sports Network acted badly in this case, it did so not by invading anyone's privacy but by humiliating a person publicly (assuming the fan was humiliated, which may not be true).

If we define privacy broadly as a right to be let alone we could regard public humiliation as a violation of privacy. But some philosophers and legal scholars, troubled by appeals to a "right to privacy," take the position that what is regarded as the wrong of violating privacy is usually reducible to some distinct wrong that need not refer to privacy. For example, spreading false gossip about someone can be regarded as the wrong of lying, or of damaging someone's property interests in their reputation. Intruding upon one's seclusion could be regarded as a trespass that violates a property right.[51] The philosopher Judith Jarvis Thomson argued in a well-known

---

48 See, e.g., *E.B. v. Verniero*, 119 F.3d 1077 (1997); and *Wallace v. State*, 905 N.E.2d 371 (2009).

49 Cf. *Muir v. Ala. Educ. Television Comm'n*, 688 F.2d 1033 (5th Cir. 1982). But see David Fagundes, "State Actors as First Amendment Speakers," *Northwestern University Law Review* 100(4):1637–1688 (2006).

50 *Chief Constable of Humberside Police v. Information Commissioner* [2009] EWCA Civ 1079 (rejecting the Information Commissioner's effort to delete certain past criminal records because of the need of police and courts to have a complete record of convictions spent and otherwise); cf. *R (L) v. Commissioner of Police of Metropolis* [2009] UKSC 3 (allowing police to disclose information about claimant and her son's past conduct in an "Enhanced Criminal Records Certificate"); but see *R(F) and Thompson v. Secretary of State for Home Department* [2010] UKSC 17 (finding that Sec. 82 of the Sexual Offences Act 2003 violates Article 8 of the ECHR because it allows no exception to a lifetime notification requirement of reporting to the police when anyone sentenced to at least 30 months for a sex offense moves or travels abroad); and *M.M. v. The United Kingdom* [2013] ECHR Case 240 29/07.

51 See William L. Prosser, "Privacy: A Legal Analysis," in Ferdinand Schoeman, ed. *Philosophical Dimensions of Privacy* (New York: Cambridge University Press, 1984):104–155.

paper on privacy that we have a right not to be tortured to have personal information extracted not because we have a right to privacy: rather, we have the so-called right to privacy because we have a right not to be tortured.[52] Thomson does not think there is a right that information about ourselves not be known to others unless acquiring or sharing that information violates some right other than a right to privacy, such as a property right, or a right not to be annoyed or caused distress.[53] Others, however, find it helpful to refer to a distinct right to privacy, or to inviolable personality.[54] I shall discuss the question of how privacy is to be defined in Chapter 2. While I shall appeal to the concept of privacy throughout this book, I hope to avoid directly confronting the position that a so-called right to privacy is reducible to other rights, by regarding rights as interests and by recognizing that interests in not receiving unwanted attention—which I shall refer to as privacy interests—can involve a variety of distinct interests such as reputation, dignity, autonomy, and property interests.

Formulating principles of privacy ethics

In deciding whether someone should be permitted to gather or share information that intrudes upon another's privacy we must take into account a variety of considerations. One of my goals is to identify a number of principles that can help guide us both in deciding whether privacy is implicated and if it is, in evaluating its relative importance. Among the principles I will defend in Chapter 3 are that one can sometimes reasonably expect privacy even in public places or in public facts. If the term "public fact" refers only to information that is known or readily accessible to the general public through legitimate means, then one could not reasonably expect privacy in a public fact. But we do sometimes speak of what one does in front of just a few strangers as a public fact even if it is not made known to the general public. I will argue that I can have a legitimate privacy interest that a public fact in this latter sense not be memorialized (by being photographed or videotaped) and then shared, as doing so could give others access to me in a way that violates my dignity; and that it not be spread to broader circles of people than the circles I willingly exposed myself to by being in a public place or in view of strangers, as that would diminish my ability to define who I am in the eyes of others. If we agree, we may say that even though Dog Poop Girl's behavior is a public fact, it is not readily accessible to the general public by legitimate means: it may not be legitimate to upload her photo to the Internet.

52   Judith Jarvis Thomson, "The Right to Privacy," *Philosophy and Public Affairs* 4(4): 295–314 (1975).
53   Thomson, pp. 311–312.
54   Edward Bloustein, "Privacy as an Aspect of Human Dignity," in Schoeman, ed., 156–202; Warren and Brandeis, in Schoeman, ed., p. 82.

The case for free speech is especially strong when the information in question is newsworthy; this can tip the scales in favor of allowing its publication. Another principle I shall defend is that not all public facts are newsworthy, and I shall explore various considerations that can help us distinguish what is and is not newsworthy. There are also more general principles, such as the principle of social utility (that we ought to choose that action or resolve on that policy that promotes more social utility than alternative actions or policies), and John Stuart Mill's harm principle (that society should not interfere with an individual's liberty except to prevent harm to others) that may be helpful guides and which I shall refer to in later chapters, though one of my central arguments is that we cannot weigh interests adequately using the sort of calculation of net utility envisioned by some utilitarians, or by relying just on the harm principle.

Grounding privacy

There are many circumstances in which free speech is not in conflict with privacy and the two values go hand in hand. Sometimes to be free to communicate one needs assurance of confidentiality or anonymity.[55] But there are circumstances in which the two values conflict and we need to assess their relative importance. As I noted above, one of the difficulties in trying to weigh the importance of privacy against the importance of having access to information is that people value privacy differently. Consider again the case of the baseball fan. He may not care that he was shown on television; or he may take the broadcaster's comment in good cheer. Or consider Tyler Clementi. Many people would be disturbed if their roommate secretly video-recorded them; but there also will be a wide variation in responses, and some people in Clementi's position might brush off the attention, or resignedly accept that they are now "outed." Privacy can be regarded as a preference and people's preferences vary. How, then, can we draw general conclusions about whether an interest in privacy is more important than an interest in free speech: won't the result of a weighing of these competing values differ for different people?

Addressing this question is another of my goals. A large proportion of court opinions, especially in the United States, favor free speech over privacy. In several of these cases my intuition is that this outcome is not desirable and that either privacy is at stake when a judge thinks it is not, or that it should be given more weight—though, as I shall discuss, the ethically desirable outcome may not be the legally desirable outcome. But the argument of this book is not: "I prefer privacy and therefore so should you." Intuitions can be an appropriate starting point in forming judgments about

---

55   See Eric Barendt, "Privacy and Freedom of Speech," in Kenyon and Richardson, eds., *New Dimensions in Privacy Law* (Cambridge: Cambridge University Press, 2006), pp. 24–30; and Solove, *Future of Reputation*, ch. 6.

ethical and legal controversies. Intuitions are "immediate," by which I mean they are not mediated by critical reflection. They may be based on feelings, instincts, or on implicit rules that we unconsciously use when we process information and make decisions. In the latter case, intuitions have some ground and are not arbitrary. But it will not do to settle upon judgments solely based on intuitions. For why should anyone who does not share your intuition be compelled to agree with you? Intuitions are not helpful in persuading those who disagree with us unless we can articulate grounds for them, or support them with plausible reasons. I will attempt to anchor intuitions that privacy should in some cases receive greater weight than free speech by pointing to reasons for valuing privacy. This is not necessarily to say that everyone ought to care deeply about privacy and that people who like to exhibit themselves are making some sort of ethical mistake.[56] But it is to say that one can have objective reasons for valuing privacy, beyond "that is just my preference"; and in resolving conflicts in which privacy is at odds with free speech, we should give due weight to these reasons.

It is important to distinguish my position that there are good reasons to respect people's privacy from the position that privacy has an objective foundation that can be empirically established. In Chapter 2 I will take up the argument of Adam Moore, who agrees that privacy can be as important as free speech. Moore also agrees that we cannot plausibly defend privacy merely by appealing to intuitions that rest on subjective desires, as these can be arbitrary and subject to manipulation.[57] Moore tries to establish an objective foundation for privacy rights by arguing that privacy is essential for sustaining life and that without it, populations self-destruct. This is a claim that Moore believes is vindicated by empirical evidence. As we shall see, I do not think the evidence clearly supports Moore's conclusion. But I do think there are good reasons for valuing privacy. One reason is that to give someone unwanted attention when they have a legitimate privacy interest is to fail to respect them as a person. But there are others as well. One of the reasons I point to that has not been emphasized by others is that privacy lets people such as "Dog Poop Girl" or Mr. Briscoe avoid undeserved or disproportionate punishment.

Reevaluating case law

Another of my goals is to make the case that courts, especially in the United States, tend not to sufficiently recognize the weight of privacy interests. For example, we shall see that U.S. courts rarely allow for the possibility that one can reasonably expect privacy in a public place. In stark contrast,

---

56 Anita Allen takes the interesting position that because privacy is what she calls a "foundational" value, the government can sometimes coerce people to not waive their privacy, in *Unpopular Privacy* (New York: Oxford University Press, 2011).

57 Moore, *Privacy Rights*, pp. 40–43.

courts in some other countries have recognized a right of a person not to have their image taken in a public place and shared with others without their consent. In *Aubry v. Editions Vice-Versa*, Canada's Supreme Court, in a 5-2 ruling, required a magazine publisher to pay $2,000 in damages after it published a photograph of a 17-year-old girl sitting on the stairs in front of a public building, without her consent, though there was nothing defamatory or even uncomplimentary about the photo.[58] In *Campbell v. MGN Ltd*, England's House of Lords ruled, 3-2, that *The Mirror* should not have published photographs of supermodel Naomi Campbell leaving a drug treatment facility even though she was in plain view in a public place (though it ruled that the paper was permitted to report the fact that she was being treated for drug addiction).[59] In another U.K. decision, *Murray v. Big Pictures*, counsel for the 19-month-old child of J.K. Rowling—the author of the *Harry Potter* series—claimed an infringement of the child's right to respect for privacy when photos of him being walked by his parents along a public street in Edinburgh were taken using a long lens camera, without his parents' consent or knowledge, and were eventually distributed, with one photo appearing in the *Sunday Express*. A lower court ruled that privacy was not implicated, referring to U.S. cases establishing that there is no right to privacy on a public street; but the Appellate court reversed that judgment.[60] In still another case involving a prominent figure photographed in a public place, the European Court of Human Rights agreed with the judgment of the German Federal Constitutional Court, in *von Hannover v. Germany (no. 2)*, that privacy rights were violated when two photos of Princess Caroline of Monaco, one of her walking in St. Moritz and the other of her on a ski lift, were taken and published without her consent.[61] Such decisions would be almost unimaginable in the United States. In addition, U.K. courts have held that in some cases the right to free expression does not justify reporting the identities of criminals;[62] some other European countries shield the identity of criminals as a rule. But as we shall see, courts in the United States do not recognize a right to privacy in information about one's criminal past.

58   [1998] S.C.J. No. 30.
59   [2004] UKHL 22.
60   [2008] EWCA Civ 446.
61   *Von Hannover v. Germany (no. 2)* [2012] ECHR 228.The Court agreed that a third photo could be published as it bore on the health of Prince Rainier and was a matter of legitimate public interest.
62   *Venables v. News Group Newspapers Ltd* [2001] 1 All ER 908 (granting an injunction to prevent publication of the identity of two boys convicted of murdering 2-year-old James Bulger, on the ground not of privacy but of ECHR Article 2's "right to life," since revealing their identities could endanger the lives of the convicted criminals); and [2010] HQ0004737 (QB) (continuing an injunction). But for a contrasting ruling, see *In re S* [2003] EWCA Civ 963 (refusing to prevent the press from reporting that a boy's brother was allegedly murdered by his mother, even though this could harm the boy).

I will be critical of a number of opinions in which courts have reached what I take to be an ethically mistaken outcome because they fail to value privacy sufficiently. As a preview, consider the following cases:

In *Florida Star v. B.J.F.*, the U.S. Supreme Court overturned a lower court ruling that had required a newspaper to pay $100,000 in damages when it published the name of a rape victim. The Court held that the newspaper should pay no damages and that a Florida law making it unlawful to publish the name of a rape victim violates the First Amendment as applied in this case. The rationale was that the news article addressed a matter of public significance and the rape victim's name was in public court records.[63]

In *Paul v. Davis*, the U.S. Supreme Court held that there was no violation of civil rights when a Police Chief handed out flyers that included a mugshot of Davis and indicated that he had been arrested for shoplifting. That charge was eventually dismissed, and Davis was concerned about the effect of the flyer on his reputation, but the Court held that there is no privacy violation in disclosing the fact that someone had been arrested.[64]

In *Gates v. Discovery Communications*, the Supreme Court of California ruled that a television production company may properly air an account of a man's crime that took place more than 12 years earlier, even though the man had served his time, was trying to lead a new life, and was not a public figure. The Court's reason was that the information that was broadcast was truthful and was taken from public court records. The Court declared that media defendants have an absolute right to broadcast such information regardless of how unwanted the attention is for the plaintiff.[65]

In *U.S. v. Vazquez*, a federal district court allowed the release of video tapes that the defendant took of people entering an abortion clinic, making them potentially available for public broadcast. The Court held that no one can reasonably expect privacy in the fact that they entered a building in plain view from a public street.[66]

In *McNamara v. Freedom Newspapers*, a state Appellate court in Texas held that a newspaper was shielded from tort liability by the First Amendment after it published a photo that revealed the accidentally-exposed genitalia of a student athlete who was playing soccer, as there was no intent to embarrass the young man and he was in a public place.[67]

Two further cases—highly influential U.S. Supreme Court cases on the Fourth Amendment—do not concern publications that give unwanted attention to anyone, but are important because they rest on assumptions about privacy that I will argue are flawed and that violate one or more principles of privacy ethics I will defend. I single out these cases because they

63   491 U.S. 524 (1989).
64   424 U.S. 693 (1976).
65   101 P.3d 552 (2005).
66   31 F.Supp.2d 85 (1998).
67   802 S.W.2d 901 (1991).

have been used as precedents that later courts rely on. In light of the threats to privacy in the age of social media, it is important to reconsider their key assumptions.

In *U.S. v. Knotts*, the Supreme Court held that the police do not need a warrant in order to use a beeper to track a car's movements, because one cannot reasonably expect privacy in one's location on public roads.[68] I shall argue that we do not forfeit all expectations of privacy when we are in a public place—we can reasonably expect not to be followed.

In *U.S. v. White*, the government, without a warrant, placed a wire on an informant who was conversing with a criminal suspect, enabling law enforcement agents to hear the conversation from a distance. The Court permitted this on the ground that the suspect could not reasonably expect that his interlocutor would not eventually reveal the contents of their conversation to the police.[69] I shall argue that recording and transmitting a conversation can be fundamentally different from hearing a conversation and relating it to another person based on one's recollection.

Of course courts in the U.S. do not always hold that free speech or other interests outweigh privacy interests, just as European courts do not always hold that privacy interests outweigh the right to free expression.[70] Nor should privacy interests always prevail; in some cases courts fail to give due weight to free speech interests. One such example is *Commonwealth v. Hyde*, in which the Massachusetts Supreme Court upheld the conviction of a man who had secretly audio-recorded the police during a routine traffic stop. The Court apparently was not concerned that the state law that prohibited individuals from secretly recording oral conversations in this case may have implicated a legitimate interest in news gathering.[71]

Distinguishing ethical and legal judgments

I believe that with the exception of *Commonwealth v. Hyde*, in all of the above cases whoever gave unwanted attention to someone acted badly. But it does not follow that the courts who ruled otherwise necessarily issued bad legal decisions. The ethically appropriate outcome might not be the legally appropriate one. Judges are bound by relevant laws and precedents, and their commitment to the rule of law may force them to arrive at outcomes that they might agree are not desirable. Sometimes a judge will say as much and urge legislators to modify the law.[72] Clarifying this

---

68   460 U.S. 276 (1983).
69   401 U.S. 745 (1971).
70   Moreover, in the U.K. in particular, the media has considerable political power that, it has been argued, accounts for policies that tend to be pro-media; see David Smith, "Oxford Privacy Information Conference" (2012).
71   434 Mass. 594 (2001); but see the dissent, at 613–614.
72   See, e.g., *T v. Greater Manchester Police et al.* [2012] EWHC 147, Par. 36; *State v. D.H., B.D.*, 9 P.3d 253, 258 (2000).

distinction between ethical and legal judgments is another of my goals. Because of the importance of this distinction, some further words are appropriate here.[73]

Sometimes a conflict between privacy and free speech raises a question of ethics, as when we are deciding whether to publish information about someone and, being conscientious, want to know if doing so is ethical in light of the consequences the publication can have to their privacy. But many of the conflicts that arise when people receive unwanted attention become legal issues requiring resolution by a court. When that happens, another layer of complexity is introduced. When someone who receives unwanted attention makes a legal challenge, they need to indicate a "cause of action," or identify existing laws or legal precedents that give them a legal right not to have their privacy violated. To decide if their claim is successful, we may need to engage in disputes about the meaning of the laws as well as theories about how these laws are best interpreted.

There are a variety of legal restrictions on what one may do to uncover or share information. In the United States, federal and state statutes restrict the ability of people to record conversations. The federal Electronic Communications Privacy Act, for example, provides for punishment of those who eavesdrop on my phone call, oral conversation, or electronic communication in situations where I exhibit an expectation of privacy, unless a court authorizes an interception.[74] States have similar laws: some states require that all parties to a conversation consent to its recording, while other states require only that at least one party consents.

Tort law provides legal remedies in cases where someone uncovers or shares information in a way that: 1) intrudes upon one's seclusion (as when a Peeping Tom uses a ladder to peer into or photograph the inside of your second floor bedroom); 2) publicly discloses private facts (as when someone uses social media to share the contents of your secret diary without your consent); 3) appropriates one's name or likeness for commercial benefit (as when a beverage manufacturer secures a photograph of a famous athlete drinking their product and publishes it without the athlete's consent as part of a magazine ad); or 4) puts one in a false light (as when someone creates a Facebook profile using my name, photographs, and other information about me, and then publishes as part of the profile a sordid list of perverse interests I supposedly but in fact do not have).[75]

The Fourth Amendment prohibits state actors from violating an individual's privacy by conducting unreasonable searches without a warrant. (The

---

73 For a brief treatment of the relation of ethics and law, see Mark Tunick, "Ethics, Morality, and Law," in Kermit Hall, ed., *Oxford Companion to American Law* (New York: Oxford University Press, 2002), pp. 275–277.

74 U.S. Code Title 18, ch. 119, §2511.

75 This last example is similar to the facts in *J.S. v. Blue Mountain School District*, 650 F.3d 915 (2011), discussed in Chapter 4.

Fourth Amendment does not apply to private actors, so it offers no protection if, for example, a private security guard searches your purse. It applies only if the search is conducted by a state actor such as a police officer.) In interpreting the Amendment, courts must decide whether a search is unreasonable, which they do by asking whether it violates an expectation of privacy that society regards as objectively reasonable.[76] Even the First Amendment, which protects one's right to speak freely, has been interpreted as limiting the ability of state actors to intrude upon the privacy we have in our homes. In *Stanley v. Georgia*, government agents searched Stanley's home for evidence of illegal bookmaking. They found none, but in a desk drawer they found three reels of film. Upon viewing the films they found them to be obscene, and arrested Stanley for violating a Georgia law that prohibited the possession of obscene material. The Court indicated that the First Amendment not only protects the press in its ability to report the news, but also gives each of us a right to be free from unwanted governmental intrusions that keep us from satisfying our intellectual and emotional needs, and so they struck down the Georgia law.[77] Of course the First Amendment also limits privacy. For example, it may protect Fox Sports Network if it gives unwanted attention to the portly baseball fan; or it may protect me if I secretly record the police giving me a speeding ticket.

England, in contrast, has not had a "right to privacy" per se though some of the interests associated with privacy have been protected by the tort of breach of confidence.[78] Thus in 1979, Sir Robert Megarry wrote, in ruling against a plaintiff who was suing because his telephone was tapped by the police, that there is no right to privacy in England.[79] Some self-regulatory mechanisms were established to hear complaints about an invasive media, including the Press Complaints Commission for complaints about newspapers and magazines, and Ofcom, for radio and television broadcasters, though these are often criticized for being ineffective.[80] But in what Raymond Wacks has called "the New Order," privacy is now receiving substantial protection through application of the European Convention on Human Rights, which has member states apply a proportionality test to weigh the Article 8 right to respect for private and family life and the Article 10 right to free expression.[81] The U.K.'s Data Protection Act 1998 has also

---

76   *Katz v. U.S.*, 389 U.S. 347, 361 (1967), concurring opinion of Justice Harlan.
77   *Stanley v. Georgia*, 394 U.S. 557, 564–565 (1969).
78   See Dawes, "Privacy and the Freedom of the Press"; *Hoskings v. Runting* [2004] NZCA 34; and Wacks, *Privacy and Media Freedom*, ch. 3.
79   *Malone v. Commissioner of Police of the Metropolis* [1979] 2 All ER 620. This decision was reconsidered by the Strasbourg Court, which found that a right to privacy was violated, [1985] 7 EHRR 14.
80   See Wacks, chs. 5, 7; and Dawes.
81   Wacks, ch. 4. The European Charter of Fundamental Rights entrenches the same rights to respect for private life (Article 7) and to freedom of expression (Article 11) and includes a right to protection of personal data (Article 8).

been used to protect privacy; it was drawn on to shut down the "Solicitors From Hell" website that encouraged disgruntled clients to name and shame their attorneys.[82] And there are other legal protections in place including Directive 95/46/EC of the European Parliament, which provides that national laws on the processing of personal data should protect the right to privacy as recognized in Article 8 of the ECHR while also protecting the free movement of data.[83]

While there are legal remedies available for those who suffer an invasion of their privacy, not everyone who acts badly should face legal sanctions.[84] If your friend posts unflattering remarks about your personal life on Facebook for your mutual friends to see, you should not necessarily have a legal remedy; the state should not intervene in all of our interpersonal relationships.[85] In deciding whether giving someone unwanted attention is to act badly, it is helpful to turn to court opinions, but not because they provide an authoritative guide in making ethical judgments. As I have already indicated, in many cases I think courts have not arrived at an ethically satisfying resolution. But judicial opinions present rich details of actual and not merely hypothetical conflicts, and judges, often drawing on briefs from counsel on both sides and other interested parties, do provide thoughtful arguments about the relative importance of privacy and free speech. I believe that answering the ethical question convincingly can in turn be helpful to courts as well as to legislators struggling to balance these competing interests. A persuasive account of the relative value of privacy and free speech and of the value of toleration in a liberal society is essential for getting the balance right.

The book's layout

I begin by discussing the competing values that are at stake when someone receives unwanted attention. I examine why privacy is valuable (Chapter 2), how we determine whether someone's interest in privacy is legitimate (Chapter 3), why free speech is valuable (Chapter 4), and then discuss a framework for weighing the competing values (Chapter 5). In Chapters 4 and 5 I take up perhaps the most prominent argument in defense of free speech that is made in the United States—the slippery slope argument—that holds that if we allow some restrictions of speech for the

---

82   *The Law Society v. Kordowski* [2011] EWHC 3185.
83   Text available at http://eur-lex.europa.eu. For discussion of recently proposed regulations on data protection, see Thomas Zerdick, "Oxford Privacy Information Conference" (2012).
84   Cf. Sir Robert Megarry's example in *Malone*, discussed in Chapter 3, "Conclusion": surreptitious lip-reading may be unethical but that does not mean it should be illegal.
85   Cf. David Smith, "Oxford Privacy Information Conference" (2012) (arguing that data protection laws are primarily to protect individuals from the state or businesses, and not to regulate relationships between individuals in their personal lives).

sake of privacy, we open the door to all-out censorship; and in Chapter 5 I argue that to adhere to the liberal values of toleration and respect for persons we must be sensitive to legitimate privacy interests. In Chapter 6 I then apply the framework to a variety of cases, such as those involving upskirt videos, the use of smartphones to film city council meetings, and the broadcast of perp walks. I distinguish cases involving private facts in private places, newsworthy private facts, private facts in public places, public facts that are not newsworthy, and newsworthy public facts. Chapter 7 concludes with a discussion of remedies both legal and non-legal, in which I emphasize the limitations of market solutions and stress the need for us to develop new social norms now that we live in the Age of YouTube and Google Glass.

2 The value of privacy

When people receive unwanted attention they may feel violated. In extreme cases, they may feel their life is no longer worth living, as Tyler Clementi apparently felt when his roommate shared a video he secretly took of Tyler kissing another man. Or they may simply feel put out and inconvenienced, as you might feel when inundated with unwanted junk mail or when interrupted at dinner by a phone solicitation. Some people might not mind the attention. But for those who do, something valuable is taken away.

There is another side to consider. The salesperson who makes a pitch over the phone conveys information that some people might find worthwhile. Publishing the photograph and address of a sex offender who lives across the street might help keep your children safe. Exposing a man's secret that he is gay after he performs a brave deed can help to correct false perceptions some people may have about gay men.[1] Or sharing photos of people in embarrassing situations may simply be entertaining. In each of these cases, giving unwanted attention to someone has some value to some people. In the next four chapters I discuss the values at stake when privacy and free speech come into conflict and how we might weigh their relative importance.

In this chapter, I take up the question "why is privacy valuable"? A compelling answer is needed if one is to argue convincingly that free speech should be restricted for the sake of privacy. But there is no simple answer. When someone refers to privacy they may refer to a number of distinct interests. A violation of my privacy might involve a threat to my security, or to my economic or psychological well-being; it might involve a mere annoyance; it might affect my ability to interact with family and friends; or it might have repercussions for society as a whole, for example, by deterring people from freely associating with others.

In answering the question "why is privacy valuable?" I will address the objections of critics who believe privacy is not that important and that we can do without it. One such critic might ask why we should care about

---

1   *Sipple v. Chronicle Publishing Company*, 154 Cal.App.3d 1040 (1984).

DOI: 10.4324/9781315763132-2

privacy if we have nothing to hide.[2] Privacy is of course valuable to criminals or deceivers in letting them avoid capture or detection. Yet it can be of value even to ordinary people who are not criminals but who want to conceal indiscretions; and to people who have no crimes, deceptions, or indiscretions to hide. Privacy can also be a valuable shield against unwanted attention for people who do have something to hide but who do not or no longer deserve to be punished.

A critic might also wonder why we should assume, as a matter of policy, that privacy is very important given that some people seem quite comfortable freely exposing all aspects of their lives to anyone who wants to observe;[3] and given that gossip "is considered gainful employment that may be honorably pursued."[4] The critic might think that when someone values privacy they merely have a subjective preference or taste for it, and that we really cannot say that objectively privacy has value. I shall address the question of whether privacy can be given an objective foundation, and if not, whether that means that privacy should necessarily lose out if we have to choose as a society between it and free speech.

Defining privacy

It seems appropriate to begin a discussion of privacy's value by defining what privacy means. Many of those who have previously written about privacy undertook this task and have provided helpful accounts. But if one were to attempt to identify the essence of privacy—features common to all the different situations in which we would say that privacy is at stake—one might run into trouble. One of the best-known definitions of a right to privacy is a right "to be let alone."[5] In some circumstances, that phrase helps explain what one wants when demanding privacy, as when celebrities do not want paparazzi following them around and photographing them, or people living near London's Heathrow airport claim that their right to privacy is violated when they are deprived of sleep because of airplane noise at night. The European Court of Human Rights in Strasbourg ruled

2   David Brin, *The Transparent Society* (Reading, MA: Addison-Wesley, 1998), p. 250. Daniel Solove addresses this question in "'I've Got Nothing to Hide' and Other Misunderstandings of Privacy," *San Diego Law Review* 44:745–72 (2007).

3   See Mark Andrejevic, "The Kinder, Gentler Gaze of Big Brother," *New Media Society* 4:251–270 (2002) (on the willingness of some people to expose every aspect of their lives on reality television); cf. David Anderson, "The Failure of American Privacy Law," in Markesinis, ed., *Protecting Privacy* (Oxford: Oxford University Press, 1999), p. 141; and for a response, Brian Murchison, "Revisiting the American Public Disclosure Action," in Kenyon and Richardson, eds., *New Dimensions in Privacy Law* (Cambridge: Cambridge University Press, 2006), p. 36.

4   Rodney Smolla, "Accounting for the Slow Growth of American Privacy Law," *Nova Law Review* 27: 289–323 (2002), p. 305.

5   Warren and Brandeis, "The Right to Privacy," in Schoeman, ed., *Philosophical Dimensions of Privacy* (New York: Cambridge University Press, 1984), p. 75.

that by failing to address the noise at Heathrow the state violated the European Convention on Human Rights (ECHR) Article 8 right to respect for private and family life and awarded the claimants £4,000 pounds each.[6] But "the right to be let alone" can be an unhelpful definition of privacy because it encompasses so much. Raymond Wacks is critical of broadly construing human rights to include a right not to be disturbed by noise, and suggests that the Article 8 right to privacy should be understood more narrowly as a personal right concerning sexual matters, health, and financial and domestic arrangements.[7] I might object to someone striking me in the face with his fists, or to my neighbor making loud noises, by saying they violate my right to be let alone; but in doing so I am appealing to a right that has little to do with the sort of privacy at stake in cases of unwanted attention. Still, "to be let alone" is what we sometimes want in wanting privacy.

By wanting privacy I might want seclusion, or physical isolation.[8] Here, to have privacy is to have a personal space which enables us to engage in some activities unobserved or undisturbed. But to define privacy as seclusion or solitude is too limiting, for that definition fails to capture a feature of some common instances in which we refer to privacy, instances in which one wants not seclusion but the ability to forge intimate ties to some people by granting them access to information that is denied to everyone else.[9]

Privacy can also refer to a condition of being anonymous—of not being recognized by or known to others—which can be quite different from being secluded. I can have privacy in the form of anonymity even in a crowded baseball stadium so long as I am not singled out and made the focus of attention, or recognized by anyone who knows me. One of the threats to privacy posed by Google Glass—a computer built into eye glasses that transmits real-time information to its wearer—is that it could incorporate facial recognition software that would enable a stranger to identify your name merely by having you in their field of vision.[10] Without this technology, you might be anonymous even if you were visible to others as they would not know who you are. In April of 2013, the *New York Times* ran a front page photo in its national edition showing a man and a woman in bathing suits embracing on the beach. The caption read: "Loving the Weather: temperatures in the mid-70s drew beachgoers like Lorenzo

6   *Hatton v. U.K.* [2001] 34 EHRR 1.
7   Wacks, *Privacy and Media Freedom* (Oxford: Oxford University Press, 2013), pp. 4–5, 154, 237–40. Cf. Judith Jarvis Thomson, "The Right to Privacy," *Philosophy and Public Affairs* 4(4):295–314 (1975), p. 295.
8   Alan Westin, *Privacy and Freedom* (New York: Atheneum, 1967), pp. 31–32 (identifying "functions" of privacy that include solitude, intimacy, anonymity, and reserve).
9   Cf. Flaherty, *Privacy in Colonial New England* (Charlottesville: University of Virginia Press, 1972), p. 44 (on solitude vs. intimacy); Solove, "Conceptualizing Privacy," *California Law Review* 90:1087–1155 (2002), p. 1104; Fried, "Privacy," in Schoeman, ed.
10   See Chapter 7, "Google Glass with Face Recognition."

Zemborain and Victoria Crowbar to Coney Island on Tuesday."[11] Presumably these two individuals agreed not to be anonymous by giving their names to the *Times* photographer and consenting to their publication. But suppose the *Times* photographer never approached them and instead used Google Glass to learn their names simply by having their faces in his visual field and relying on an application that matches their faces to those in a database, and that the paper published their names as in the above caption without their consent. Suppose also that they had reasons not to have some people learn where they were or that they were embracing. They could have a legitimate interest in privacy even while on a public beach—especially if they are from out of town and would not expect anyone they know to see them at Coney Island. In this case, the use of Glass impinges on a privacy interest in remaining anonymous.

Another definition of privacy, which I shall refer to most often as it characterizes the privacy that is always at stake when someone receives unwanted attention, is the ability to control who has access to information about oneself. This is often referred to as *informational privacy*.[12] This definition of privacy has some overlap with some of the other definitions of privacy. When I want anonymity I do not want others to know a particular piece of information about me—my identity. Sometimes the desire for seclusion is a desire for informational privacy, as when we do not want others to know what we are doing; but sometimes it is not, as when we simply do not want to be disturbed. A telemarketer who asks you about your age, income, political party, religion, hobbies, sexual orientation, or what television shows you watch is potentially intruding upon your informational privacy, although merely asking you for information is not restricting your ability to control access to it. The telemarketer may also have intruded upon your seclusion by calling you at dinner time, but that is a distinct reason their call may be unwelcome. If the state were to test your DNA by swabbing your inner cheek, this would intrude upon your seclusion and fail to "leave you alone," but it would also compromise your informational privacy. No one makes a mistake in referring to privacy in these different ways; the mistake would be to think that one of these senses alone captures what "privacy" really means.[13]

A right to privacy has sometimes been understood to refer to a right to do as one pleases. This is the sense of privacy referred to in landmark judicial decisions in which the U.S. Supreme Court held that laws restricting the use of contraceptive devices (*Griswold v. Connecticut*), or prohibiting a woman from having an abortion in the first trimester of pregnancy (*Roe v.*

---

11 *New York Times*, April 10, 2013, p. A1 (National print edition).
12 See Beate Rössler, *The Value of Privacy* (Malden: Polity Press, 2005), p. 9, distinguishing informational privacy from decisional and local privacy.
13 See Solove, "Conceptualizing Privacy" (resisting the temptation to seek an essential definition of privacy).

Wade), violate a right of privacy.[14] In these cases, a right to privacy refers to a right to be let alone to make decisions about how to live one's life without undue interference from the state—it is a right to "decisional autonomy." Grant Mindle, a critic of this notion of privacy, sees it as a claim to do as one pleases in public "with little if any regard for the feelings of others."[15] The decisional privacy Mindle is critical of can be distinguished from the informational privacy at stake when one receives unwanted attention. One can be concerned about unwanted attention without taking a position about what role the state should have in regulating our decisions about how to live. Yet these distinct conceptions of privacy are certainly connected. David Flaherty shows in his account of privacy in colonial New England how a recognition of the importance of "minding one's own business" and not being a busybody served as a check against rigid enforcement of Puritan laws that prohibited, among other things, having sex outside of marriage, swearing, living alone, or dressing ostentatiously.[16] Out of a respect for privacy, the enforcers of these laws—constables, tythingmen, nightwatchmen, and grand juries—were less than diligent. Had they been as diligent as some Puritan leaders wanted them to be, and had there been little informational privacy, individual autonomy would have suffered dearly, and the pressure to conform might have stifled all but the most ardent individualists. Informational privacy—which itself can be facilitated by having seclusion or local privacy but which can be achieved by other means as well—can be an important check on the social pressures to comply with the dominant views about how one ought to live, pressures that might threaten one's decisional autonomy.

In the cases I examine, someone exposes information about a person, usually without their consent, and in lacking privacy the subject of the attention loses some autonomy or control over their life. Without the ability to keep certain information secret, one can become vulnerable. Westin argues that the "deliberate penetration of the individual's protective shell, his psychological armor, would leave him naked to ridicule and shame and would put him under the control of those who knew his secrets."[17] In extreme cases, one can be blackmailed.[18] For example, the owner of the "Solicitors from Hell" website referred to in Chapter 1 had contacted the solicitors who were named and shamed on the website, offering to remove the defamatory postings for a fee.[19] In another case, a claimant who had a

---

14   381 U.S. 479 (1965) (*Griswold*); 410 U.S. 113 (1973) (*Roe*).

15   Grant Mindle, "Liberalism, Privacy, and Autonomy," *Journal of Politics*, 51(3):575–598 (1989), p. 579.

16   Flaherty, *Privacy in Colonial New England*, ch. 7.

17   Alan Westin, *Privacy and Freedom*, p. 33.

18   Solove, "A Taxonomy of Privacy," *University of Pennsylvania Law Review* 154:477–564 (2006), pp. 542–544.

19   *The Law Society v. Kordowski* [2011] EWHC 3185 (QB), Pars. 45, 119.

weekly show on BBC Radio 1 was harassed for money by individuals threatening to share with the press photographs they had of him in a brothel.[20] In China, government officials have repeatedly been blackmailed by those who threaten to publish incriminating and sometimes doctored photos or video of them to the Internet.[21] But we have an interest in privacy even if we are not subject to blackmail or other sorts of manipulation. We sometimes have an interest simply in not being humiliated or exposed against our will.

One can be humiliated without having one's privacy intruded upon. It is tempting to think that this is how to characterize what happened to the baseball fan discussed in Chapter 1 who is singled out in a crowded stadium by a television network's camera and made the brunt of a joke about his weight. One might think that he had no privacy interest except in the very broad sense that he was not "let alone," and that he could not possibly expect informational privacy. But that view is too simplistic. Unless he conceals himself, he cannot prevent people in the stadium from looking at him; but social norms or laws could conceivably permit him to control whether his image is memorialized by being broadcast on television or whether someone could capture his image and post it to YouTube. His ability to control access to information about himself may be compromised if he loses complete control over who his image is presented to even though he was plainly visible to hundreds of people.[22]

Because the notion of controlling access to information will play so central a part in the argument of this book, it is worth considering another example to illustrate how one might lose control of information in one respect yet have an interest in retaining control in other respects. In a case widely discussed by privacy theorists, Oliver Sipple became a national hero when he grabbed the arm of Sara Jane Moore as she attempted to shoot

---

20   *Theakston v. MGN Limited* [2002] EWHC 137 (QB), Par. 5.
21   Dan Levin and Amy Qin, "True or Faked, Dirt on Chinese Fuels Blackmail," *New York Times*, June 18, 2013.
22   Compare this case to another: in a nationally televised college football championship game, ESPN cameras singled out a young woman in the stadium, quarterback A.M. McCarron's girlfriend, who was crowned as Miss Alabama, while announcer Brent Musburger commented that she is "a lovely lady," with what struck some viewers as inappropriate enthusiasm. See Mary Pilon, "Musburger Criticized for Remarks About Star's Girlfriend During Title Game," *New York Times*, January 8, 2013. One reason the case is different is that "Miss Alabama" and star quarterbacks have reduced expectations of privacy. Musburger's comments might have been inappropriate, but not as an intrusion upon privacy.
23   The Sipple case is discussed in Lever, *On Privacy* (New York: Routledge, 2012), pp. 31–33; Jeffrey Rosen, *The Unwanted Gaze* (New York: Random House, 2000), pp. 47–48, 63; Ferdinand Schoeman, *Privacy and Social Freedom* (New York: Cambridge University Press, 1992), pp. 154–155; Rodney Smolla, *Free Speech in an Open Society* (New York: Alfred Knopf, 1992), pp. 130–132; and Adam Moore, *Privacy Rights* (University Park: Pennsylvania State University Press, 2010), pp. 147–148.

President Ford in Union Square, San Francisco in 1975.[23] After a news article mentioned that he was gay, he claimed his privacy was violated by publication of what he regarded as a private fact. A federal appellate court held that Sipple could not control access to this fact given that he was a prominent member of the San Francisco gay community whose name had appeared in gay magazines, who marched in gay parades, and whose sexual orientation was known by hundreds of people in several cities.[24] But Sipple could have agreed to reveal his homosexuality to members of some gay communities without wanting to grant access to this fact to his family in Detroit. He became estranged from his family after they learned he was gay, and led a troubled life. He was found dead at the age of 47.[25] Controlling *who* had access to this information was deeply important to him. Privacy, as the interest in controlling access to information about oneself, includes an interest in controlling which circles of people have access to particular information.[26]

Several of the above senses of privacy refer to a condition in which we control access to ourselves: either *physical* access (seclusion), or access to *information* about who we are or what we have done. Controlling access to information about me and controlling access to me are both instances of privacy, but there is a subtle difference between the two. Jeffrey Reiman, Elizabeth Paton-Simpson, and Charles Fried each have emphasized that an image of me in an embarrassing situation does not just reveal the fact that something embarrassing happened to me; it conveys the embarrassment. A picture of someone's tattoo on a part of their body they normally cover does not merely convey information (that this person has that tattoo); it gives continued access to something the person wants to keep unobserved.[27] Fried notes the difference when he observes that "a good friend may know what particular illness I am suffering from, but it would violate my privacy if he were actually to witness my suffering ..."[28] This distinction is particularly important when we consider the impact of video sharing technologies on privacy. Suppose I am fond of sunbathing nude but keep this a secret from everybody I know. I make sure to go to remote beaches where nude sunbathing is permitted but where I am unlikely to run into

24   *Sipple v. Chronicle Publishing Company*, 154 Cal.App.3d 1040 (1984).
25   Rosen, in *The Unwanted Gaze*, p. 48, says Sipple committed suicide; but a newspaper account says he died of pneumonia—see Lynne Duke, "Caught in Fate's Trajectory," *Washington Post*, December 31, 2006.
26   Smolla uses the metaphor of "circles" in discussing Sipple's case in *Free Speech in an Open Society*, p. 132. For further discussion of the connection between privacy and autonomy see Rössler, pp. 52, 62–63, 71–72; and van den Hoven, "Privacy and the Varieties of Moral Wrong-Doing in an Information Age," *Computers and Society*, September 1997:33–37.
27   Elizabeth Paton-Simpson, "Private Circles and Public Squares," *Modern Law Review* 61(3):318–340 (1998), pp. 333, 337, citing Reiman's work.
28   Fried, "Privacy," p. 210.

any of my friends or acquaintances. Even if someone at the beach recognizes me and tells my friends, I can still have an interest in not having a picture taken of me at the beach and posted on the Internet. This interest in privacy is not merely an interest in keeping information about me from others; it is an interest in not being continually exposed.

A distinction should also be made between surveillance and disclosure. Outcries against the massive collection of people's phone records by the National Security Agency reflect concerns with how informational privacy is threatened by surveillance, concerns that would persist even if that information were never revealed to the public.[29] Daniel Solove has noted that surveillance in itself can destroy a person's peace of mind and inhibit daily activities even if whatever is found out is never disclosed.[30] Surveillance and disclosure are obviously related when what is disclosed is first uncovered through surveillance. But they can involve distinct wrongs. The focus of this book is unwanted attention and so my greater concern is with the interests in avoiding disclosure; but several of the arguments I will consider as to why privacy is valuable help explain why we should be concerned about surveillance as well.[31]

When one is given unwanted attention either by being exposed to others or by losing control over who has access to information about oneself, something that one may value—privacy—is lost. I now turn to accounts of why controlling access to oneself or to information about oneself is valuable.

Why privacy is valuable

It is easy to see why criminals on the lam may want to keep certain information about themselves out of the public eye. But people who are not criminals also value informational privacy. It is the rare person who, like Dostoyevsky's Marmeladov, delights in telling complete strangers about their deepest secrets and moral depravities—and Marmeladov is usually quite drunk when he confides in others.[32] If we were enveloped by a mysterious gas with the peculiar quality of compelling us to answer questions with complete openness and honesty, many of us might start avoiding other people so that they do not find out about things we would prefer to keep hidden from them. A teacher might fear revealing her conviction for a past

---

29   For a report on court rulings concerning the N.S.A. policy see Adam Liptak and Michael Schmidt, "Judge Upholds N.S.A.'s Bulk Collection of Data on Calls," *New York Times*, December 28, 2013.

30   Solove, "Conceptualizing Privacy," p. 1130.

31   I address threats to privacy posed by some forms of surveillance in Tunick, "Privacy in Public Places: Do GPS and Video Surveillance Provide Plain Views?", *Social Theory and Practice* 35(4):597–622 (2009).

32   Feodor Dostoevsky, *Crime and Punishment* (New York: Norton, 1989), Pt I, ch. 2.

crime that she hid from her family and her employer: she could lose her job and alienate her children. A quarterback might not want his teammates to know he is gay.[33] A businessman might not want his religious clients or even his neighbors to know he is an atheist, or any of his clients or colleagues to know he is being treated for drug abuse. Someone might not want people in the community to know their annual income, or that they own guns.[34]

But even someone with nothing to hide may object to receiving publicity. Some people simply do not like to be an object of attention; they may be shy, blush easily, and get embarrassed when strangers' eyes are turned to them. They may instinctively run from cameras, not because they are guilty of anything but because they cannot bear being a spectacle for others.[35] Not everyone is like this, and some people might regard excessive shyness as a defect of character and perhaps something to be held to account for, though there is some evidence it may have a biological basis.[36] If asked why they do not want attention, shy persons might not be able to provide an explanation other than to say that this is just how they feel. In many situations there may be no reason not to respect such feelings even if we do not understand them. But in deciding how much privacy we should grant as a matter of social policy, those who are leery of restricting free speech for the sake of privacy may be unwilling to make concessions merely to accommodate an unjustified preference that some people have for being left alone. When we have to justify a pro-privacy policy to people who disagree and who can point to the social costs of the policy, we need an account of why privacy is valuable that is more persuasive than "just because." I now consider a number of distinct reasons people with or without something to hide may have for valuing privacy and objecting to unwanted attention.

Reputation

Having information about oneself exposed to others can obviously affect one's reputation, and when one's reputation is damaged and one's standing is reduced in the eyes of one's friends, family, coworkers, or

---

33 Cf. "Truth," *Smallville* season 3, episode 18.

34 Many residents of a New York suburb were upset when a newspaper posted their names and addresses on a webpage identifying people who owned guns; see Christine Haughney, "After Pinpointing Gun Owners, Paper is a Target," *New York Times*, January 6, 2013.

35 See *Aubry v. Editions Vice-Versa* [1998] S.C.J. No. 30 (Canada), Par. 69, quoting J. Ravanas, "La protection des peronnes contre la realization et la publication de leur image" (1978): "A person surprised in his or her private life by a roving photographer is stripped of his or her transcendency and human dignity, since he or she is reduced to the status of being a 'spectacle' for others."

36 See Jerome Kagan, J. Reznick, N. Snidman, "Biological Basis of Childhood Shyness," *Science* 240:167–171 (1988).

community, one can suffer a number of setbacks, including monetary loss and emotional or physical distress.

The loss of one's reputation can yield economic harms. For example, Food Lion Stores suffered massive losses when the fraudulent, unsafe, and illegal practices of some of its grocery store employees were exposed on national television.[37] One study that attempted to quantify the economic value of a good reputation found that people are willing to pay on average 7.6 percent more for items sold on eBay by sellers with good reputations.[38] Reputation has obvious economic value for businessmen, doctors, lawyers, teachers, engineers and other professionals; it is important for anyone entering what some economists refer to as the dating or marriage markets.[39]

But reputation can also be an important source of self-esteem that may have more than monetary value.[40] As we have seen, some people have judged that a life with a stained reputation is not worth living. A striking fictional example of the non-economic value a good reputation can have is presented in Vincent Sherman's 1947 film *Nora Prentiss*. Dr. Richard Talbot, a respected San Francisco doctor and family man with two children, by chance runs into Nora Prentiss, a nightclub singer, after she is slightly injured when hit by a car across from where he works. They are immediately attracted to each other and he courts her for some time, lying about his whereabouts to his family as he enjoys his trysts. He wants to run off with Nora, but he lacks the courage to tell his wife about the affair and ask for a divorce. When a patient of his has a fatal heart attack in his office—after hours, so nobody else is in sight—and he observes that he and the patient, Mr. Bailey, are the same age, height, and weight, he has the idea of faking his own death. He puts his personal effects on Bailey, places the body in his car, and drives the car off a cliff after setting it afire. He then follows Nora across the country to New York, using the name Robert Thompson. After he gets in a scrape in New York and the police take his fingerprints, the prints are matched with those found at the scene of Dr. Talbot's "death," and so Mr. Thompson is arrested and goes on trial for murdering Talbot. But Thompson, who had been disfigured in a car crash in New York so that he is no longer recognizable as Dr. Talbot, refuses to reveal who he really is or vindicate himself by establishing that he committed no murder because Talbot never died. He even extracts a promise from Nora never to reveal who he really is. Why? Talbot would rather face death and be remembered as a good man (since it is "Thompson" who will be

37   *Food Lion v. ABC*, 194 F.3d 505 (1999).
38   Resnick, *et al.*, "The Value of Reputation on eBay," *Experimental Economics* 9:79–101 (2006); cited in David Ardia, "Reputation in a Networked World," *Harvard Civil Rights-Civil Liberties Law Review* 45(2):261–328 (2010), p. 322.
39   See, e.g., Gary Becker, "A Theory of Marriage: Part I," *Journal of Political Economy* 81(4):813–846 (1973).
40   Ardia, p. 274 (noting that some members of the open source software community believe a good reputation among one's peers can have more value than money).

executed) than be known as an adulterer, liar, and schemer in the eyes of his wife and children.

In cases where someone puts you in a false light in a way that damages your reputation, we might think that the wrong done to you can be explained without appealing to the concept of privacy: it is wrong to defame because it is wrong to lie. But that may not be the only wrong involved: at the same time, one is casting unwanted negative attention on you, which will have the consequence that you will need to defend yourself by correcting misjudgments and reestablishing your good name. This implicates privacy in several ways: valuable time is taken from you; and you may be forced to reveal information about yourself to correct the lie. Perhaps you need to show paycheck stubs, bank account information, or provide alibis to refute the impression that you acquired funds illicitly or committed a crime on a particular day.

One's reputation can be affected also by truthful information. If a wrong is involved in such cases, it is not the wrong of lying. A prisoner who snitches on another inmate has a reputation interest in keeping his informer status private. A fellow inmate who exposes the informer commits no defamation since the accusation is true; but the exposure could be deadly.[41] Publishing the name of a rape victim is not defamation if the person named really was raped. Even so, and while an enlightened society might not regard the victim of rape as deserving a diminished reputation, the rape victim has interests in not having the fact that she was raped broadcast to the public. In the case of *Florida Star v. B.J.F.*, the woman who had been raped claimed that after a newspaper published her name she received threatening calls that forced her to change her phone number and residence and seek mental health counseling.[42] There is also a sense, which I will discuss further in a later section on intimacy and relational harms, in which reporting B.J.F.'s status as a rape victim affects her privacy by taking out of her control how she is presented to others. If one of the first things someone wearing Google Glass with face recognition learned when looking at B.J.F. was her status as a rape victim, this would not be the identity she wants to convey.

Avoiding unjust punishment, and the "right to be forgotten"

One important set of cases involving reputation interests concerns individuals who either committed past crimes for which they already received their just punishment, or who were arrested but not convicted, or who were not accused of a crime but nevertheless acted badly at one point in their lives. In each of these cases, one may have a legitimate interest in keeping this

41 Cf. Ardia, pp. 300–301.
42 491 U.S. 524, 528 (1989).

information private in order to avoid undeserved or excessive punishment.[43] Punishment here refers to non-legal punishment by non-state actors. While only the state can mete out legal punishment, there is a socially recognized practice of non-legal punishment that individuals often invoke to enforce social norms.[44] Punishment in both its legal and non-legal forms is unjust if it is undeserved or disproportionate. The principle of proportionality provides an important limiting principle that may help avoid cycles of escalated reprisals.[45] It demands that punishment should have an upper limit, or an endpoint, unless the crime being punished is so severe as to deserve a life sentence. Once someone receives their due punishment for their past offense they should not suffer further punishment for that offense. But when information about someone's past crimes or misdeeds is available to the general public essentially forever, it may expose them to widespread and perpetual punishment. By its very nature, non-legal punishment, in contrast to punishment by the state, cannot be issued as part of a coordinated response, and there can be no assurance it will be fairly measured.[46] If the public has perpetual, ready access to this information it can be difficult for individuals to shed a past marred by a mistake they may now regret; it makes it harder for them to reinvent themselves and form new ties, and reintegrate into society.[47] In some rare cases, it exposes them to life-threatening risks.[48]

This interest in avoiding unjust punishment has weight not only for former criminals but for people who have been accused but not yet convicted, such as Louis Conradt, the Texas state prosecutor who engaged in sexually explicit online chatroom exchanges with someone purporting to be underage, and who was about to be confronted by an NBC reporter and camera crew when he shot himself. While Conradt is hardly a sympathetic figure, he has a legitimate privacy interest in not being publicly shamed by

---

43   See Mark Tunick, "Privacy and Punishment," *Social Theory and Practice* 39(4):643–668 (2013), from which parts of this section are drawn.

44   See Leo Zaibert, *Punishment and Retribution* (Aldershot, England: Ashgate, 2006), and Christopher Bennett, "The Varieties of Retributive Experience," *Philosophical Quarterly* 52(207):145–163 (2002). Some courts have taken into account the non-legal punishment one already received in the form of shaming to reduce a convicted person's sentence, see *R v. Philip Oliver* [2011] EWCA Crim 3114.

45   But the principle has its critics: see Louis Kaplow and Steven Shavell, *Fairness versus Welfare* (Cambridge, MA: Harvard University Press, 2002); and Larry Alexander, "The Doomsday Machine: Proportionality, Prevention and Punishment," *The Monist* 63(2):199–227 (1980).

46   Tunick, "Privacy and Punishment," p. 649.

47   On the importance of privacy to our capacity for self-presentation and identity formation, see Rössler, p. 116; Helen Nissenbaum, *Privacy in Context*, (Stanford: Stanford University Press, 2010), pp. 81–82; and van den Hoven, "Privacy and the Varieties of Wrong-Doing in an Information Age," p. 36.

48   Charles Parker was murdered by someone who found him on a sex offender registry and mistakenly assumed he had been convicted of child molesting. See Alan Blinder, "Double Murder Seen as Part of Man's Quest to Kill Sex Offenders," *New York Times*, July 27, 2013.

NBC before he has an opportunity to defend himself in court. Even if he deserved punishment and would not have received it from the state, the punishment of being exposed on national television might have been grossly disproportionate to his offense.[49] The interest in avoiding unjust punishment also has weight for non-criminals who behave badly in public but do not deserve repeated punishment for the rest of their lives. The Korean woman who did not clean up after her dog on a subway acted badly, but she did not deserve the widespread public humiliation that reportedly forced her to leave her university, and that may cast her forever as "Dog Poop Girl."

The interest in avoiding unjust non-legal punishment is sometimes associated with an interest in not being subjected to manipulation. In the U.S. there are websites that draw on local law enforcement databases to post mugshots and booking information of people who were arrested. The information can be indexed and made readily accessible to anyone who googles an arrested person's name. In 2011, the owner of one such website, florida.arrests.org, placed a prominent banner ad at the top of the main page that read "Mugshot problems? We remove mugshots" and linked to http://www.removemymug.com, where individuals could have their mugshot removed in 24 to 48 hours for a fee.[50] The owner of floridaarrests.org was reported to receive payments from websites such as removemymug.com in exchange for removing the offending mugshots.[51] A person who gathers and displays my mugshot and then charges me to remove it is effectively blackmailing me, though it might not technically be blackmail as long as it is within his rights to gather and post the mugshots.[52] Courts are just beginning to address this issue. A recent lawsuit in Ohio resulted in a settlement and agreement to stop charging for the removal of mugshots;[53] and class action suits are being filed in other states. One California suit is resting on a claim not of reputational injuries but of misappropriation of people's likeness for commercial gain, in violation of state law.[54]

One may think that if you truly did something that damages your reputation you have no one to blame but yourself—you earned your bad name. A person convicted of drunk driving years ago but whose mugshot now appears online might think that his past mistake should be buried and that

---

49   See Tunick, "Reality TV and the Entrapment of Predators," in Robson and Silbey, eds., *Law and Justice on the Small Screen* (Oxford: Hart Publishing, 2012).

50   http://florida.arrests.org/, accessed August 4, 2011.

51   David Kravets, "Mug-Shot Industry will Dig up Your Past, Charge You to Bury it Again," *Wired.com*, August 2, 2011; cf. Gregory Wolfe, "Smile for the Camera," *Columbia Law Review* 113:227–275 (2013), p. 2243.

52   Tunick, "Privacy and Punishment," pp. 651–652.

53   John Caniglia, "Ohio lawsuit over online mug shots reaches settlement," *The Plain Dealer*, January 7, 2014.

54   Ricardo Lopez, "Lawsuit targets website that posts mug shots," *Los Angeles Times*, January 22, 2014.

he should not live under a dark shadow for the rest of his life because of it. Yet, one might respond, he did make this mistake, and having to explain himself, perhaps by showing that he has not made the same mistake since, might continually deter him and others from driving under the influence. We might even think it wrong to try to erase such truths about the past. We might share the sentiment expressed by the poet James Fenton that "[a] man should face what he has been, this is the ideal, this is hard."[55] Or we might be committed to the view that we should strive to maintain as thorough a record of the past as is possible.

These sorts of considerations are at the center of the debate in Europe about whether there should be a "right to be forgotten."[56] For example, a plastic surgeon in Spain has fought Google in the EU Court of Justice because references to his allegedly botched surgery over twenty years ago keep appearing when one googles his name, setting back his professional career.[57] In Germany, two half-brothers who were convicted in 1993 of killing a famous Bavarian actor, Walter Sedlmayr, in a case that received extensive media coverage at the time, filed a suit to have their full names removed from the Internet in connection with the crime that took place over twenty years ago. The German Federal Court of Justice recognized a privacy interest in not having information about the Sedlmayr murderers actively pushed out to the public, but held that the information can appear on the Internet if an active search is required to access it, or if it is plainly identified as an archived report.[58]

If there were a right to be forgotten, there could be dire consequences for those who want to gather information they have a legitimate need to know. Restricting access to information about a person's past conduct, economists have argued, facilitates fraud and makes it harder to determine whether someone is reputable.[59] An employer who is hiring someone for a

55 Quoted by Rosemary Jay, Oxford Privacy Information Conference: "The 'Right to be Forgotten' and Beyond," June 12, 2012. Online at www.csls.ox.ac.uk/conferences/oxpilsconference2012.

56 See Mayer-Schoenberger, *Delete: The Virtue of Forgetting in the Digital Age* (Princeton, NJ: Princeton University Press, 2009); Daley, "On its Own, Europe Backs Web Privacy Fights," *New York Times*, August 10, 2011; and Jeffrey Rosen, "The Right to be Forgotten," *Stanford Law Review Online* 64:88 (February 13, 2012). For criticism of a right to be forgotten, see Bill Dutton, "Oxford Privacy Information Conference" (2012).

57 An advocate general ruled for Google, see David Roman and Frances Robinson, "Google Gets Boost in EU Privacy Case," *Wall Street Journal*, June 25, 2013; cf. Karen Eltis, "Breaking through the 'Tower of Babel': A 'Right to be Forgotten'," *Fordham Intellectual Property, Media and Entertainment Law Journal* 22:69–95 (2011), pp. 85–86. But the European Court of Justice has since ruled that Google can in some cases be required to remove personal data that is no longer relevant from the results list produced by its search engine, see *Google Spain SL v. AEPD* [2014] Case C-131/12, discussed in Chapter 7.

58 See Siry and Schmitz, "A Right to be Forgotten?," *European Journal for Law and Technology* 3(1)(2012); and [2012] VI ZR 217/08.

59 Richard Posner, "The Economics of Privacy," *American Economic Review* 71(2):405–409 (1981); and Richard Murphy, "Property Rights in Personal Information," *Georgia Law Review* 84:2381–2417 (1996), pp. 2385–2386.

sensitive position that requires the utmost financial responsibility might legitimately decide never to hire someone who had ever been convicted for absconding funds. Granting doctors a right to erase records of their past misdeeds would not serve the interests of potential patients who might reasonably choose not to see a doctor who ever was guilty of serious malpractice.[60] But if we adopted a blanket rule that individuals forever forfeit their good reputation because of their past misdeeds we would violate a principle of justice that requires that punishment be proportional to the offense and therefore have an endpoint; and when we continually stigmatize former criminals we could impede their reintegration into society.

Resolving the question of whether there should be a right to be forgotten will require a nuanced approach—we must balance interests in privacy with interests in the free flow of information. We almost certainly do not want to erase accounts of past crimes from archived newspaper records or police databases, but there may be other ways to preserve privacy. One possibility is to require search engines to be modified to limit the prospect of certain embarrassing information appearing at the top of a results page. Courts are beginning to address the legal arguments for and against holding companies like Google or web portals liable when someone's reputation is damaged as a result of their services.[61] In later chapters I will turn to these cases, and address the question of how we might weigh the competing interests of privacy and free speech and arrive at remedies that take both interests properly into account.

Property

Another interest one may have in controlling information about oneself that is related to the interest in reputation is a property interest. Richard Murphy argues that "personal information is, in fact, property."[62] Our interest in (or in his terms our preference for) privacy can be assigned an economic value that reflects a willingness to pay to protect it. People spend money to increase their privacy by purchasing paper shredders, more expensive phones that provide extra security, software that encrypts their electronic messages, or soundproofing materials, and this suggests privacy is a preference that has an identifiable value.

According to Murphy's "law and economics" approach, we can decide which information about me is private and which instead belongs to the

---

60 Cf. Jacobs and Larrauri, "Are Criminal Convictions a Public Matter?," *Punishment and Society* 14(1):3–28 (2012), p. 5.

61 *Google Inc. v. Agencia Española de Protección de Datos* [2012] ECJ EUR-Lex LEXIS 1014, and [2014] Case C-131/12; *Trkulja v. Google* [2012] VSC 533 (Australia); *Payam Tamiz v. Google* [2012] EWHC 449 (QB); *Metropolitan Intl Schools v. Designtechnica* [2010] EWHC 2411; *Delfi AS v. Estonia* [2013] 64569/09 (Strasbourg Court). Several of these cases will be discussed in Chapter 7.

62 Murphy, p. 2393.

public by viewing the question as an economic problem of how best to distribute rights so as to yield the greatest societal good. The approach draws on utilitarian theory, which we will consider in more detail in Chapter 5 but which essentially holds that we should resolve disputes about public policy—such as whether information should be made public or kept private—so as to increase the net overall happiness or utility of the members of society. On Murphy's view, we decide whether the right to control information about myself should be assigned to me or the public by devising a rule that would benefit most parties and "minimize the costs associated with contracting out of the rule."[63]

How the economics approach to privacy might work in practice is clearly spelled out in an article by Joseph Siprut. Siprut focuses on the question of whether an image of me may be published without my consent. His answer is that individuals should by default possess rights in their image except in the case where the image is newsworthy. This will maximize the odds that the right will be put to its most valued use.[64] He explains by considering the case of a nude bather on a public beach who would prefer not to be photographed. If she is assigned the property right to her image, a photographer would need to get her consent to publish her picture. If she prefers not to be photographed, the photographer might need to pay to gain her consent. Siprut assumes that the transaction costs in arriving at an agreement are not prohibitive. If the photographer offered the woman $500 and she refused, and he is not willing to pay more than that amount, then the woman values her privacy more than the photographer values publishing her image and he would need to seek out another nude bather, or hire a model. Society would still receive the benefit of a photo of a nude bather, while the woman's privacy preference would be respected. If the woman were a celebrity, using another person's image might not be a suitable substitute; but Siprut allows for a "newsworthy" exception: if an image is newsworthy, the right to it belongs to the public by default.[65] If, in contrast, society assigned the right to the public and not the individual, the photographer could either simply take the photo and publish it or, Siprut argues, if the photographer is an astute businessman, he might try to bargain with the woman to see what she would be willing to pay to acquire the right to her image. She might agree to pay $500. The photographer could agree and then acquire a photo of someone else. A problem arises in this scenario because if the woman agrees to pay the photographer not to publish her photo, a second photographer, seeing the economic possibilities, has an incentive to snap a similar picture and extort money from her. The woman would need to bargain with this photographer as well; and possibly with a

63   Murphy, pp. 2395–2396, 2412.
64   Joseph Siprut, "Privacy Through Anonymity: An Economic Argument for Expanding the Right of Privacy in Public Places," *Pepperdine Law Review* 33:311–334 (2006), pp. 312–313, 322.
65   Siprut, p. 325.

third, and a fourth, and so on. Siprut writes that "clearly, as a practical matter if not a theoretical one, value-maximizing bargaining or negotiations will not take place when the right is assigned to the public domain." Giving the public the right puts the image in a lower-valued use and this leads to "highly inefficient results." By granting the initial right to the individual, Siprut concludes, "the party or parties who value the right the most will end up with it—and from society's perspective, that is a good thing."[66]

We need not rely on the possibility of numerous photographers extorting money from the woman to reach Siprut's conclusion, though that possibility makes the case for assigning her the property right that much stronger. It might be worth a great deal to the woman not to have her picture published; we need not ask why she values her privacy so much: we just accept that this is her preference. We also assume that there is nothing outstandingly distinctive about her such that the value to society of seeing a picture of her as opposed to someone of similar appearance would be anything but negligible. The disutility she would suffer of paying that amount to just one photographer (let alone n times that amount if she is confronted by n photographers) or of having her picture published if she could not afford to pay may never be outweighed by the utility to society of having her picture published as opposed to a similar picture of someone who consents at no or little cost. Even if it takes the photographer half a day to find a willing subject, the value of his time is unlikely to approach the value to the woman of not being exposed.

There may be a practical difficulty with the solution Siprut recommends. Suppose an individual really did not care whether her photo was published. Yet because she would by default have the right to veto its publication, she could act strategically and hold out for money in exchange for waiving her right, even though what she might agree to accept does not really reflect the value she places on her privacy. Of course if she holds out for too much, the photographer will just find someone else; and it seems unlikely that so many people will act strategically that it would become difficult for publishers to acquire such photos.

There is another difficulty with the law and economics approach that I regard as more serious. According to Siprut's argument, the reason the photographer must get the person's consent is that giving individuals the right to control the use of their image increases aggregate social utility so long as the image is not newsworthy. But one might think that someone's privacy should not be something for which one has to bargain, and that, and not the goal of promoting economic efficiency, explains why the individual retains the right to her image. In other words, the law and economics approach arrives at the right outcome but for the wrong reason. Solove

---

66 Siprut, pp. 324–326. In Chapter 5 I consider a possible qualification to Siprut's argument: whether an outcome is efficient may depend on the distribution of privacy preferences. If very few people would care about their image being published, there may be greater utility in leaving the right to the public.

argues that to appropriate my image without my consent can interfere with my self-development and right to choose whether or how to expose myself in public: when another person exhibits me without my leave, I am a "slave" under their control. Even if the exposure is not degrading or humiliating, it is an "exploitation."[67] This argument draws on some other accounts of the value of privacy that we shall explore soon.

Viewing privacy interests as property interests can be helpful. The property account of privacy convincingly explains the primary wrong involved in appropriating a public figure's image for commercial gain. When you use a photograph of a famous athlete drinking your company's product, without the athlete's consent, you profit from the fame of someone else who had made the effort to earn that fame.[68] There are possibly other wrongs involved: the athlete may strongly prefer a rival product and so your advertisement would mislead the public and cast the athlete in a false light. But the property account points to one reason it is wrong.

The property account can also be convincing in cases where intrusions upon privacy create risks the avoidance of which requires one to expend resources. Boudewijn de Bruin argues that invasions of privacy can lead to a decrease in "negative freedom."[69] For example, revealing the fact that a headmaster is gay could decrease the headmaster's freedom because he might be pressured to resign; or if my bank's computer server is hacked into, I am more subject to identity theft, which will decrease my negative freedom by making me devote substantial amounts of my time and money to remedy the problem. While the possible harms of the privacy invasion are speculative, my negative freedom is diminished simply because I do not know what uses will be made of the information.[70] Privacy promotes a property interest by letting us preserve our resources rather than expend them to compensate for or avoid injuries that result or might result from unwanted attention.[71] But the property account fails to capture some other important reasons for valuing privacy. Consider the example of a man with an embarrassing tattoo on his back. The possibility that someone would capture and share an image of his shirtless back without his consent might require him to expend resources to purchase window curtains or more shirts, but that might not best explain why it would be wrong to take and publish the photo.

67   Solove, "A Taxonomy of Privacy," pp. 547–549.
68   See, e.g., *Abdul-Jabbar v. General Motors Corp.*, 85 F.3d 407 (9th Cir. 1996). Cf. Eugene Volokh, "Freedom of Speech and Informational Privacy," *Stanford Law Review* 52(5):1049–1124 (2000), p. 1075: When you take the product of someone else's labor you create disincentives for them to work, which as a rule would be detrimental to society.
69   Boudewijn de Bruin, "The Liberal Value of Privacy," *Law and Philosophy* 29:505–534 (2010).
70   De Bruin, pp. 509–510, 516.
71   Cf. Murchison, "Revisiting the American Public Disclosure Action," p. 39: privacy is a "security interest against possible physical harm resulting from mass disclosure of identity."

A lack of privacy is objectively harmful

On the law and economics approach to privacy, privacy is a mere subjective preference or taste, its value measured solely by what one is willing to pay to satisfy this taste. To say my desire for something is subjective is to say that the only reason I can give for my wanting it is that I prefer it and that if someone demanded to know *why* I preferred it I could not give any reason other than "I just do." My judgment that x is better than y cannot compel universal assent.[72] In contrast, if I have an objective basis for preferring x, then if challenged as to why I prefer x I can offer a plausible, non-arbitrary reason that potentially persuades others to form the same judgment. The law and economics view that privacy is merely a subjective preference might at first glance seem to be plausible given that individuals appear to have widely varying preferences for privacy. The fact that individuals vary in their desire for privacy is something that will need to be addressed when we think about how much privacy society should guarantee as a matter of public policy. It might be unfair for everyone to bear the burdens of a strongly pro-privacy regime that benefits what might only be a small subset of the population with strong subjective preferences for privacy that most people in society might regard as unreasonable or idiosyncratic, especially given that pro-privacy policies have social costs. This is an important issue that draws us into questions of political theory that I take up in Chapter 5. But there is an alternative to the law and economics position that privacy is merely a subjective preference or taste: that we have an interest in having privacy—even if we do not desire privacy—because without it we are objectively less well off.

Even if my desire for privacy were subjective in the way I have described above, it might nevertheless be the case that without privacy I will be objectively worse off. Suppose I am so disturbed by unwanted attention that I cannot bear living anymore, so that the result of my lack of privacy will be either that I take my own life or I act erratically and endanger myself involuntarily; or suppose I so dread unwanted attention that I am ready to give in to someone's threat that unless I meet their demands they will share embarrassing information about me with my friends and colleagues. My preference for privacy may be subjective in the sense that I cannot offer convincing reasons why I cannot bear the attention; but the fact that a lack of privacy is dysfunctional may provide an objective grounding for privacy. A person with a strong subjective preference might suffer harm if that preference is not satisfied, and avoiding harm is a non-arbitrary reason for judging privacy to be of value.

---

72   Cf. Immanuel Kant, *Critique of Judgment*, sections 7 and 8; cited in Stanley Cavell, *Must We Mean What We Say?* (New York: Charles Scribner's Sons, 1969); and discussed in Hanna Pitkin, *Wittgenstein and Justice* (Berkeley: University of California Press, 1972), pp. 232–236.

I now want to pursue an even stronger claim for privacy being an objective value: that a lack of privacy is objectively harmful not just to the supersensitive person with unusually strong privacy preferences who may suffer objectively harmful consequences because of those preferences, but to a typical person, and that while subjective desires for privacy may vary, humans objectively need privacy whether they know it or not.

Intuitively the claim that privacy is important for a typical person's psychological well-being may seem plausible to most people who reflect on what it would be like to have their deepest secrets permanently and widely exposed.[73] Some anthropologists and historians have suggested that privacy is not an idiosyncratic desire but a widely shared need of humans in different historical periods and across cultures.[74] Shame and embarrassment are emotions that encourage individuals to conform with cultural norms, and having the fact that one diverged from these norms exposed may, depending on one's culture, lead to one's being rejected by family, peers, or the entire community, which could be devastating. The psychologist Karl Menninger argued that for our mental well-being we all may sometimes need to put aside our social roles and engage in minor noncompliance with social norms.[75] Privacy can make it easier to do that. But it is difficult to gather systematic empirical evidence that would demonstrate or quantify the effect a loss of privacy would have on a typical individual's well-being.

Adam Moore musters evidence that he thinks establishes privacy's objective value. Moore thinks that we need to establish an objective foundation for privacy because a defense based on subjective desires is inadequate: subjective desires can be arbitrary or may be the result of having been manipulated by others. So he takes what he calls an "objectivist" perspective that sees privacy as essential to human flourishing and objectively as valuable as food, water, and shelter.[76] For Moore, privacy has objective value because of its role in sustaining life itself. Without it, both human and nonhuman animal populations self-destruct.[77] For evidence to support this claim, Moore refers to studies by social scientists conducted in the 1950s and 1960s which purport to show that a lack of privacy results in physical and mental impairment. One study concludes that when put in overcrowded settings, rats suffer disease, heart failure, stress, and experience

---

73   In addition, Solove has observed how many of us may feel some discomfort simply if strangers were to stare at us, in "A Taxonomy of Privacy," p. 493.

74   See Thomas Gregor, "Exposure and Seclusion," in Tefft, ed., *Secrecy: Cross-Cultural Perspectives* (New York: Human Sciences Press, 1980) (on the practice of seclusion among the Mehinaku); and Flaherty, pp. 73–75 (on the need for occasional solitude in colonial New England).

75   See Karl Menninger, *The Crime of Punishment* (New York: Viking Press, 1966).

76   Moore, *Privacy Rights*, pp. 6, 43.

77   Moore, pp. 33–34.

alienation.[78] More recent studies of humans in prisons reach similar conclusions: putting people in overcrowded situations can be damaging both physically and mentally.[79] One problem with this evidence is that while it may show the value of seclusion or isolation (although in a prison setting there are other plausible variables that might explain impairment), it does not establish the value of the sort of privacy for which Moore later argues we need greater legal protection—privacy against unwanted attention, such as protection against having one's photo broadcast to the world against one's will.[80]

It is not that difficult to measure the extent to which people subjectively value privacy. One might conduct a survey or design an experiment in which subjects reveal their privacy preferences. A survey, for example, might ask "how much would you be willing to pay to avoid having a photo taken of you sunbathing nude at a public beach published in a magazine?"[81] But discerning the objective value privacy has in avoiding psychological harm is another matter. Apart from the above studies that look at the consequences of overcrowding on lab rats and prisoners, and a few studies addressing work performance in situations where office workers have more or less privacy defined as isolation from others, I am aware of no study that tries to measure harm as a variable dependent on privacy.[82] Imagine what such a study might have to look like and it will become apparent why it might never have been done. There are a large number of potential causes of psychological impairment, and to determine to what extent a lack of privacy was a cause, one would have to control for these other variables. This might require that we observe subjects with similar mental health in dissimilar environments, one with privacy and one without. Some people who are forced to live for a significant period of time with strangers in close confines will no doubt

---

78   Moore, pp. 48–49, citing John Calhoun, "The Study of Wild Animals Under Controlled Conditions," *Annals of the New York Academy of Sciences* 51:113–122 (1950); Moore also cites John Christian, "Phenomena Associated with Population Density," *Proceedings of the National Academy of Sciences* 47:428–429 (1961).

79   Moore, pp. 55–56, citing studies conducted primarily in the 1970s and 1980s on prison crowding.

80   This paragraph draws on Mark Tunick, "Review of Adam Moore, *Privacy Rights*," in *Social Theory and Practice* 37(3):510–517 (2011).

81   For an example of survey-based research see Acquisti and Grossklags, "Privacy and Rationality in Individual Decision-Making," *IEEE Security and Privacy* 3(2):26–33 (2005); for discussions of measuring privacy, see Kosa and El-Khatib, "Measuring Privacy," *Journal of Internet Services and Information Security* 1(4):60–73 (2011); and H. Jeff Smith *et al.*, "Information Privacy," *MIS Quarterly* 20(2):167–196 (1996).

82   For some empirical research that associates a lack of privacy with increased stress, see Stephen Webb, "Privacy and Psychosomatic Stress: An Empirical Analysis," *Social Behavior and Personality* 6(2):227–234 (1978); Michael O'Neill and Pascale Carayon, "The Relationship between Privacy, Control, and Stress Responses in Office Workers," *Human Factors and Ergonomics Society Annual Meeting Proceedings* (1993), 479–483. See also Eric Sundstrom *et al.*, "Privacy at Work: Architectural Correlates of Job Satisfaction and Job Performance," *Academy of Management Journal* 23(1):101–117 (1980).

exhibit stress and even breakdown, but we would need a sufficiently large sample size to determine if this were a result of the particular dynamics among the subjects or of other factors besides a lack of privacy.

If we conducted experiments with a large enough number of subjects and consistently observed a significant increase in psychological impairment in people put in close confines with others, we still have not established what aspect of privacy is needed to avoid harm: there are a number of reasons why overcrowding or a lack of physical isolation can cause harm that have nothing to do with informational privacy. To measure the effect of a loss of informational privacy, one might need to manipulate subjects in disturbing ways, such as by seeking out embarrassing information about some subjects and observing their response as the information is exposed. It is doubtful that an institutional review board would or should approve such treatment of human subjects. Comparative studies attempting to measure mental well-being as a function of privacy face the difficulty of measuring the level of privacy in different societies and controlling for other factors that might explain variations in psychological outcomes.

That it is difficult to measure the objective value of privacy systematically does not mean there is no value to be measured. But we may need to assess the relative value of privacy as against free speech without compelling empirical evidence about the consequences of a lack of privacy to the typical person's well-being. Several of the accounts of why it is reasonable to want privacy that I consider in this chapter suggest privacy is not a mere arbitrary taste but serves compelling purposes.

Intimacy, relational harms, and the need to compartmentalize

One reason privacy has value is that it lets us maintain intimate relationships with friends and loved ones.[83] One of the identifying features of an intimate relationship is that those involved share things between themselves that they do not share with just anyone. At the same time, intimate relationships can sometimes only be preserved by keeping certain information from one's partner: revealing to your spouse that you once committed adultery might end the marriage. In either case, a relationship is maintained by carefully controlling access to information about oneself.

Publicity can take this control away; it may force someone to address matters "at a time or in a context that they would not choose" and "preempts the first telling of facts."[84] That a person has been raped could have

---

83   See Charles Fried, "Privacy"; James Rachels, "Why Privacy is Important," *Philosophy and Public Affairs* 4(4):323–333 (1975); and Schoeman, *Philosophical Dimensions of Privacy*, p. 3.

84   Murchison, "Revisiting the American Public Disclosure Action," pp. 53–54.

a traumatic effect on their relationship with family and loved ones. Some rape victims may choose to keep the fact that they were raped secret, especially in cultures where being raped brings dishonor on one's family; others may choose to share it with those closest to them. But if word gets out publicly of the rape, the victim no longer has this choice. Mr. Briscoe, who was involved in a hijacking and had completed his sentence over a decade prior to the publication of an article that mentions his crime, chose to keep his crime from his daughter and friends; when they learned of it from the article they abandoned him. He might have been ill-advised to keep this fact about his past a secret from them, but this was his way of forging his intimate relationships. When *Reader's Digest* exposed his past crime, he was forced to explain himself, and this created a tension that damaged those relationships beyond repair.

I want to develop the argument that privacy is important for preserving intimate relationships by casting it more generally: privacy is important in allowing us to compartmentalize information about ourselves.

We share information about ourselves selectively. There are some things some of us might not tell anyone except perhaps a therapist: thoughts we would not want anyone and especially not our most intimate friends to know we have. There are also some things we would share only with dear friends and not with casual acquaintances or colleagues at work. Our lives have different compartments. You might share details about a romantic fling with friends but not your parents or coworkers, and if you were a teacher, not with your students. A person conducting secretive research in a secure laboratory facility will not share information about work with his friends or even family. Very few of us indiscriminately share any and all information about ourselves with everyone we know; instead, we consider the nature of our relationships with others in deciding what information they should have access to.[85]

This crucial fact has prompted Google to develop "Google +" to address a problem that had become apparent with the social networking website Facebook prior to changes that Facebook went on to institute in 2011. Facebook allows one to connect with people that are termed "friends": these may be close friends—to be distinguished from "Facebook friends," of which close friends may be a subset; or they may be family, casual acquaintances, colleagues at work, students, members of a club or religious organization, fellow fans of Lady Gaga, or Facebook friends of any of these people. The problem is that at least prior to 2011, Facebook did not easily let you selectively distribute information to a subset of your friends for

---

85 Cf. Irwin Altman, *The Environment and Social Behavior* (Monterey, CA: Brooks/Cole, 1975) (seeing privacy as a set of interpersonal boundary-control processes to assert control over how much we open up to various others); discussed in Zynep Tufekci, "Can You See Me Now? Audience and Disclosure Regulation in Online Social Network Sites," *Bulletin of Science, Technology and Society* 28(1):20–36 (2008).

whom that information is appropriate, and exclude access of that information to other Facebook friends who have no business knowing about it. Google + addresses this problem by allowing you to form "circles." As its website explained when Google + was first introduced, forming a circle is "the easiest way to share some things with college buddies, others with your parents, and almost nothing with your boss." More recently the website explained that circles let you "share the right things with the right people."[86] Just as we do in our face-to-face interactions, we still take the risk that information we share with someone is then spread by them to someone in a different circle. Similarly, YouTube allows a user who uploads a video to designate it as "public" (a setting which YouTube recommends); but it also allows the user to limit access of the video only to people to whom the user emails the link to the video. Once you email a link to someone else, you cannot control who they pass it on to.

Selectively granting access to private information about yourself can be valuable not just for preserving intimate relations but in other ways. Suppose an employee facing a family crisis is unable to meet a deadline at work and seeks an extension. While the employee would prefer to keep his family problems private, by revealing his situation to his boss he impresses upon her that he has a valid reason for his request and is not just being lazy, and that may convince her to grant it. Consider a more complicated scenario. I assign my class a group project to be done in teams of four. Suppose a member of one of the groups approaches me and says that he just learned that his sister has a serious illness and so he needs to fly home every other week to be with her and the rest of his family. As a result, he will not be able to work as much on the project. For the group to succeed, the other members will have to work harder. What would motivate them to do that? It would be important for them to know that the student has a good reason for not doing his fair share and is not shirking responsibilities because he prefers to surf at the beach. The reason may motivate other group members to make sacrifices so that the group will succeed. In this situation, the student may well want to convey very private information selectively to his group members, and ask them not to tell anyone else. This illustrates a more general principle: individuals benefit from the ability to give a select group of people access to information they need to know while keeping it from others who have no such need to know.

The argument that people who have nothing to hide need not care about privacy should now be exposed decisively as a red herring. There is nothing inherently dishonest or immoral about keeping information about yourself in different compartments and not being equally open to everyone. Of course sometimes there is: you might not want photos of your summer cycling vacation that you share with your Facebook friends to get into the

86   https://plus.google.com, accessed August 1, 2011 and January 18, 2013.

hands of an insurance company if the photos reveal that the claim you filed with the company falsely depicts the severity of your injury.[87] But if we shared information about ourselves indiscriminately with everyone, an important basis for intimate relationships and friendships would be lost;[88] and we would also find it more difficult to manage our social roles.

I am aware of no empirical, controlled studies that quantify how a loss of privacy affects interpersonal relationships, but I think what was said earlier about the lack of empirical studies on the link between privacy and psychological well-being should be said here: the lack of systematic empirical evidence may be a result of the ethical objections to conducting experiments that could establish an objective effect and does not imply that there is no significant relation between privacy and the ability to manage our relationships.

No harm no foul?

In the above accounts, a violation of privacy might be thought to be harmful in some way: a loss of reputation can cause monetary losses; unwanted exposure can cause psychological harm; a loss of solitude or anonymity might bring intrusions that are annoying or steal away one's time; and a loss of privacy may damage relationships that are meaningful to us. In each of these situations we might think of privacy as a guard against possible harms, and its value something that we can measure by tallying up the costs of those harms. Privacy invasions are not typically "visceral harms" or sensationalistic; Solove writes that seldom are there "dead bodies." As we have seen, though, sometimes there are. Solove's point is that more typically one confronts a series of relatively minor intrusions that can add up, like gradual pollution, resulting in a serious harm.[89]

I now want to be more precise than I have been in characterizing the loss of privacy as a harm. Not just in philosophical circles but even in ordinary language, "harm" can carry a special meaning such that to say that something causes harm is not to say that it is merely disagreeable. When a bee stings me or an ant bites me, it causes me pain, and perhaps I would say it hurts me, but it would be odd to say it harms me. So too, receiving unwanted junk mail may annoy me, and knocks on my door from religious proselytizers during dinnertime may be upsetting. But they do not harm me. As Joel Feinberg explains in analyzing the concept of harm, even when

---

87 Compare four cases from Canada: *Murphy v. Perger* [2007] O.J. No. 5511 and *Leduc v. Roman* [2009] O.J. No. 681 (allowing access to relevant photographs posted to Facebook for purposes of discovery in cases involving claims for damages) with *Stewart v. Kempster* [2012] O.J. No. 6145 and *Knox v. Nathan Applebaum Holdings Ltd.* [2013] O.J. No. 5981 (recognizing a privacy interest in what one posts only for one's Facebook friends).

88 Charles Fried, "Privacy."

89 Solove, "I've Got Nothing to Hide," p. 769.

you are dealt a serious setback to your interests—and not even that typically happens when you are stung by a bee or disturbed by spammers—you have not necessarily been harmed. If the person who you love with all your heart and soul tells you they do not feel the same way about you, they have not harmed you. You *want* their love, and not receiving it may change your life for the worse. But to be harmed, one must be wronged—that is, there must be a violation of a right. You are not wronged when you are stung by a bee because you have no right not to be stung. You are not wronged when the person you love does not reciprocate because you have no right to their love. Feinberg identifies a few important criteria for determining if someone has been wronged and therefore harmed: A wrongs B by acting culpably and without B's consent so as to cause a setback to interests B has which are regarded as rights. Harming someone, on this definition, requires acting culpably. If A does something to B accidentally, without acting recklessly or negligently, A has not acted culpably and has not wronged B. (This is another reason why the bee does not harm me.) Nor does A harm B by striking B with a heavy blow if B consented to A's doing so.[90]

In some cases, unwanted attention can set back my interests, interests that are regarded as rights, so that whoever intruded upon my privacy wronged and harmed me. Whether I was harmed will depend on whether society recognizes that I had a right that was violated. In other words, to say that something harms me requires us to have already established that I have a right to certain things. I will eventually take the position that we should say that a right to privacy has been violated only after we determine that a legitimate interest in privacy was at stake and is more substantial than competing interests.

Whether I am harmed by unwanted attention may depend not only on whether I have a right not to receive the attention that results in a setback to my interests, but on whether I had a right not to have those interests set back, and on whether the attention was the morally relevant cause of the setback. If I spy on you and learn that you are an adulterer, and I spread the word, and the word gets to your spouse, who leaves you as a result, I might not have harmed you in the sense of harm that Feinberg delineates even if you had a right not to be spied on. Even though you might still be married if I never spied on you, I may not be the morally relevant cause of your wife leaving you; nor do you have a right that she not leave you. As another illustration, take again the case of Mr. Briscoe, who served a prison term for hijacking a truck and who hid this fact from his family and friends. Is he harmed when *Readers Digest* publishes a story that mentions his past crime? Briscoe has a privacy interest in keeping it a secret. Whether society recognizes this interest as a right will depend, according to the framework

---

90　Joel Feinberg, *Harm to Others* (New York: Oxford University Press, 1984), Chapter 1.

I will present, on the result of a balancing test. Depending on how we decide to carry out that test, we might weigh society's interest in having access to information about past crimes in general, or Briscoe's crime in particular, against his privacy interest or those of former criminals in general, and against society's interest in allowing ex-convicts to get a new start (for it will be difficult for them to find jobs and become productive members of society if they wear a permanent badge declaring them to be forever untrustworthy).[91] If we were to agree that Briscoe had a right to privacy that was violated, it still might seem questionable to conclude that *Reader's Digest* was the morally relevant cause of the consequences Briscoe suffered when he was abandoned by his loved ones. While he might have been abandoned only because *Reader's Digest* published his secret, we might say he brought that result on himself by keeping secrets from loved ones who might reasonably expect to know about his past. They might choose to leave him not because of the past that *Reader's Digest* exposed, but because he had lied to them about that past. The point I want to emphasize, however, is that privacy still has value to individuals like Briscoe even if invasions of their privacy are not the morally relevant cause of harm.

There are situations in which intruding upon someone's privacy through surveillance, or giving them unwanted attention by disclosing information about them, clearly exposes them to harm and can reasonably be regarded as culpable. An example of the former wrong would be sifting through someone's garbage to find credit card information which one then uses to commit identity theft and fraud, though in such cases we could appeal to rights against theft and fraud without needing to appeal to a right of privacy to explain the wrong. An example of the latter wrong is presented in *Planned Parenthood v. ACLA*. A coalition distributed posters that identified doctors who performed abortions, and included their photos, addresses, and used language intended to encourage acts of violence against them. The 9th Circuit Court of Appeals refused to protect this speech because it could foreseeably lead to acts of violence.[92] The avoidance of foreseeable harm was the rationale also of the Queen's Bench in *Venables* when it issued an injunction against the world prohibiting the publication of information that could lead to the identity of the individuals who brutally killed James Bulger.[93]

If the only reason privacy was valuable was that by protecting it we avoid harm, one might want to conclude that when no harm results from an invasion of privacy there is no foul. But as we see in the case of Mr. Briscoe, there are circumstances in which there is value in having privacy

---

91   See e.g. Devah Pager, *Marked: Race, Crime, and Finding Work in an Era of Mass Incarceration* (Chicago: University of Chicago Press, 2007).
92   290 F.3d 1058 (2002).
93   [2001] HRLR 19.

though it may be difficult to establish that one was strictly speaking harmed by the unwanted attention. Suppose that someone, without my consent, and acting with the purpose only of humiliating me and not blackmailing or otherwise harming me, took a video of me in an embarrassing situation and uploaded it to YouTube using a pseudonym. Suppose the person who did this set the permissions on YouTube so that the video was accessible to the public, but the person did not describe the video or provide a tag that would identify me as its subject and so it was not readily accessible to someone typing my name in a search engine. If the video received no views by anyone other than the person who uploaded it, have I been harmed in any sense? It may seem unlikely. I had a desire that no one know about my embarrassing situation, and perhaps even an interest in this. Taking the video might have violated an existing legal right if it was secured by a trespass or by violating an anti-eavesdropping statute. But if no one views the video, I appear to suffer no setback to my interests. Even if the person who did this did intend to harm me, that intent does not make harmless activity harmful. But that I am not harmed does not mean there is no value in protecting my privacy in this case.

There is the possibility that someone may eventually watch and draw attention to the video and this possibility might be thought to vindicate the no harm no foul principle: we still may want to prevent such unwanted attention not because we disagree with that principle but because we cannot be sure that there will be no harm in the future. So consider now another example that eliminates this possibility. Suppose a device was invented that detected one and only one thing: the presence of a substance it was illegal to possess. Much like when a trained canine detects whether someone possesses an illicit drug by sniffing them, when the police point the hypothetical device at someone it reacts only if the person has the illegal substance; otherwise it does nothing. It reveals no other information.[94] Unlike with use of a trained canine, people may be unaware they are being searched when police point the device at them, as it works from a distance. A few authorities have argued that use of such a device does not constitute an unreasonable search.[95] Anyone who is not breaking the law experiences no ill effects of having the device pointed at them; and anyone who is breaking the law had no right to do so and can hardly claim they were

---

94   See Arnold Loewy, "The Fourth Amendment as a Device for Protecting the Innocent," *Michigan Law Review* 81:1229–1272 (1983), pp. 1246–1247; Rosen, *Unwanted Gaze*, p. 39 (on the "worm"); and Stanley Benn, "Privacy, Freedom and Respect for Persons," in Pennock and Chapman, eds., *NOMOS XIII* (New York: Atherton Press, 1971), p. 230 (arguing that it is wrong to secretly watch someone though this may cause no actual harm, as it violates a dignity interest). I discuss Benn's argument in Chapter 5.

95   Loewy, pp. 1246–1247; cf. *U.S. v. Jacobsen*, 446 U.S. 109, 123 (1984) (arguing that the interest in privately possessing cocaine is not legitimate); but see Justice Brennan's dissent (446 U.S. 109, 138–139); and Mark Tunick, *Practices and Principles* (Princeton, NJ: Princeton University Press, 1998), p. 190.

harmed by being detected: no harm, no foul. But this argument seems unsatisfying. If the device were used against me, something of value is taken from me, just as something of value is taken from me when video of me in an embarrassing situation is surreptitiously taken and posted online but viewed by nobody. I now turn to some accounts of privacy that might help us articulate just what of value is taken, accounts that suggest it might be wrong to invade someone's privacy even if doing so does not cause harm in the strict sense of being the morally relevant cause of a setback to interests that are regarded as rights. Some of these accounts explain why it may be wrong to violate my privacy through surveillance even if I am unaware that I am being observed.

Trust

On one such account, violating someone's privacy can signal that we do not trust them, or breach an existing relation of confidence, and this can be damaging insofar as trust is essential for society to function smoothly. One thoughtful version of this argument was given by Scott Sundby in a law review article written in 1994. Sundby, who focuses on surveillance rather than disclosure, and on invasion of privacy by government rather than by private actors, argues that "[t]rust that the citizenry will exercise its liberties responsibly … is jeopardized when the government is allowed to intrude into the citizenry's lives without a finding that the citizenry has forfeited society's trust."[96] On his view, the reason we should not allow the government to search through people's garbage without a search warrant based on probable cause is that such searches signal a lack of trust between government and citizens.[97]

Sundby's argument is most convincing in a few specific contexts, such as when the government conducts suspicionless searches. His argument might, for example, provide a powerful criticism of government use of specially trained canines to conduct random drug searches of high school students. As Justice Brennan noted in his dissent in *Doe v. Renfrow*, "Schools cannot expect their students to learn the lessons of good citizenship when the school authorities themselves disregard the fundamental principles underpinning our constitutional freedoms."[98] When governments conduct searches without probable cause, they fail to show trust in citizens and this may lead to a reciprocating lack of respect and trust on the part of citizens.[99] This might occur even if an individual is unaware that they in

---

96 Scott Sundby, "Everyman's 4th Amendment: Privacy as Mutual Trust Between Government and Citizen," *Columbia Law Review* 94:1751–1812 (1994), p. 1777.
97 Sundby, p. 1792.
98 *Doe v. Renfrow*, 451 U.S. 1022, 1028 (1981).
99 Mark Tunick, "Does Privacy Undermine Community," *Journal of Value Inquiry* 35:517–34 (2001), p. 528.

particular have been searched, so long as people are generally aware that there is a policy of conducting such searches.

While Sundby applies the trust argument to government surveillance, the idea that it is wrong to breach trust can help explain why it is wrong for partners in an intimate relationship to publicize private, embarrassing information such as descriptions of their sexual activity. Andrew McClurg has argued that in such situations there is an implied contract of confidentiality. People tacitly agree "not to humiliate or otherwise abuse intimate partners (or ex-partners) by giving widespread publicity" to such information.[100] While one assumes risks in entering into intimate relationships, McClurg believes the assumption of risk is not absolute; there is an implied promise that intimate partners will not cruelly expose the other to the world.[101]

One can easily imagine some questions that might arise if we put this approach into practice. Are Platonic friends who share deep secrets "intimate partners" with an implicit contract of confidentiality? Or people who have a one-night stand? It might be difficult for courts to provide clear and consistent answers, though courts in England have not avoided the challenge. In *Theakston v. MGN*, Mr. Justice Ouseley reasoned that a celebrity could not expect a prostitute he had sex with in a brothel to treat their relationship as confidential in part because such relationships are so transitory.[102] In *Mosley v. News Group Newspapers*, Mr. Justice Eady suggested a principle that might seem at odds with the *Theakston* standard when noting that "*anyone* indulging in sexual activity is entitled to a degree of privacy" as long as it is between "consenting adults (*paid or unpaid*)."[103] Another court appeared to apply a further standard for determining whether a relationship gives rise to an expectation of confidence, distinct from the test of non-transitoriness, in holding that a well-known sports figure could not expect a woman with whom he slept multiple times to keep their extramarital relationship in confidence.[104] Each court based its judgment on a variety of considerations that took into account the unique facts presented to it and so the opinions do not necessarily conflict. But

---

100 Andrew McClurg, "Kiss and Tell: Protecting Intimate Relationship Privacy through Implied Contracts of Confidentiality," *University of Cincinnati Law Review* 74:887–939 (2006), pp. 888–889. Cf. Jacqueline Lipton, "We, the Paparazzi: Developing a Privacy Paradigm for Digital Video," *Iowa Law Review* 95:919–984 (2010), pp. 962–964; Steven Biba, "A Contractual Approach to Data Privacy," *Harvard Journal of Law and Public Policy* 17:591– 611 (1994); and Randall Bezanson, "The Right to Privacy Revisited," *California Law Review* 80:1133–1175 (1990).

101 McClurg, pp. 925–926.

102 [2002] EWHC 137 (QB), Pars. 60–64.

103 [2008] EWHC 1777 (QB), Par. 98, my emphasis. This is not so say the rulings are inconsistent. In *Mosley* privacy was implicated by a clandestine video recording; in *Theakston* it was similarly held that publication of photographs of the claimant in the brothel might be restricted, as opposed to descriptive accounts of his behavior.

104 *A v. B plc* [2002] EWCA Civ 337.

they do indicate the difficulty in determining which relations generate implied promises.

McClurg recognizes that it will be difficult to define precisely who has implied contracts and what they stipulate, but he does not think the task is insurmountable. He suggests that the intimate relationships that give rise to these contracts need not have a sexual but must have an emotional component, so that purely physical relationships do not generate an implied contract.[105] As to what matters are agreed upon to be private, McClurg would appeal to the "general, customary expectations of parties to intimate relationships." For example, a person's "favorite color, music, or brand of soft drink" are not customarily the types of information divulged only in confidence. Revealing your partner's favorite place to dine is therefore no invasion of privacy, but revealing their sexual preferences would be.[106] McClurg suggests that partners who want to leave no doubt as to what information between them must remain private could enter into express confidentiality agreements and even specify damages should one of the partners breach the contract. He concedes that "presenting a partner with a mutual written confidentiality agreement is not likely to be met with enthusiasm as the world's most romantic gesture," but he still thinks such an agreement "might be in the best interest of both parties."[107] Leaving aside the potential issues that would arise if we used the implied contract approach as a legal remedy for privacy invasions, I want to focus on its underlying idea, that invasions of privacy can be wrong because they involve a breach of trust.

In many cases of unwanted attention, the trust argument may be of little or no relevance. It does not explain why it might be wrong for a website to post someone's mugshot online, for *Reader's Digest* to publish a story about Mr. Briscoe, for a newspaper to publish the name of a rape victim, or for a public advocacy group to videotape people entering an abortion clinic. In virtually all of the examples of unwanted attention we have so far considered, the publicizer was a stranger. It is worth noting in this regard that in England the requirement in a breach of confidence action that there be a pre-existing confidential relationship often kept it from providing an effective remedy against invasions of privacy; but England now has other legal bases for protecting privacy.[108]

The trust argument, however, does help account for why it is wrong for someone to share information they were able to acquire only because they are in a relationship that gives them privileged access. One reason it is wrong of you to snoop through a diary of a family member is that in doing

---

105 McClurg, pp. 917–918.
106 McClurg, p. 923.
107 McClurg, p. 934.
108 See *Kaye v. Robertson* [1991] FSR 62 (on the limits of a breach of confidence action); and Wacks, pp. 67–102.

so you betray their trust. There is a difference between a robber stealing your diary and then reading it, and your spouse reading it when you are away. The robber acts badly by trespassing and stealing. The robber may also act badly in reading the diary by violating a societal understanding that diaries are private. But only your spouse acts badly by betraying your trust; only they breach an implied promise or duty of confidentiality.

When either the robber or your spouse disseminate the secrets they discover, they then give you unwanted attention. In doing so, each infringes upon an interest you have that is distinct from the property interest which the robber infringes; and your spouse does more than merely undermine the relationship of trust the two of you had shared. Each may damage your reputation and your relationships with friends or colleagues. Even if no secrets are revealed that could damage your reputation or cause you other injuries, by publicizing information you did not want to share they diminish your ability to control how you present yourself to others. In cases in which you have naked photos or video of your lover and after an unamicable breakup you publish them on a "revenge-porn" website, not only might you have violated an implied promise of confidentiality, but you have affronted someone's dignity and possibly injured their reputation.

There are different accounts of why society should protect expectations of privacy that arise from relations of trust. A utilitarian might argue that social utility is increased when people can rely upon confidants or implied promises.[109] Norms or laws that assure people that the information they reveal only to those they trust will not be exposed to third parties will encourage people to take advantage of trusting relationships, which presumably will benefit everyone in society. There are also non-utilitarian reasons for not violating someone's trust and keeping one's promise not to divulge information. A Kantian would argue that breaking a promise fails to show someone respect and that is wrong in itself regardless of the effect breaking a promise has on social utility. The Kantian, whose views I shall return to in Chapter 5, holds that we owe respect to all human beings and should treat human beings as ends in themselves and not use them as means to promote our own good.[110]

Dignity and respect for persons

The Kantian argument that we must respect the privacy of someone who has confided in us because of an imperative to respect people as human beings by treating them as ends in themselves points to a reason to respect the privacy of anyone and not just those with whom we are in a special relationship of trust. Stanley Benn in particular has defended privacy by appealing to the "general principle of respect for persons." He chooses this

109 See Chapter 5, "The Utilitarian Approach."
110 See Tunick, *Practices and Principles*, ch. 2.

principle over the principle of utility because he thinks it alone correctly sustains an objection to "secret watching, which may do no actual harm at all."[111] Jonathan Wolff, also drawing on the idea of respect, has argued that every human being can reasonably expect some privacy against prying eyes insofar as seeking out certain information about someone may imply that they are not trusted or respected as a human being. He argues that asking a stranger to justify themselves can be insulting and undignified, and that if you do not trust someone in areas in which you would hope to be trusted yourself, you do not respect them as an equal.[112] In this section I consider the argument that violating someone's privacy fails to show them respect and in some cases affronts their dignity. But it is important to recognize that while respect is due to all human beings, expectations of privacy can be greater in information shared by people in special relationships of confidence or trust.

Some intrusions upon privacy are deeply invasive and an obvious affront to one's dignity. Consider body cavity searches. After inmates in jail or prison are visited by friends or family, men are sometimes required to lift their genitals and bend over to spread their buttocks for visual inspection to ensure that nothing is being smuggled in; female inmates may have their vaginal and anal cavities visually inspected. Sometimes this has been done in the presence of other inmates.[113] The U.S. Supreme Court upheld such searches in *Bell v. Wolfish*, but Justice Marshall dissented, characterizing body cavity searches as "one of the most grievous offenses against personal dignity and common decency" and as "so unnecessarily degrading that it 'shocks the conscience.'"[114] None of the reasons for valuing privacy that we already considered quite captures why these searches should give us pause. The searches are particularly troubling but not merely because they violate one's trust, and not because they undermine one's property rights, or make it difficult for one to maintain intimate relations. The demand that we respect someone's personhood is sometimes associated with the idea of decisional privacy that is central in *Roe v. Wade*.[115] But while body cavity searches or urine testing may limit one's ability to conceal criminal activity and in that sense restrict the liberty people have to make decisions about how to live their lives, that is not why they are so intrusive. In some

111 Benn, pp. 228–230.
112 Wolff then reaches the more controversial conclusion that we must stop asking humiliating questions of and collecting data on welfare recipients as to why they are unemployed, even if this means some people receive a subsidy unfairly: "this can be a price worth paying: sometimes unfairness is to be tolerated if fairness conflicts with respect"—in Wolff, "Fairness, Respect, and the Egalitarian Ethos," *Philosophy and Public Affairs* 27(2):97–122 (1998), pp. 108–109, 117.
113 *Bell v. Wolfish*, 441 U.S. 520 (1979).
114 441 U.S. 520, 576–578.
115 Solove, "Conceptualizing Privacy," pp. 1116–1117; cf. the section "Defining Privacy," above.

circumstances, a body cavity search may well be reasonable; but if so, this would be because the need for information is so compelling that it outweighs the substantial interest in being treated with dignity and having one's personhood respected.

One well-known defense of the argument that privacy is a means to preserve human dignity was given by Edward Bloustein. Bloustein argues that there is a distinct interest in privacy that is not a reputation interest or an interest in avoiding harm and is not reducible to a monetary value: "A woman's legal right to bear children without unwanted onlookers does not turn on the desire to protect her emotional equanimity, but rather on a desire to enhance her individuality and human dignity."[116] He argues that when one suffers a certain kind of exposure or surveillance, one is no longer respected as a human being. "A man whose home may be entered at the will of another, whose conversation may be overheard at the will of another ... is less of a man, has less human dignity on that account."[117] A person whose every thought and desire is subject to public scrutiny "has been deprived of his individuality and human dignity" and is "not an individual."[118]

One challenge presented by the argument is that it requires us to identify when an intrusion upon privacy amounts to an indignity. Bloustein, as have other philosophers, characterizes an indignity as a failure to show a person respect.[119] But I might be said to fail to respect someone whenever I violate their moral or legal rights, be it by lying to them, stealing their property, violating their privacy, or breaking a promise. Surely not every violation of a right involves an indignity. Murders are the most egregious rights violations, yet there are ways to commit murder that do and that do not affront the victim's dignity. Some of the particular invasions Bloustein identifies as affronts to a person's dignity—such as viewing a woman giving birth, and entering another's home as one pleases—may not be indignities in all times and places. In recent decades, live childbirths have been publicly broadcast, suggesting that observing this event is less taboo than it once was;[120] and in some cultures one commonly enters a neighbor's home

---

116 Edward Bloustein, "Privacy as an Aspect of Human Dignity," in Schoeman, ed.:156–202, p. 164.
117 Bloustein, p. 165. Flaherty, drawing on a remark by John Adams, also characterizes an intrusion into one's home as an indignity, in *Privacy in Colonial New England*, p. 88.
118 Bloustein, p. 188.
119 See Thomas Hill, *Dignity and Practical Reason in Kant's Moral Theory* (Ithaca: Cornell University Press, 1992); and Denise Réaume, "Indignities: Making a Place for Dignity in Modern Legal Thought," *Queen's Law Journal* 28:61–94 (2002), p. 79.
120 See, e.g., Robert Altman's film *Dr. T and the Women* (2000); http://blip.tv/live-birth-birth-live (accessed January 14, 2013); and *Daily Mail Online* (September 23, 2013), www.dailymail.co.uk/news/article-2429968/Today-Shows-Born-Today-series-air-live-births-week.html (on NBC broadcasts of live births on its morning show).

without knocking.[121] There are historical and cultural variations in what people in a given society regard as invasions of privacy, or as an affront to dignity, or as behavior that fails to show respect for someone's personhood, and within a culturally diverse society individuals may have differing views as well.[122]

That may not be an intractable problem. But there is a more serious challenge in adopting the dignity argument: it is hard to know its force in cases in which an interest in privacy conflicts with other values. Its advocates do not seem to want to assign dignity a measurable value. Their point is that privacy has such great importance, in that without it we are no longer human beings, that it should not be put on a scale of costs and benefits. But that position is unhelpful if we think, as I do, that privacy needs to be weighed against competing values. A body cavity search of a terrorist is an indignity but may be justified if it produces evidence that could save many lives. Even Bloustein recognizes that we must "submit to some minimum scrutiny of our neighbors as a very condition of life in a civilized community." His concern is that a person who is "compelled to live every minute" of his life among others and is constantly under public scrutiny "is deprived of his individuality."[123] But the dignity theorists say little about how to determine *which* privacy protections are needed to preserve our personhood. Jeffrey Reiman argues that the point of social practices that provide privacy is to grant "an individual's moral title to his existence": to be a person, I must be recognized as having an exclusive moral right to shape my destiny.[124] Reiman recognizes that to shape my own destiny it is essential only that I can control "whether and by whom my body is experienced, *in some significant places.*"[125] But that demand may well be satisfied even in a society that permits body cavity searches or the sharing of images through social media as long as I can sometimes retreat into my home and draw the curtains and password-protect my computer.[126]

While it may be difficult to know what weight to give the dignity argument, it does effectively characterize what is wrong with specific sorts of intrusions. Body cavity searches, urine testing, or showing an image of a person naked or engaged in sex without their consent are indignities at least in societies in which it is shameful to be naked or to have conventionally hidden bodily functions exposed. I think we can say more generally that it is an affront to dignity publicly to expose vulnerable

---

121 Tunick, *Practices and Principles*, p. 170 (referring to practices of colonial New Englanders and the Javanese).

122 See Tunick, *Practices and Principles*, ch. 5.

123 Bloustein, pp. 188–189.

124 Reiman, "Privacy, Intimacy, and Personhood," in Schoeman, ed., p. 312.

125 Reiman, "Privacy, Intimacy, and Personhood," p. 314, my emphasis.

126 Cf. Volokh, p. 1111: "Claims about what would happen if privacy were totally destroyed tell us nothing about which particular privacy rules … are indispensable."

people against their will in ways that are likely to produce strong feelings of shame or humiliation.[127] Recall the reality television show "To Catch a Predator," discussed in Chapter 1. Hidden cameras film Chris Hansen, a reporter for NBC, unexpectedly emerging out of a backroom to publicly humiliate the adult males who showed up at a house to meet someone who they were told is underage. Hansen asks his squirming target a barrage of questions: "What are you doing here?" "How old is she?" "How old are you?" "Why did you bring condoms and lotion?" Catching them when they are in a state of shock and most vulnerable, Hansen gets many of these men to reveal their deepest inner thoughts, often before they are aware they are talking to a journalist and being filmed. This intrusion does not merely tarnish their reputation prior to their having an opportunity to defend themselves in a court of law; it imposes the indignity of being publicly shamed. That they suffer an indignity is apparent from the sting targets' reactions to Hansen's revelation that they are on national television. One man was put into diabetic shock; another had an asthma attack; still another man collapsed. One man said he wanted to kill himself and poked himself with a pen in a half-hearted attempt. Texas prosecutor Louis Conradt did kill himself.[128] While the sting targets are not sympathetic figures, when their depravities are exposed on national television they suffer an indignity.

When someone is unwillingly exposed they might be injured in their relations with others, or suffer economic setbacks or other reputational injuries. But the argument based on dignity and respect for persons points to a distinct interest. Warren and Brandeis, in their famous paper on privacy, argued that exposure may effect one's reputation but that there is also the effect upon one's "estimate of himself and upon his own feelings," which they refer to as a "spiritual" rather than a "material" interest.[129] They characterize this as an interest in avoiding an "injury of feelings" or violation of one's "honor," and as a right of "inviolate personality."[130] A few examples are helpful in understanding this distinction between material and spiritual interests. Suppose someone is horribly disfigured and goes around with a protective mask to avoid being looked at;[131] or consider a Muslim woman who always wears a veil in public. Being unwillingly exposed to the gaze of others would injure them, and while I am not sure that referring to what is at stake here as a spiritual interest clarifies precisely what is at stake, I think it is clear that what is at stake is not primarily an interest in property or even in reputation. One might argue that in the former

---

127 Solove, "A Taxonomy of Privacy," pp. 536–538.
128 Tunick, "Reality TV and the Entrapment of Predators," pp. 289, 293.
129 Warren and Brandeis, p. 78.
130 Warren and Brandeis, pp. 78, 82.
131 See Thomson, p. 304 (giving examples of a man whose face had been badly disfigured in a fire, or who woke up and discovered he had grown fangs or no longer had a nose).

example the injury is indeed reputational in that one wants to hide defects. Perhaps as a result of evolutionary pressures people are resistant to having flaws exposed that might inhibit their reproductive success.[132] But the person who, like "Elephant Man," goes about with a mask has already resigned himself to reputational injuries; and the Muslim woman who does not want her face exposed is not concerned with exposing defects that would hamper her success in the marriage market.[133] Even if the Muslim woman wears the veil to avoid being accused of being a loose woman, to remove her veil would not hurt her reputation in the way that her not wearing a veil in the first place would. Unmasking and exposing such individuals may well damage their reputation but it also violates them. If we see this difference and recognize its significance, we have felt the force of the dignity argument.

How we assess the weight of the dignity argument when other values besides privacy are at stake is something I will address in Chapter 5.

Privacy, toleration, and community

The reasons so far explored for why privacy should be valued focus on the value that privacy has to individuals: to their reputation, autonomy, well-being, property interests, relations of trust, and dignity. But privacy is not just an "individualistic" value.[134] It has value for communities as well, a point that is sometimes ignored on the mistaken premise that privacy, in protecting criminals and deviants, can only harm a community.[135]

Communities with democratic forms of government have good reason to ensure that people can keep secret the fact that they belong to various organizations; without this assurance of privacy people may be reluctant to associate with others in ways that are essential to the functioning of democracy.[136] Privacy can promote community in other ways as well. People may

132 I thank Celine Rodriguez for this suggestion. The evolutionary psychology explanation would not necessarily diminish the ethical force of the dignity argument or the weight the utilitarian would give to the privacy preference not to be looked at.
133 For a related case, see *Freeman v. Department of Highway Safety and Motor Vehicles*, 924 So.2d 48 (Fla.5th DCA 2006), in which a state court ruled that a Muslim woman seeking a driver's license could be required to remove her veil so that an image of her face could appear on the license; and for further discussion see Allen, *Unpopular Privacy*, ch. 3.
134 Priscilla Regan, *Legislating Privacy* (Chapel Hill: University of North Carolina Press, 1995).
135 "The Responsive Communitarian Platform: Rights and Responsibilities," in Amitai Etzioni, ed., *Rights and the Common Good: The Communitarian Perspective* (New York: St. Martin's Press, 1995). For a more detailed discussion of the connection between privacy and community, see Tunick, "Does Privacy Undermine Community?," *Journal of Value Inquiry* 35:517–34 (2001).
136 Solove, "A Taxonomy of Privacy," p. 532; on the value privacy has for democracy, see Annabelle Lever, *On Privacy*, ch. 1; and "Mill and the Secret Ballot," *Utilitas* 19(3):354–378 (2007).

be more amenable to the positive interactions with others that help forge a strong sense of community if they have a private realm to which they can retreat.[137] More abstractly, we might say that fruitful interaction among members of a community requires their mutual recognition and respect, and privacy can play an essential role in developing the capacity to recognize and respect others as equals.[138]

Privacy is important in maintaining the stability of large, pluralistic, culturally diverse societies. One distinguishing feature of a liberal society is its toleration of people with lifestyles, cultural practices, and religions that diverge from those of the majority. Michael Walzer has argued that by permitting people to keep certain parts of their lives private, the state can more readily tolerate minorities.[139] Without privacy, behavior that the majority might find objectionable would be in public view, creating tensions that could undermine the stability of the society and test its commitment to toleration. It is easier for a society with a fundamentalist Christian majority to tolerate homosexuals if people can engage in intimate behavior in private; it is easier for a society with a majority of Muslims to tolerate the use of alcohol or pornography if these can be distributed and consumed in private.

While privacy can promote community, it is also an important protection for individuals particularly within small, relatively homogeneous communities. Some small towns of colonial New England had just a few hundred people, with very little change in the population from year to year, so that anonymity was impossible. As Flaherty writes, "anyone who stood out would be subject to attention."[140] This is especially so in societies in which face-to-face interaction was the primary means of finding out what is going on in one's world. People living in isolation might be the object of suspicion or scorn. Privacy might have its most meaningful role in such contexts, by allowing people to challenge social conventions and moral norms at least in their own lives, protected from the glare of others and therefore from what could be the oppressive social pressure to conform to a prevailing lifestyle that might be far from ideal.

Summary

Privacy need not be regarded purely as a subjective preference which can be defended only by asserting "that is just my taste." There are objective

---

137 Wilson and Baldassare, "Overall 'Sense of Community' in a Suburban Region," *Environment and Behavior* 28(1):27–43 (1996), p. 38; cited in Tunick, "Does Privacy Undermine Community?," p. 526.

138 Tunick, "Does Privacy Undermine Community?," pp. 528–9; drawing on Hegel, *Elements of the Philosophy of Right* , tr. Allen Wood (Cambridge: Cambridge University Press, 1991).

139 Michael Walzer, *On Toleration* (New Haven: Yale University Press, 1997), pp. 26, 77–78.

140 Flaherty, *Privacy in Colonial New England*, p. 110.

reasons for wanting privacy, though I have argued that the available empirical evidence purporting to show that privacy is necessary for human societies to survive and flourish is not particularly compelling. Failing to respect one's privacy can damage one's reputation; result in the loss of property rights; subject one to unjust punishment, or blackmail; signal a lack of respect or impose an indignity; damage relations of trust or intimacy; compromise one's ability to control how they present themselves to the world or reinvent themselves and forge new ties; discourage nonconformity; and undermine community. These are non-arbitrary reasons for protecting privacy as distinct from the subjective reason that my privacy should be respected simply because that is my preference or taste.

3 Legitimate privacy interests

There are compelling reasons to value privacy; in Chapter 4 we will review some of the compelling reasons to value free speech. But before we weigh these competing values we first need to establish that privacy truly is at stake. One may desire privacy but that desire may be misplaced.

Welsh soccer star Ryan Giggs did not want his identity revealed as the unnamed footballer having a six-month adulterous fling with a reality TV star, as reported in a *Sun* newspaper article, and sought an injunction to keep the press from revealing his name or publishing photos in connection with the affair, appealing to the European Convention on Human Rights (ECHR) Article 8 right to respect for one's private life. Mr. Justice Eady, who at the time was under the apparently mistaken impression that Giggs was being blackmailed by the woman, issued a controversial injunction after applying what he calls the "new methodology." The new methodology is a two-stage process that begins by asking whether Giggs could reasonably expect privacy in this information. Even though word had quickly spread through Twitter that Giggs was the subject of the article, Eady's answer was yes, as the information concerned "conduct of an intimate and sexual nature"; and though word was already out, there can still remain "a reasonable expectation of *some* privacy." The next stage in the process is to weigh the claimant's Article 8 right to respect for private life against the ECHR's Article 10 right that the newspaper and the public have freely to express or receive information serving the public interest, and Mr. Justice Eady had no reason to think that publication would serve the public interest.[1] While one might challenge Mr. Justice Eady's answer to the question of whether Giggs could reasonably expect privacy, the method of beginning the analysis by posing that question is sound: if a relationship between a star athlete and a television celebrity is not one that the athlete could legitimately expect to keep private then no private fact is at stake and there would be no need to balance privacy and free speech interests.[2]

1   *CTB v. News Group Newspapers Ltd* [2011] EWHC 1323 (QB), Pars. 23–26.
2   Cf. *Campbell v. MGN Ltd* [2004] UKHL 22: the question of whether privacy is implicated is a threshold issue that is addressed before turning to the balancing test (Lord Nicholls, dissenting, at Par. 21; and Baroness Hale, at Par. 137).

DOI: 10.4324/9781315763132-3

A similar methodology can be employed when approaching the cases of unwanted attention introduced in Chapter 1. Before we can say that the person who took the photo of the inconsiderate pet owner on a Korean subway and shared it on social media sites, or Tyler Clementi's roommate, Dateline NBC, or Fox Sports Network have acted badly, we must establish not just that privacy is valuable but that there was an invasion of privacy in the first place. If, for example, the portly man attending a major league baseball game cannot reasonably expect privacy in the fact that he is eating a salad in a stadium with thousands of people present, we might want to say that Fox Sports Network did nothing wrong in airing his image.

What information or experiences can we have a legitimate privacy interest in or reasonably expect to keep private? Surely, we might think, not what is in plain view or earshot, or what we voluntarily convey to others. But as will become apparent in this chapter, the answer to this question is not so straightforward, for there are ways in which one can expect privacy in public places even though one is in plain view; and we might have a legitimate privacy interest that certain information that we voluntarily convey to others not be further disseminated.

Terminology: Legitimate privacy interests and reasonable expectations of privacy

Before addressing this question, I want to point to a subtle difference between the concepts of a legitimate privacy interest and a reasonable expectation of privacy (REOP). The latter concept is central in Fourth Amendment jurisprudence.[3] The Fourth Amendment to the U.S. Constitution holds that "[t]he right of the people to be secure in their persons, houses, papers, and effects, against unreasonable searches and seizures, shall not be violated, and no Warrants shall issue, but upon probable cause …" The Amendment prohibits not all searches, only unreasonable ones, and the Supreme Court determines whether a search is unreasonable by determining if it violates a reasonable expectation of privacy. A search is unreasonable not merely if the person affected by a search had an expectation of privacy; that expectation must be one society regards as objectively reasonable.[4] For example, if police officers enter a public restroom and see a drug transaction take place in front of their eyes, they have not conducted an unreasonable search. Those involved probably had no expectation that they would not be observed. But even if they did,

3   But not always; in a recent Fourth Amendment privacy case, the U.S. Supreme Court held that when police, without a warrant, attach a GPS device to a car to track its movements, they violate the Fourth Amendment not because they violate a reasonable expectation of privacy but because attaching the GPS device amounts to a trespass. See *U.S. v. Jones*, 132 S.Ct. 945 (2012).
4   *Katz v. U.S.*, 389 U.S. 347, 361 (1967).

a judge would respond that they were in a public place in plain view and should have known that anyone could legitimately enter the facility and see them—their subjective expectation of privacy was objectively unreasonable.[5] If they wanted privacy, they could have gone into a windowless toilet stall, closed the door, and made sure that no one outside could peer in.

In Fourth Amendment jurisprudence, having a reasonable expectation of privacy implies one has a right to privacy against government searches unless there is a special government need that would justify an exception. The distinction I want to draw is this: in asking whether one can legitimately expect privacy one is not reaching the question of whether a legitimate privacy interest is so weighty as to be regarded as a right, whereas courts deciding whether one has a reasonable expectation of privacy sometimes blur these distinct questions. To say one has a legitimate privacy interest is to say privacy is implicated but it is not yet to say one has a reasonable expectation of privacy; one does if the interest is weighty enough. One can have a legitimate interest in privacy even if, taking all things into account including society's interests in free speech or in fighting crime, one should not be able reasonably to expect privacy.

That an expectation of privacy is reasonable against a police search need not mean it is reasonable against a snooping private citizen. It may be that we should want to hold the police to higher standards than we hold non-state actors as a means to check their awesome power, so that while a private citizen might get away with sifting through my garbage or putting a GPS device on my car to track my movements, police could not do this without a search warrant. Or we might take a very different view, and allow police more leeway to engage in surveillance than we would give to citizen-snoops so as not to hamper them in their pursuit of criminals. Or we might think that the police should be held to exactly the same standards we apply to the average citizen. I shall not take sides in that debate.[6] But according to the distinction I am drawing, whether one's interest in privacy in certain information is legitimate does not necessarily depend on whether uncovering that information would be helpful in fighting crime or achieving some other valuable social end. In any given situation informational privacy either is or is not at stake or implicated; if it is at stake, then we can say one has a legitimate interest in keeping information private. But if, given the circumstances, there are compelling reasons for exposing the information, it might be unreasonable to expect privacy even though one's privacy is implicated. In some cases, a legitimate interest in privacy is outweighed by other competing interests.

---

5   Cf. Mark Tunick, "Privacy in the Face of New Technologies of Surveillance," *Public Affairs Quarterly* 14:259–277 (2000).
6   It has been said that the paradigm case where the European Convention on Human Rights Article 8 right to respect for private life applies is "where the putative violation is by the State itself"—see *Wood v. Commissioner of Police for the Metropolis* [2010] 1 WLR 123, Par. 28.

The plain view principle, modified

All individuals living in a well-ordered society should expect that some information about themselves will be revealed to others. When we walk down the street talking to a friend it would be unreasonable to expect others to avert their eyes or cover their ears. If we do not want them to see us together we should wear good disguises; if we do not want them to hear us we should make sure we are out of earshot. But we should not have to retreat to a windowless and soundproof room whenever we want privacy. Society has norms of permissible and impermissible methods of gathering information, and we should have to protect what we do not want exposed only against permissible or legitimate methods of exposure.[7]

It is usually thought to be permissible to observe what is in plain view or what is knowingly exposed and so courts in the U.S. have held that police do not need a warrant to peer into an uncurtained window from a public sidewalk. Nor do they need a search warrant in order to overhear a conversation of someone who is talking at a non-enclosed public phone; or to point a video camera at a front yard to reveal what is in plain view (though in this case the use of video to permanently record events may make a difference ethically).[8] However, if one is in a location traditionally accorded privacy, such as the home, or an enclosed stall in a public restroom, one typically has a right against a warrantless search.[9]

Courts in the United States have arrived at these conclusions by adopting what they call the "plain view" principle. However, they have not provided a satisfying account of what constitutes a plain view. In several cases courts have held that so long as it is possible for information to be exposed by an observer who is not trespassing or otherwise violating any laws, the information is in plain view. For example, the Supreme Court held that a person could not reasonably expect privacy in the fact that he grew marijuana in the backyard of his California home even though he had an inner and outer fence that kept the marijuana from being seen by passersby or neighbors, because the marijuana could be seen by someone who flies overhead in a plane at 1,000 feet or who stands on top of a double-decker bus that is passing by. The marijuana was said to be in plain view even though it is rare for planes to fly so low over a residential area, and though double-decker buses in California were virtually unheard of, because it is legal to assume that vantage point.[10] In another case, *California v.*

---

7   Tunick, "Privacy in the Face of New Technologies."
8   *Katz v. U.S.*, 389 U.S. 347 (1967); *State v. Constantino*, 603 A.2d 173 (1991) (non-enclosed public phone); *State v. Holden*, 964 P.2d 318 (1998) (camera pointed at a front yard).
9   *Kyllo v. U.S.*, 533 U.S. 27 (2001) (homes receive special protection); *Bielicki v. Superior Ct of L.A.*, 371 P.2d 288 (1962) (invalidates a search where an officer looks through a ceiling pipe into a private toilet stall in a public restroom); cf. *People v. Heydenbeck*, 430 N.W.2d 760 (1988) (allowing use of a camera at the entrance of a public restroom).
10   *California v. Ciraolo*, 476 U.S. 207 (1986).

Greenwood, the Court diverged from the rule that to be in plain view information must be observable through permissible means of inquiry. The majority held that because the trash I leave out on the curb for pickup could be rifled through by "snoops," leaving the contents exposed to any passerby, I cannot reasonably expect privacy in my garbage and the police may therefore search it without a warrant.[11] Given that the Court also relied on the possibility that animals or children might expose the contents of one's garbage, the Court's appeal to what snoops might do as a standard for permissible means of exposure might charitably be understood as an unintended lapse in its adherence to the plain view principle.

Another court held that I cannot reasonably expect privacy in what I do inside a building if I am visible through an uncurtained window to someone outside who uses a ladder to get a vantage point enabling them to peer inside.[12] According to the logic of the plain view principle, since window cleaners, painters, and other maintenance workers might legitimately use a ladder outside my apartment that enables them to see inside, if I want privacy inside my home, I must take appropriate precautions, such as closing the blinds. Whether I should forfeit privacy because of those unlikely situations is something I shall shortly address. But it is important to note that presumably, on this view, use of a ladder to peer into the second-floor window of a private home is not legitimate insofar as a homeowner could exclude anyone from using a ladder on their property—something apartment tenants cannot do. So homeowners, but not tenants, would have a legitimate privacy interest in what they do in a room on the second floor, assuming that what they do cannot be seen by anyone using legitimate means of observation. In this circumstance, what they do in their homes is not in plain view.

Let us return to the case where a second-floor apartment dweller is observed by someone atop a ladder. Assume that my apartment is situated so that it would not be possible for someone without a ladder to peer through my windows even using a telescope from a distance. It seems troubling to conclude that because it is legitimate for a window cleaner or painter to be there, I can never legitimately expect privacy unless I curtain the windows. Usually on the rare occasions where work is done on the exterior of my unit I would have notice, and could adjust my expectations of privacy accordingly. One might argue that I should not have to adjust them, because it would be wrong of workers to divert attention from their job in order to get a good look inside. But since privacy can be lost by an accidental passing glance, if I really care about privacy, it would behoove me to adjust my expectations in such cases. However, I should not have to adjust my privacy expectations all the time merely because for a few hours

11   486 U.S. 35, 40 (1988).
12   *Commonwealth v. Hernley,* 263 A.2d 904 (1970).

every several years someone might legitimately have access to a vantage point from which they could observe me inside my home. To reach this conclusion we need to modify the plain view principle.

On the plain view principle as it is presently understood by courts, I have no legitimate privacy interest in information that is observable by one or more people from a vantage point it is permissible to be at, unless the only people who could ever be at that vantage point are ones I could trust to keep the information private. So long as it is possible for information to be exposed by an observer using legitimate means of observation, the information is in plain view. Instead, we should understand the plain view principle to hold that information is in plain view only if it is *readily accessible* using legitimate means of observation.[13] One can have a legitimate privacy interest not only in information that can be exposed only by illegal or other illegitimate means but also in information that can be exposed through legitimate means of observation but only in highly improbable circumstances, so that the information is not readily accessible. Such information can legitimately be observed but is not in plain view.

One compelling reason to modify the traditional formulation of the plain view principle in this way is that unless we do so, police or unsavory snoops might be permitted to engage in highly intrusive surveillance to uncover information so long as that information could possibly be uncovered using legitimate means of observation, even though that information would almost certainly not be exposed without use of intrusive surveillance techniques. Suppose, for example, that I want to keep private the route that I drove from point A to point B a hundred miles away at a particular day and time. My reasons do not matter in deciding whether I have a legitimate privacy interest, though they might if we need to weigh my interest against competing interests in deciding whether my expectation of privacy is reasonable. Since I am travelling on public roads and people in nearby cars could observe me, I take special precautions to ensure I am not being followed. I am very good at this and so if the police did try to follow me they would fail. Still, despite all my precautions, it is conceivable that my movements could be detected by legitimate means. While I do not think it is legitimate to follow me for a hundred miles without my consent, it is not impossible that five or six different people who know me and are at various points between A and B see me drive by, recall the time and place, and convene and put the pieces together to learn my route. If I were a person of great interest to the police and they were trying to follow me, they could

---

13 In an earlier article I defended a somewhat different principle, what I called the "mischance principle": where information is intentionally exposed to reveal what could not be accidentally discovered by a non-snoop (someone not intending to uncover information) using legitimate and normal means of observation, there is a reasonable expectation of privacy against such exposure; otherwise there is not. See Tunick, "Privacy in the Face of New Technologies."

not hope to use this method as they would not know where to plant various officers since they would not know where I was headed: my movements could be traced this way only with incredible luck. If we used the traditional formulation of the plain view principle, that slimmest possibility means I am in "plain view" and cannot reasonably expect privacy; that in turn means the police need no search warrant to use some other system of surveillance that is sure to work, perhaps one that employs a satellite tracking system or GPS device. But with the modified version of the plain view principle, I retain a legitimate privacy interest in my movements as they are not "readily accessible." Consequently police would need a warrant to use a tracking system unless my privacy interest was outweighed by more compelling interests. According to this argument, *U.S. v. Knotts*, discussed in Chapter 1, was wrongly decided.[14] The fact that someone could conceivably uncover information about me using legitimate means of observation should not in itself entitle them to use illegitimate means on the premise that I can no longer expect privacy.

Which means of observation are legitimate?—the Careful and Carefree societies

The modified plain view principle holds that we cannot have legitimate privacy interests, or reasonably expect privacy, in information that can be readily observed by someone using legitimate means of observation who could not be expected to keep that information to themselves. Whether something is readily observable by legitimate means will depend on numerous factors including accepted social practices of observation, architecture, technologies of surveillance, the level of trust within a society, the amount of freedom accorded its citizens by the laws, and attitudes toward sexuality and the body. In a society in which doors are not locked and one does not knock before entering a neighbor's home, one may not have a legitimate privacy interest in all the activities that take place in one's home.[15] In many societies when one enters a toilet stall in a public restroom, closes the door behind and latches it, one has a legitimate interest in privacy. The architecture of restrooms makes it difficult to observe someone in a stall, and social understandings of what it means to close a door and the private nature of evacuation dictate that in these societies it is not legitimate to stare fixedly through the space under the stall door, or peek through a hole in

---

14   460 U.S. 276 (1983). See also Tunick, "Privacy in Public Places," *Social Theory and Practice* 35(4):597–622 (2009) (arguing that police use of GPS devices without a warrant to follow someone's movements over time violates a reasonable expectation of privacy).

15   See Tunick, *Practices and Principles* (Princeton, NJ: Princeton University Press, 1998), ch. 5.

the partition or ceiling.[16] To do so might be regarded as outrageous.[17] One can imagine other societies with different architecture and different attitudes toward evacuation in which this was not the case. For example, in the "Dinner Scene" in Luis Buñuel's film *The Phantom of Liberty* (1974), people perform excretory functions together around what we would regard as a "dinner table" in a common living area and regard eating as a deeply private activity done in a special room that provides seclusion.

But the reasonableness of expectations of privacy cannot wholly depend on prevailing practices and existing understandings. While social practices are important sources for determining which methods of observation are legitimate, it is important that we be able to criticize practices that undermine important values, even if those practices have become widely shared. People living in Nazi Germany could expect little privacy in their homes given widespread surveillance practices;[18] but that those practices were widespread does not mean they were legitimate.[19] While the prevalence of a practice or technology of observation is an important indicator of its legitimacy, not all practices or uses of popular technology are acceptable. If they were, people would forfeit privacy in the face of rapid development of advanced surveillance technologies that take hold before society and the legal system are able to formulate and enforce norms against their widespread use.[20]

Imagine a society in which people never shaded their windows because they enjoyed the breathtaking scenery, but even so, one could not clearly

<hr/>

16 See *Ward v. State*, 646 So.2d 68 (1994); *Britt v. Superior Court of Santa Clara County*, 374 P.2d 817 (1962); *Bielicki v. Superior Court of L.A. County*, 371 P.2d 288 (1962); *Brown v. State*, 238 A.2d 147 (1968); *State v. Bryant*, 177 N.W.2d 800 (1970). But for a contrary view see *Smayda v. U.S.*, 352 F.2d 251 (1965) (finding no unreasonable search when a park ranger looked through a ceiling hole into a public restroom stall); and *U.S. v. Billings*, 858 F.2d 617 (1988) (finding no unreasonable search when a police officer looked through the gap between the floor and bottom of the stall door).

17 See Carl D. Schneider, *Shame, Exposure and Privacy* (New York: W.W. Norton, 1992), p. 72: "If one wants to find assured privacy in our culture, one flees to the bathroom ... [I]t symbolizes utmost privacy. Intrusion into the bathroom symbolizes violation of the private sphere of the person." See also Robert C. Power, "Technology and the Fourth Amendment," *Journal of Criminal Law* 1:1–113 (1989), p. 89: "our society demands privacy for evacuation and nudity."

18 Bernt Engelmann, *In Hitler's Germany* (New York: Schocken Books, 1986).

19 Tunick, *Practices and Principles*, p. 155.

20 Anthony Amsterdam, "Perspectives on the Fourth Amendment," *Minnesota Law Review* 58:349–477 (1974), p. 384; *State v. Young*, 867 P.2d 593, 597 (1994). Cf. Warren and Brandeis, "The Right to Privacy," in Schoeman, ed., *Philosophical Dimensions of Privacy* (New York: Cambridge University Press, 1984), p. 85: advances in photography that allow surreptitious pictures to be taken mean there is a greater need to protect privacy; and *U.S. v. Kim*, 415 F.Supp. 1252, 1256 (1976) (rejecting the argument that increased use of telescopes by private citizens means government can use high-powered telescopes without a warrant).

see into a neighbor's home with the naked eye without being invited or trespassing onto their property because homes are sufficiently distant from each other and from public pathways and roads. Suppose also that people in this society commonly used pocket telescopes to observe passing ships or monitor their neighbors' crops.[21] Now suppose, hypothetically, that people came to widely use these devices to peer into their neighbors' windows. Knowing that others did this, more people started doing it them- selves, and over time this became an accepted practice, a practice that came to be known as "homeviewing." Most people who become aware that they are being observed in their home by their neighbor do not react with outrage, and no law suits are filed any more for invasion of privacy as the courts had early on rejected such suits on the ground that one could not reasonably expect privacy against being observed by one's neighbor given the prevalence of homeviewing and given that if one wanted privacy one could simply curtain the windows. Pocket telescopes, after all, could not penetrate walls, shades, or blinds.

Now imagine two possible trajectories for this society. In the first, it becomes what I call the "Carefree Society." The vast majority of people stop caring about privacy in their homes. They no longer bother to reorder their lives to avoid certain activities in their homes, or curtain their windows. In fact they came to enjoy displaying themselves to their neighbors or for that matter to anyone. At one point, there were television shows devoted to showing people doing amusing things in their home as seen from a distance as if through a neighbor's pocket telescope, but after a while ratings dropped as the novelty of these shows wore off. Some unsavory individuals started using high-powered lenses to discern information such as credit card or bank account numbers from papers that people left lying on tables near windows in their homes; but the response was additional checks on identity theft rather than a call to discourage or ban homeview- ing. Eventually people who did curtain their homes were ridiculed, to the point where drapes and blinds are now virtually unknown.

The second trajectory differs in subtle and not so subtle ways. It is still the case that few people express outrage when they learn that their neigh- bors peer into their homes; many people even join in, using their own pocket telescopes to peek at their neighbors. But unlike in Carefree Society, here many people do reorder their lives by avoiding certain activities in their own homes; and many people curtain their windows and keep them drawn when they want privacy. For this reason let us call it the "Careful Society." Unlike in Carefree Society, in Careful Society some people (perhaps it is many) are unhappy when they are observed or have to cover their windows, though they seldom express their unhappiness. They

---

21   See the discussion of the use of pocket telescopes on the Shetland Islands in Erving Goffman, *Behavior in Public Places* (New York: Free Press, 1963), p. 15, n. 3; discussed in Tunick, *Practices and Principles*, pp. 158–160.

resignedly accept homeviewing. Some people truly do not value keeping the activities in their home private, at least from their neighbors—though even they might be upset if their activities were video-recorded and broadcast, or viewed by strangers—something that does not bother many people in Carefree Society.

I will concede for now that in Carefree Society one cannot reasonably expect privacy in activities one does in one's home in the line of sight of anyone who can see inside using a pocket telescope. However, in Careful Society I think we should say that despite prevailing practices, one can. To make this case, we might appeal to the value of being free to act uninhibitedly in one's home without having to shade one's windows or retreat to a windowless room. In Chapter 5, I will explore two different ways of supporting that conclusion—one that would support pro-privacy policies that augment the total utility within society; and a non-consequentialist approach that insists we give due respect to all human beings. I will also reconsider whether we should so readily concede that in Carefree Society one can have no legitimate privacy interest in not being homeviewed, in light of the argument that a liberal society should be sensitive to the needs of even a very small minority to whom the practice may be oppressive.

I do not think the legitimacy of practices of surveillance necessarily hinges on whether special technology is used to enhance one's natural observational abilities and so it is not the fact that pocket telescopes as opposed to the naked eye are used that bears on whether homeviewing is legitimate. Suppose we modify the scenario so that in Careful Society people's eye lenses by nature have the ability to magnify images with a concentrated effort. It may be that if this were the case it would be more likely for the society to adopt the ways of Carefree Society; but if it did not, the fact that homeviewing could occur without the aid of technology does not matter. A people can adopt ethical norms requiring them in certain situations to refrain from using their natural abilities. Even if such norms were frequently ignored, there is still as good a case to regard privacy interests in one's activities within the home as legitimate regardless of whether homeviewing does or does not require sense-enhancing technology.

Qualifying the plain view principle

According to the plain view principle as I have modified it (and from now on all my references to the plain view principle will be to the modified version), we cannot have a legitimate privacy interest in information that is *readily* accessible through legitimate means of observation to one or more persons who could not be expected or trusted to keep this information to themselves. In the rest of this chapter, I offer qualifications to the plain view principle, qualifications that are essential if the principle is to be persuasive in dealing with some important cases of unwanted attention.

Before turning to these qualifications, I want to make two observations. First, the converse of the plain view principle may not be true. While we may not have legitimate privacy interests in information readily accessible through legitimate means of observation (except for qualifications such as the ones I will soon discuss), we do not necessarily have a legitimate privacy interest in all information that is not in plain view. There is quite a lot of information about me that is not readily accessible but the exposure of which would not implicate my privacy. It would take some doing to discover the address of the house in which I lived when I was eight, or the name of my third grade teacher, or the funny way I used to pronounce "macabre." But someone who takes the trouble to find out using legitimate means of inquiry does not violate my privacy—unless of course they collect this information to develop a dossier on me or to assume the position of someone who knows me. They do not injure my reputation, property interests, or relations with others, or affront my dignity, diminish my autonomy, or expose me to unjust punishment.

The second observation is that I can still have a legitimate privacy interest in information that is accessible but not readily accessible and which therefore should not be regarded as in plain view. Someone's past criminal record may be in a sense a "public fact" in that it is accessible by visiting a court building during business hours and searching through filing cabinets of past cases; but if the only way to access that information is by going to the brick and mortar building, because the information is not online or otherwise published, then it might not be readily accessible; it is not really in plain view, and so there is a sense in which it is not a public fact.[22]

Elizabeth Paton-Simpson makes a similar point. She notes that public record information is public in the descriptive sense that any of us can look it up. But it can remain descriptively private to the extent it remains "practically obscure."[23] An item appearing in a local newspaper with a low circulation may be a public fact but, Paton-Simpson argues, "there can be a vast difference between a matter being mentioned in passing on page 4 of a suburban rag, and the same information being featured on nationwide television ten years later."[24] When Mr. Justice Eady issued the injunction in the Giggs case, he noted similarly that one might still reasonably expect privacy in information that might have been published on a limited scale but was not published in the national media.[25] Paton-Simpson argues that some of these facts, such as the identity of a rape victim who is named in a court record, normatively ought to remain private.[26] Courts sometimes

22 I will discuss the different ways one might define a public fact and a private fact in Chapter 6.
23 Paton-Simpson, "Private Circles and Public Squares," *Modern Law Review* 61(3):318–340 (1998), pp. 327, 336.
24 Paton-Simpson, p. 330.
25 *CTB v. News Group Newspapers Ltd* [2011] EWHC 1323, Par. 28.
26 Paton-Simpson, pp. 321–322.

impose legal restrictions on publications of some details of judicial proceedings even though theoretically anyone could have attended the proceeding and learned them.[27] England's Queen's Bench, for example, issued an injunction against reporting the new identity of one of the killers in the notorious case in which 2-year-old James Bulger was brutally murdered, even though that killer's identity was referred to at one point in open court.[28]

Mr. Briscoe was convicted of a criminal offense in the 1950s and that information was accessible to anyone who went to the public building that housed the record of his conviction. But when *Reader's Digest* published a brief account of his conviction in 1968, it made what had been an obscure fact readily accessible, and subjected Briscoe to consequences he would not otherwise have faced. Perhaps he could not reasonably expect his prior conviction to be deleted or kept secret; but he could have a legitimate interest in not having new attention cast on his past crime. If we do not regard it as legitimate for *Reader's Digest* to have made this information readily accessible, then the fact that Briscoe committed the crime might have been normatively private even after the *Reader's Digest* article appeared. It might have eventually become descriptively private once again since *Reader's Digest* articles from 1968 are not freely available online, had Briscoe not taken legal action that resulted in published court opinions that revealed this fact.

In Chapter 2 I noted that competing interests are at stake in debates about whether there should be a "right to be forgotten," including the privacy interests of former criminals and the public interest in accessing information about past crimes. One way to take each interest into account would be to maintain the information but require some nontrivial effort to retrieve it. In this way, it could be available to those with a need to know but not readily accessible to the general public so as to cast new attention on an individual's past misdeeds. While the information would be available to some, it would not be in plain view and one could have a legitimate privacy interest in it. This is the approach the German Federal Court of Justice took in the Sedlmayr case mentioned in Chapter 2. The Court held that information about the men convicted for the 1990 murder should not be literally pushed to the public over two decades later, but it can be made available on the Internet as long as the information is readily identifiable as a dated news report, or requires an active search. The Court suggested that creating a link to a pay-to-view archive containing an original report of the case would be appropriate—the information would reach only a small audience; but it might not be legitimate to produce a new TV documentary

---

27 Paton-Simpson, p. 329.
28 *Venables and Thompson v. News Group Papers Ltd* [2010] Case nos. HQ0004737 and HQ0004986 (QB).

that presents the story afresh in prime time.[29] The discussion of privacy's value in Chapter 2 points to one rationale for this position: producing the TV documentary would make information that is and ought to be accessible to those with a need to know readily accessible to many more people, thereby implicating a privacy interest in avoiding disproportionate non-legal punishment.

The qualifications to the plain view principle which I will now consider are called for because information that is readily accessible to one or a few people by legitimate means may still be information in which one has a legitimate privacy interest. I shall focus on two ways in which this might be the case. First, what one wants to keep private may be of so personal a nature that its exposure to others may implicate one's dignity. Second, while I may not have a legitimate privacy interest that certain information not be known to those to whom it is in plain view at a given time and place, I can have a legitimate privacy interest that this information not be disseminated to a broader audience or that it not be *memorialized* in the form of an audio or video recording the access to which I cannot control.[30]

One may reasonably expect privacy when one's dignity is implicated

On June 24, 1990, Ms. Shulman and her son were injured in a car accident in California when their car tumbled into a drainage ditch. Ms. Shulman was pinned, and eventually cut free by the jaws of life. A camera filmed her extrication from the car and a flight nurse's efforts in transporting her by helicopter to a hospital. The flight nurse wore a microphone that picked up her conversation with Ms. Shulman, and that audio as well as videotape of Ms. Shulman in transit to the hospital was used for a television segment that lasted about nine minutes as part of the show "On Scene: Emergency Response" which was repeatedly broadcast about three months after the accident. The tape shows Ms. Shulman several times. She is heard to reveal that she is 47 and thinks she is old. Viewers hear her ask if she is dreaming and say, twice, "I just want to die." She saw the broadcast and was shocked.[31]

Ms. Shulman could not expect privacy in the fact that she was in an accident on a public road and was promptly transported to a hospital. She was in a public place, visible to numerous people. Showing her being

---

29   BGH, Urteil vom 8. 5. 2012 – VI ZR 217/08, at Pars. 38–42; online at http://lexetius.com/2012,2122; cf. *Google Spain SL v. AEPD* [2014] Case C-131/12 (requiring Google to delete personal information about an individual that appears in its search engine results even though the information still is accessible on a newspaper's website); cf. Siry and Schmitz, "A Right to be Forgotten?," *European Journal for Law and Technology* 3(1) (2012).

30   The ensuing sections expand on ideas I first laid out in Mark Tunick, "Privacy and Punishment," *Social Theory and Practice* 39(4): 643–668 (2013).

31   See *Shulman v. Group W Productions*, 18 Cal.4th 200, 210–212 (1998).

transported could serve a legitimate public interest by demonstrating that tax revenues are used to good effect. But the thoughts Ms. Shulman conveyed to the flight nurse are another matter. She can retain a legitimate privacy interest in some of the details of an event that is a public fact when exposure of those details would be an affront to her dignity or violate her trust.

It may be that no qualification to the plain view principle is needed to arrive at this conclusion. The plain view principle holds that one cannot expect privacy in information readily accessible by legitimate means of observation to persons one cannot expect or trust to keep this information private, and while the car accident itself was readily observable using legitimate means of observation, what Ms. Shulman said to a flight nurse was not. Ms. Shulman conveyed that information to a medical professional and any further conveyance to other parties might be a violation of professional codes of conduct and a breach of trust. So suppose, now, that Ms. Shulman's words were recorded not on a helicopter transport but while she lay on the side of the road, and not by a flight nurse but by a journalist who had a right to be at the scene as it was a public place. Even though Ms. Shulman's words might be readily accessible, she retains a privacy interest that her words not be conveyed to others, an interest that is explained by appealing to the value of human dignity. Ms. Shulman is not concerned with her reputation: nobody is likely to think badly of her for being in an accident, or for feeling so vulnerable. Still, she has a legitimate claim not to be exposed in this way.

In some cases, being exposed even though one is in plain view can be an affront to one's dignity as well as a source of embarrassment. McNamara was a student playing in a high school soccer game at which a picture was taken by a photographer for the *Brownville Herald* that revealed McNamara's genitalia as one of his legs was raised. A court found that there was no intent to embarrass him, as none of the persons involved in the publication apparently noticed that the genitalia were visible.[32] But embarrassed he was when the picture was published. A Texas Court of Appeals dismissed McNamara's suit on the ground that anything connected with a newsworthy event such as a soccer game may be disclosed, and the picture revealed what was in plain view, McNamara being in a public place. Here, too, we need to make an exception to the plain view principle. One can retain a legitimate privacy interest in details of a public event. While McNamara has to deal with the embarrassment that his fellow athletes or onlookers might have caught a glimpse of his private parts, the picture that was published casts attention on what for anyone who was actually there would have been observable only fleetingly. If the picture was never taken and published, people who were not there still might have heard about the embarrassing incident. But by publishing the photograph, the newspaper

32 *McNamara v. Freedom Newspapers, Inc.*, 802 S.W.2d 901 (1991).

subjected McNamara to a qualitatively different and more severe intrusion upon his privacy. It is one thing to hear about what happened to him, or to be told what Ms. Shulman said as she was being transported to a hospital; it is quite another to see McNamara in his indelicate position, or hear Ms. Shulman's words from her own mouth at a moment when she is so vulnerable.

Courts in England have recognized that publishing a picture of an event can be more intrusive than publishing a descriptive account of it. Max Mosley, former chief executive of Formula 1's governing body, prevailed in his suit against a newspaper that arranged for him to be secretly videotaped while he participated in a sex orgy with an alleged Nazi theme and that posted video clips on its website. He was awarded £60,000 but denied exemplary damages. One reason his privacy interest prevailed was, Mr. Justice Eady implied, that putting a video of him on the Internet increases the magnitude of the intrusion and was therefore not a "reasonable method of conveying" information.[33] Recently, a French court ruled that Google must prevent its search engine from providing links to images showing Mosley's involvement in the orgy.[34]

The distinction between conveying information by telling others and by showing them was discussed in Chapter 2. There we saw that Charles Fried illustrates this distinction by noting the difference between a good friend of mine knowing I am sick, and her actually seeing me in that condition. For her to actually witness my suffering would violate my privacy in a way that her merely having information about my condition would not.[35] In Chapter 2, we also saw that Elizabeth Paton-Simpson, drawing on Jeffrey Reiman's work, characterizes the distinction as the difference between conveying information about a person and giving an audience an experience of that person. People may have already seen the tattoo on your back, but still you can legitimately claim a privacy interest in now keeping the tattoo unobserved even by those who have already seen it.[36] The dignity interest here is not in limiting access to information about oneself, but in limiting access to oneself.

---

33   *Mosley v. News Group Newspapers Ltd* [2008] EWHC 1777 (QB)(Par. 21); cf. *Theakston v. MGN Ltd* [2002] EWHC 3185 (QB), granting an injunction against publishing photographs taken inside a brothel while permitting publication of verbal descriptions.

34   Ian Burrell, "French Court Orders Google to block Max Mosley Orgy Pictures," *The Independent*, November 6, 2013.

35   Fried, "Privacy," in Schoeman, ed., p. 210. In addition, this unwanted exposure to my friend could damage the friendship.

36   Paton-Simpson, pp. 337–338; drawing on Jeffrey Reiman, "Driving to the Panopticon," *Santa Clara Computer and High Technology Law Journal* 11(1):27–44 (1995). See also Tunick, "Privacy and Punishment," Section IV.

One can have a legitimate privacy interest that information not be spread to circles wider than one willingly exposed oneself to

Another reason it may be wrong to publish the photo of McNamara's exposed genitalia is that it makes a fact known to a small circle of people readily accessible to a wide audience. When photos or video are uploaded to the Internet, that audience can extend not only across geographical borders but to future generations.[37] Individuals can have an interest in not facing the consequences of widespread and permanent exposure of what they do in a public place. In some cases, such as when someone is photographed while sunbathing nude at a clothing-optional public beach, such exposure would cause them to suffer an indignity, though in many other cases it may not.

In the McNamara example it may be hard to see any distinction between these two reasons to qualify the plain view principle: publishing the photo at once affronts his dignity and memorializes the incident and makes it available to a wide audience. But the reasons are conceptually distinct. Posting photos to the Internet of people who are rude, drive badly, or talk too loudly on cellphones does not treat those people without dignity.[38] They may even deserve some degree of shaming. But while their bad behavior took place in public places and so they cannot expect that nobody will know what they did or relate it to others, they do have an interest that this information not be broadly disseminated and permanently available and searchable online.[39] They have a legitimate privacy interest in avoiding unjust punishment; in not suffering undue burdens on their friendships and intimate relationships; and more generally an autonomy interest in not being defined by others and in being able to reinvent themselves.[40]

It is especially important to recognize these interests in the age of social media, in which people can capture and share images of me without my consent and anyone who googles my name can access them for the rest of my life. Before this technology became widely available, people retained significant control over information about their activities even if they were observed in public. Gay men could go to locales frequented by other gay men without risking that friends and family living thousands of miles away

37 See Tufekci, "Can you See me Now?," *Bulletin of Science, Technology and Society* 28(1):20–36 (2008).
38 See Solove, *Future of Reputation* (New Haven: Yale University Press, 2007), pp. 87–89, for discussion of websites devoted to such postings.
39 Cf. Moore, *Privacy Rights* (University Park: Pennsylvania State University Press, 2010), p. 124, on the magnitude of an intrusion bearing on its wrongness.
40 See Nissenbaum, *Privacy in Context* (Stanford: Stanford University Press, 2010), pp. 81–82; Rössler, *The Value of Privacy*, tr. Glasgow (Malden, MA: Polity Press, 2005), p. 116; and van den Hoven, "Privacy and the Varieties of Moral Wrong-Doing in an Information Age," *Computers and Society* September 1997:33–37, pp. 35–36.

would discover their sexual orientation. Someone who got frustrated with a waiter and could not help making a scene and using vulgar language must have understood that anyone within earshot would see what she can be like when she is upset, but did not have to worry that someone with a smartphone might record the scene and make it available on the Internet so that it could forever define the kind of person she is. Like this person, many of us have to struggle to be the sort of person we want to be. Someone might normally be kind, gracious, and patient, but belie these virtues now and then. If I am always under public scrutiny whenever I go outside or appear before strangers, I may be judged and punished for behavior that may not accurately reflect my character. I might have succumbed to pressures not visible to others.[41] Even if the judgment is accurate, I still have an interest in controlling who sees which aspects of me. Mr. Sipple had an interest in controlling who knew of his sexual orientation. When a newspaper outs him to the general public without his consent, it takes this control away from him.[42]

Ms. Shulman could not expect that paramedics would not relate the thoughts she shared with them to their spouses; McNamara could not expect that people at the soccer game would not tell his friends that his private parts were exposed; and a woman sunbathing nude at a public beach cannot expect that an onlooker will not see her and then tell the woman's coworkers. But that they exposed themselves in a public place does not mean they have no legitimate privacy interest in not having these particular moments in their lives memorialized and made readily accessible to the general public. McNamara has an interest in not being defined as "the soccer flasher"; the woman has an interest in not being defined as "the nude sunbather"; Briscoe has an interest in not being defined as "the hijacker"; but this is how they may be defined for the rest of their lives if the incidents they want to be forgotten are the first thing one learns when one looks at them with Google Glass or types their name in a search engine.

There is a difference between being photographed in a place where one would not expect to be recorded, as when on a bus or subway or at a public beach, and being photographed in a public place where the media are clearly present. During a playoff game in 2013 between the Miami Heat and the Chicago Bulls in Miami, a woman later identified by a local newspaper was caught on camera thrusting her middle finger in the face of Bulls center Joakim Noah as he left the floor after being ejected. She should have known that cameras would be focused on Noah as he exited, and so she should not be surprised that the photo was featured the next day on several

41   Tunick, "Privacy and Punishment," p. 651.
42   Annabelle Lever adds that it is "invidious" to single out one person to be a lesson for others when perhaps thousands might have been chosen, in *On Privacy* (New York: Routledge, 2012), p. 38.

popular sports websites;[43] and given that she was a widow of a prominent public figure, she should perhaps not even be surprised that one newspaper published a story the next day with details about her "intriguing past."[44] In contrast, being at a beach or on a bus or subway should not entail that one can be the subject of the next viral YouTube video.

With few exceptions, courts in the United States have refused to recognize that one can have a legitimate privacy interest in information that is in a court record viewable by the public, or in what you say or do in a public place.[45] They assume that once I go outside I cannot expect not to be seen or followed and so it is permissible for the police to track my movements or for me to be videotaped.[46] The Supreme Court ruled, in a case in which the defendant revealed incriminating evidence to an acquaintance who turned out to be a police informant, that you cannot expect that your interlocutor will not repeat what you said to the police;[47] then in a later case the Court reasoned that since you cannot reasonably expect that, it makes no difference whether the police rely on your interlocutor's memory of your words, or on a surreptitious recording or transmission of them, since you knowingly exposed the information to others.[48]

The position that one cannot expect privacy in the fact that one was accused or convicted of committing a crime does not reflect a conceptual truth. In continental Europe, public disclosure of a criminal past is not the norm; access to conviction records is restricted, and an accused person's real name may not even appear on the docket.[49] As we have seen, there are proposals in the European Union to recognize a "right to be forgotten" which would give people a legal right in some cases to demand that even facts about one's past that were once public be deleted from the Internet.

Nor is it a conceptual truth that one cannot expect privacy in a public place. The European Court of Human Rights ruled in *Peck v. U.K.* that

---

43 Doug Padilla, "Joakim Noah Shows Composure," ESPNChicago.com, May 10, 2013; also http://nba.si.com/2013/05/09/filomena-tobias-joakim-noah-flip-bird-heckler-miami-heat-chicago-bulls/.

44 Ihosvani Rodriguez, "Heat bird-flipper is millionaire with intriguing past," *Sun Sentinel* May 9, 2013, online at www.sun-sentinel.com/news/palm-beach/fl-heat-fan-finger-20130509,0,1623453.

45 *Gates v. Discovery Communications Inc.*, 101 P.3d 552 (2005) (overruling *Briscoe v. Reader's Digest* based on intervening Supreme Court precedents holding that one cannot expect privacy in information taken from public court records); *McNamara v. Freedom Newspapers*, 802 S.W.2d 901 (1991).

46 *U.S. v. Knotts*, 460 U.S. 276 (1983) (allowing use of a beeper to track movements); *U.S. v. Vazquez*, 31 F.Supp.2d (1998) (allowing the release of a video recording of people entering a public building).

47 *Hoffa v. U.S.*, 385 U.S. 293 (1966).

48 *U.S. v. White*, 401 U.S. 745 (1971). Cf. *In re. John Doe Trader No. 1*, 894 F.2d 240 (1990); and *Commonwealth v. Eason*, 427 Mass. 595 (1998).

49 James B. Jacobs and Elena Larrauri, "Are Criminal Convictions a Public Matter? The USA and Spain," *Punishment and Society* 14(1):3–28 (2012).

although a man who attempted suicide on a public road was visible to people who happened to pass by, this does not mean that it was legitimate to make a surveillance photo of him available to the general public.[50] Peck was caught on CCTV holding a knife. An operator monitoring the camera alerted the police, who arrived, took the knife from Peck, and gave him medical assistance. Photos of Peck with no masking were shared with local papers and video footage was provided for various programs including the BBC's "Crime Beat," which has 9.2 million viewers. Trailers for the show did not mask Peck's features. Peck sued, claiming his privacy was violated. The High Court in England had ruled against Peck on the ground that there was no right to privacy in England, and there was no breach of confidence, defamation, or trespass. But Peck appealed, relying on Article 8 of the European Convention on Human Rights, and prevailed at the Strasbourg Court. The Court held that there is a zone of privacy even in public contexts: "Private life considerations may arise [o]nce any systematic or permanent record comes into existence of such material from the public domain."[51] Having established that Article 8's right to respect for private life was implicated, the Court then reasoned that disclosure of the footage was disproportionate and unjustified. Other non-U.S. courts have similarly recognized legitimate privacy interests in public places.[52] Some have not, instead adopting the dominant position in the U.S.[53] But that dominant position can be challenged, because exposing oneself to the view of passersby when walking down a street need not entail that one exposes oneself to the world for all time.

Some commentators who reflect on the rapid spread of social media technologies seem to take it for granted that because so many people are uploading embarrassing videos and intimate photos online where over 2 billion users can access it, we just have to accept that the public sphere is "more public than ever before."[54] But the prevalence of technologies allowing one to broadly share images or text need not mean that their use is always acceptable. My argument is that we can still have a legitimate privacy interest in retaining control over access to information that is accessible using legitimate means of observation, and even to some information

---

50   [2003] 36 EHRR 41.
51   [2003] 36 EHRR 41, Par. 58.
52   *Aubry v. Editions Vice-Versa* [1998] S.C.J. No. 30 (Canada) (discussed in ch. 1); *Campbell v. MGN Ltd* [2004] UKHL 22; *Murray v. Big Pictures* [2008] EWCA Civ 446; *Von Hannover v. Germany (no. 2)* [2012] ECHR 228.
53   *Hoskings v. Runting* [2004] NZCA 34 (while declaring that New Zealand now recognizes a privacy tort, the court ruled that in this case the claimant, twin 18-month old children of well-known public figures who objected to a photograph of them being published in a magazine without their consent, cannot reasonably expect privacy when walking down a public street).
54   Brian Stelter, "Upending Anonymity, These Days the Web Unmasks Everyone," *New York Times*, June 21, 2011.

that is readily accessible to one or more people and therefore in "plain view." If we recognize the weight of this privacy interest, we might conclude that it would be wrong of a reporter to sift through old newspaper archives and write an article about a person's crime decades earlier so as to make the information readily accessible to any member of the general public who googles the person's name; or wrong of a person to take a photo of "Dog Poop Girl" on the Korean subway and share it on social media sites. But this conclusion is subject to one important proviso: that details about the crime or the activity that the camera captured are not newsworthy. If they are, the interest in free speech may outweigh the privacy interest, a consideration I address in the next two chapters.

The framework I propose in Chapter 5 will rely on a two-step process similar to the one I have just discussed: we first ask whether a legitimate privacy interest is at stake; if it is, we then weigh it against interests in free speech. It may be apparent from the preceding discussion that the process may not be simply sequential. In deciding whether a privacy interest in information is legitimate, we must determine whether the information is in plain view or whether a qualification of the plain view principle may apply. This may require us to determine whether the means used to expose the information is legitimate, and deciding that, in some cases, could depend on a balancing of privacy and free speech interests. The process may involve revision of tentatively held views based on further reflection—what John Rawls refers to as "reflective equilibrium."[55] For example, we cannot say for certain whether a person in Careful Society is in plain view when in their home near an uncurtained window until we decide whether homeviewing is a legitimate practice, and that might depend on how we weigh interests in privacy and in access to information. But we can tentatively propose that the person may have a legitimate privacy interest, with the understanding that only when we arrive at the second stage and balance the privacy interest with the interest homeviewers have in accessing information can we determine whether it was legitimate in this case. Dog Poop Girl's behavior was clearly in plain view. Here I think we can say she has a legitimate privacy interest that a photo memorializing her behavior not be taken and spread to circles wider than the one she willingly exposed herself to; but that this kind of interest may in some cases be outweighed if the information is sufficiently newsworthy.

Controlling the intended audience of one's message

Sometimes I may share words with others who then spread what I have said to people I did not intend to be recipients and who I was not addressing. Even if I cannot expect privacy in that information, I still can expect

---

55   Rawls, *A Theory of Justice* (Cambridge: Harvard University Press, 1971), p. 20.

that my words are not understood to be for those unintended recipients and in this sense I have an interest in retaining control over those words. Consider the following example.

Suppose students in a campus organization confront the University's President about the President's plan to cut funds for student groups. On one occasion, they prepare signs and demonstrate outside the administrative building. When the President leaves for the day she avoids the students and rushes to the parking lot. Some students follow her, demanding she read their signs and address their concerns. As she enters her car, a few students surround it, blocking her from exiting. The President is alarmed. After police ask the students to move away, the President drives off. But one student, who ignored the police's instructions, receives a minor bruise when the President's car brushes against him. The student notifies the local press and threatens to sue. Seeing the newspaper account, the President is furious. She notes that the demonstrators violated the code of conduct by obstructing traffic, and demands an apology. The students are upset as well—they feel the President should have gotten out of the car and spoken with them rather than abruptly drive away.

Not wanting to antagonize the President, the Dean of the College issues a public statement on behalf of the College community that apologizes to the President for the students' "utterly inappropriate behavior." Many of the faculty are upset that in the statement the Dean found no fault with the President. Some of the faculty draft an email in response that expresses complete support for the students' right to protest and blames the President for rushing away. But several faculty members are worried by the draft: the President might respond to it vindictively. If it is to be sent at all, they plead, it should be sent only to the students, since its purpose is to show that the faculty support their free speech rights. Addressing it instead to the whole University, as some faculty members propose, would be to confront and challenge the President. During the faculty's debate over this issue, someone argues that there is no point just sending the email only to the students; in the age of social media there can be no such thing as a private show of support since any of the recipients could easily forward the email to a broader group that includes the University President. The argument is the one we have just considered: once you make information available to others who are not in a special relationship of trust, you cannot expect that they will not spread the information to others. It is similar in a key respect to an argument relied on by the New Zealand High Court in *Tucker v. News Media Ownership Ltd*. A man with a heart condition was seeking donations to pay for his treatment. Years earlier, he had been convicted of indecency offenses, and he now sought to prevent publication of reports of those convictions, arguing that publication would create emotional distress that could kill him. But the convictions were already reported by some radio stations and a Sydney newspaper, and so the Court held that restraining further publication would be an exercise in futility: "in New Zealand once the proverbial cat is out of the bag her progeny spread like lightning."[56]

It is true that one cannot expect privacy in the contents of an email sent to a large list of recipients. But this does not mean that a statement of support to a select audience is no different from a public statement. Sending an inflamed President a message supporting the students is likely to be construed by her as a challenge to her authority. Several faculty no doubt have that intention, but other faculty do not. A message sent to the President will have a different meaning than the same message sent just to the students. That difference matters even though it is likely that a message to students will be passed on to the President. That an email sent to a particular person and intended only for them can be forwarded to others means that we need to be careful not to convey secrets that we would not want to be in the hands of just anyone. But we can have a legitimate interest in controlling who the intended audience of our message is even if we cannot control who ultimately receives it.

Clarifying what counts as "readily accessible through legitimate means"

With some important exceptions, one cannot reasonably expect privacy in information that is in plain view, and according to the modified plain view principle information is in plain view only if it is readily accessible through legitimate means to one or more persons who could not be expected or trusted to keep this information to themselves. The argument I have developed relies on a distinction between information that is accessible but perhaps hard to find and information that is readily accessible, and I now want to clarify what it means for information to be "readily accessible through legitimate means."

Suppose we are sitting on a bench in New York City's Central Park discussing a private matter. We are in a secluded area with very few people passing by, and so we are talking at a normal volume as opposed to whispering. Every five or ten minutes someone does walk by and so we pause until they are out of earshot. But at one point our discussion gets so heated that we fail to notice a woman approach, and she can hear us. Our words are readily accessible to her in the sense that she does not need to make any special effort to hear us. But they are not readily accessible to anyone else but her and the two of us. If she were to record our words and share them on the Internet, our words would not be in plain view or earshot of the general public insofar as it is not legitimate for her to record and share our conversation without our consent. Moreover, while we cannot reasonably expect that passers-by will not catch a small portion of our conversation, we might be able reasonably to expect that she does not stop, conceal herself behind a tree, and listen to a great deal more. In a Canadian case, *R v. Rudiger*, which I will discuss in more detail in Chapter 6, Mr. Justice Voith argues that a caretaker in a public park cannot reasonably expect not to be seen bathing or changing a child, but such observations "will be fleeting in nature"; they are akin to catching some small portion of your conversation when walking by you. The caretaker can still expect that someone not take video that focuses on the unclothed child for a sustained period of time.[57] If the eavesdropping woman could get the gist of our conversation only by stopping and listening intently, then our conversation may not be readily accessible and in plain view since stopping to listen might be to act badly—it would not be a legitimate means of observation.

But now suppose that our conversation concerns a criminal plot, and the woman passerby is a police inspector. The small portion of our conversation that she can legitimately hear are the words "set the explosion for 2." Concerned, she stops, conceals herself, and intently listens as we heatedly debate whether to blow up a bank vault at 2 or 3 in the morning. One could plausibly argue that the inspector does not violate a reasonable expectation of privacy when she uses what she heard to get a search warrant that leads to other incriminating evidence, because here the eaves-dropper does not act badly, and we should have recognized that anyone who overhears us may well go to the police. In this case, our conversation was in plain view and we needed to be more careful. Yet one might also plausibly argue that our words were not readily accessible because we were after all in a secluded place with hardly anyone around, and there-fore not in plain view, so that we had a legitimate privacy interest in them; but even if we adopt this interpretation of the ambiguous concept of "read-ily accessible," we could still eventually conclude that this interest is outweighed by a more compelling interest in preventing crime.

Suppose, instead, that we were discussing not a bank robbery but your marital problems, and the eavesdropper was sitting on a bench nearby within earshot but out of our view. If the eavesdropper did not know us, she could not relate this information in a way that would cause you any embarrassment; at best she could say that "someone is having some personal issues" but she could not connect this to you. Now suppose that by sheer bad luck she did know you, and she cannot resist spreading gossip about your difficulties to people you know. When you expose infor-mation to even one person who could not be expected or trusted to keep this information private—even when you do so unknowingly—the infor-mation may be in plain view. Ms. Shulman, in contrast, might have been able to expect or trust that the flight nurse would not further convey the personal information Ms. Shulman exposed to her to those without a need

---

57   *R v. Rudiger* [2011] B.C.J. No. 1947, Par. 107.

to know. Some information, however, is so deeply personal that we might think that ethical norms would prohibit even a person who is *not* in a particular position of trust from gossiping to others about it. We may need to invoke such norms in a situation where the eavesdropper was a stranger who wore Google Glass and had access to face recognition software enabling her to identify you and share this information with your Facebook friends. Or we could argue that use of technology to identify someone who otherwise would remain anonymous is not legitimate—an argument I will return to in later chapters.

Consent

Sometimes information is unknowingly exposed to others. Sometimes it is knowingly but unwillingly exposed, perhaps due to carelessness. In both cases, the information may now be in plain view, and unless one of the qualifications to the plain view principle applies, one may no longer be able to reasonably expect privacy in that information. An even clearer case in which one may waive a claim to having an expectation of privacy in information is when one knowingly and willingly consents to its release. But we need to be mindful about what is being consented to.

An airline passenger may consent to a body-scanner search but would not consent to certain uses of the information exposed by the scan. The consent passengers give is restricted to certain trained professionals having access to an image of their body for the limited purpose of ensuring compliance with regulations governing safe passenger transport. It is not consent for images of their body to be shared for any other purpose, or with the general public. A woman may consent to being observed by her husband from time to time in their bedroom, but this does not mean she consents to the husband covertly taping her activities there.[58] We must also be mindful that consent sometimes is not fully voluntary. A man was videotaped while he was in an emergency room in a New Jersey hospital by a camera crew working on a show called "Trauma: Life in the ER" that is broadcast on the Learning Channel. He signed a release form authorizing his appearance in the video, but he claims his consent was not genuine because he was heavily medicated at the time, and because he was coerced when he was told that doctors pay more attention to patients when they are filmed. While the case is complicated by the fact that the video was never broadcast and it is not clear that consent is required if what is shown is newsworthy, it points to how consent can sometimes be less than voluntary.[59]

Adam Moore takes consent to be the most important factor in determining whether there has been a violation of a privacy right. He argues that if

58   *In re Marriage of Tigges*, 758 N.W.2d 824 (2008).
59   *Kinsella v. Welch and NYT Television*, 827 A.2d 325 (2003).

I consent to your exposing information about me, I can hardly claim you violated my rights.[60] In this section, I suggest a proviso to this position.

I can have no legitimate privacy interest that information not be known to those with whom I willingly share it. But, I have argued, I can still expect to retain some control over that information with respect to other people with whom I did not share it, or with respect to the ways in which that information is further conveyed. Suppose, now, that at one point in time I voluntarily consent to make information about me available to the general public and not just to a select group of individuals: do I thereby forfeit any claims to privacy in that information in the future if I later change my mind?

Consider the case of former UCLA student Alexandra Wallace. She was upset by what she perceived as a tendency of Asian students to talk in the library, and made a video in which she ranted against Asians, invoking several inappropriate and offensive stereotypes. She uploaded the video to YouTube and it quickly spread and made national headlines as an example of a white person wrongly casting judgment on an entire ethnic group. The consequences were harsh: she received death threats, faced reprimands from the University, and eventually withdrew from college.[61] We might think that she brought this on herself by making the video and putting it online. But the matter is not so straightforward. Ms. Wallace took the video down from YouTube; but a number of other people soon made it available again, using software that allows one to download any Internet video and then re-upload it.[62] One re-posting had over 2.1 million views as of late December, 2013;[63] and some television news stations showed excerpts that are also available on YouTube.[64] Should Ms. Wallace be able to withdraw her consent if she comes to have regrets about having put the video on YouTube, or has she forever forfeited her right to control access to it the moment she made it available to the public?

Ms. Wallace's situation is very different from those in which a person's image is captured and uploaded by someone else. In Chapter 1 I referred to the case of "Dog Poop Girl." Another example is the case of "Bus Uncle": he was speaking loudly on his cellphone on a bus in Hong Kong, and ignored requests by others to be quiet. After someone else took and uploaded video evidence of his rude behavior, he was attacked at a restaurant.[65] In these two cases, the person receiving unwanted attention behaved

60   Moore, *Privacy Rights*, pp. 127–128.
61   See www.cbsnews.com/stories/2011/03/15/national/main20043230.shtml (March 15, 2011).
62   One example of such software, available for free, is "Keepvid," see http://keepvid.com/ (accessed February 14, 2014).
63   www.youtube.com/watch?v=FNuyDZevKrU, accessed December 28, 2013.
64   www.youtube.com/watch?v=TxQ5Q39FQ2E, accessed December 28, 2013.
65   Discussed in Lipton, "We, the Paparazzi," *Iowa Law Review* 95:919–984 (2010), citing Daniel Solove, *The Future of Reputation*, and Jonathan Zittrain, *The Future of the Internet* (New Haven: Yale University Press, 2008).

badly. But both Dog Poop Girl and Bus Uncle had a legitimate privacy interest in not having their image shared through social media, and whoever gave them unwanted attention also might have acted badly. Ms. Wallace, however, brought the attention on herself, and, for that reason, we might think that she alone of the three has no legitimate complaint. As long as printing technology has existed, people have had to face the prospect of publishing something they may later regret, with no ability to delete their mistake. One might think that once you upload a video to the Internet then you cannot have control over its use given the prevalence of video-download technology. But while it is not practicable to delete passages from books that have already been distributed, it is possible to restrict access to videos on sites like YouTube, as the film industry has done by taking legal action to protect its copyrighted films from unauthorized viewings.[66] One reason it would be problematic to delete all versions of Ms. Wallace's video is that because of the novelty of the issue her video raised, it instantly became newsworthy. I sometimes show excerpts of it when I give talks on privacy. Given the principle that one can have a legitimate privacy interest in controlling access to certain information even if that information is a public fact, Ms. Wallace could have a legitimate privacy interest in being able to remove all copies of her video from the Internet; but in her case that interest may be outweighed by the competing interest society has in the video's ready accessibility, as that accessibility contributes to discussions on matters of legitimate public concern. Chapter 4 is devoted to a more systematic discussion of the competing free speech interest.

Whether our consent to make information about ourselves available to the general public can be withdrawn so that we can restrict access to it in the future may depend on the extent to which we think the original consent was fully informed and voluntary. A 12 year old who posts an embarrassing video of himself that he will come to regret when he is older may be incapable of giving truly informed consent at his age, as is an adult who posts a similarly embarrassing video while intoxicated.[67] Another consideration may be the extent to which the person is a public figure. The comic actor Michael Richards, who played "Kramer" on the iconic comedy series *Seinfeld*, appeared before the public at a venue called the Laugh Factory, during which he made several racist remarks that shocked many people, and a video of his tirade was made available on YouTube and elsewhere.[68]

---

66 The Ninth Circuit Court of Appeals recently ordered Google to remove a controversial video from YouTube—the video offended many Muslims but the order was based not on that but on copyright interests; *Cindy Garcia v. Google, Inc.*, 12-57302 (9th Cir. 2014).

67 Consider *Neff v. Time, Inc.*, 406 F.Supp. 858 (1976): Neff sued after *Time* published a photo of him at an NFL game with his pants zipper open; the court ruled for Time as Neff "was catapulted into the news by his own action"; but the case is complicated because while Neff encouraged the photograph, he might have been drunk at the time.

68 See www.metacafe.com/watch/307809/seinfelds_kramers_racist_tirade_of_craziness/, accessed December 28, 2013.

As a professional entertainer performing in public, it would be hard for him to make a convincing case that he has a legitimate privacy interest in controlling access to the video—though if cameras were not permitted in this venue he might have a claim of appropriation based on a property interest in his performance.

Conclusion: Privacy in public places

It is often argued that there can be no privacy in public places.[69] Courts have said that "what a person knowingly exposes to the public, even in his own home or office, is not a subject of Fourth Amendment protection";[70] and that "there is no liability for giving further publicity to what the plaintiff leaves open to the public eye."[71] In one case, producers of Dateline NBC secretly videotaped a lunch meeting with representatives of a company at a restaurant in Malibu; they later broadcast excerpts of the meeting on television. A state appellate court found no invasion of privacy, reasoning that the plaintiffs spoke freely at a restaurant where even the employees could hear what they said. They could not reasonably expect privacy in the middle of a crowded outdoor patio of a public restaurant at a table that was within close proximity to other tables.[72]

I have argued against this view. There are instances in which one can have a legitimate privacy interest in what takes place in public or is known to others. The fact that waiters can hear you speak when they come to your table should not mean that you cannot expect privacy in those parts of your conversation in which you lower your voice so that you cannot be heard by anyone using legitimate means of observation apart from the person to whom you are speaking. I take it as obvious that it would normally not be legitimate for a snoop to read your lips from a distance or to use an electronic listening device in order to hear your words.[73]

Even if you were speaking loudly enough to be heard by people at other tables, this does not mean you have no legitimate interest in not having

---

69   Ardia, "Reputation in a Networked World," *Harvard Civil Rights-Civil Liberties Law Review* 45(2):261–328 (2010), p. 279 (anything that occurs in a public place is not private by definition).

70   *Katz v. U.S.*, 389 U.S. 347, 351.

71   *Virgil v. Time, Inc.*, 527 F.2d 1122, 1126 (9th Cir. 1975).

72   *Wilkins v. NBC*, 71 Cal.App.4th 1066 (1999).

73   However, in *Malone v. Commissioner of Police of the Metropolis* [1979] 2 All ER 620, in which the court found no basis in English law for providing a remedy to an individual whose phone was tapped by the police, Sir Robert Megarry writes that "those who exchange confidences on a bus or a train run the risk of a [d]istant passenger ... who is adept at lip reading." His point is not that the lip reader does nothing wrong, only that there should be no legal remedy against the lip reader: one may act dishonorably by overhearing a secret without giving some warning, but "there are, of course, many moral precepts which are not legally enforceable."

your conversation recorded and distributed to the general public.[74] Recognizing this is particularly important given the widespread use of mobile devices with built-in video capturing abilities that allow people to memorialize sounds and images in public places. Of course, when you are in a public place, there are limits to what privacy you can expect. If you are dining at a restaurant and do not want others to hear your conversation, you should speak softly. If you do not want to be recognized when walking down a street you should wear a good disguise.

Even public figures may have a legitimate interest in privacy when they dine at a public restaurant. However, as I have emphasized and will continue to do so in the ensuing chapters, legitimate interests in privacy can be outweighed by other compelling interests. Suppose a well-known politician is dining at a restaurant and a newspaper reporter sees him and decides to observe him discreetly from an adjacent table. The reporter focuses her attention on the politician's conversation. It is barely audible but she can occasionally make out some interesting words such as "payoff" and "kickback" and "kill him." Intrigued, the reporter takes out an amplifying and recording device and makes a detailed recording of the conversation that incriminates the politician in unspeakably corrupt activities. In this extraordinary situation in which there is a compelling public interest in having access to this private information, it might be reasonable to say not only that the information can be handed over to law enforcement agents, but that it could be properly conveyed to the public, even though this would frustrate what I think is clearly a legitimate privacy interest.

---

74   Cf. *R v. Wong* [1990] 3 S.C.R. 36, 62, where Chief Justice Lamer of Canada's Supreme Court writes: "A person who is situated in what would normally be characterized as a public place (a restaurant, for example) … would not reasonably expect that the police will surreptitiously monitor and record the private conversation taking place at his or her table."

4 The value of free speech

Unwanted attention can damage your reputation, affront your dignity, erode trust, make it difficult to reinvent yourself and form new relationships, subject you to identity theft or other fraud, and cause psychological harm. Why ever allow it? Because there can be great value in conveying or having access to information. In this chapter, I consider another value at stake in cases of unwanted attention, the value of free speech and expression. I use "speech" broadly to encompass the sharing of images or conveying of information or data, including information about what an individual has said or done.[1] My purpose is not to attempt a comprehensive analysis of the substantial scholarship on free speech, but to highlight some of the important reasons for valuing speech so that we are better equipped to weigh the interest in free speech against the interest in privacy when they conflict. The point I will emphasize is that not all speech has the same value. A conscientious weighing of free speech and privacy interests will require us to think about which speech is so valuable that it might outweigh legitimate privacy interests but also which speech is not so valuable.

Reasons free speech is valuable

One starting point for considering the value of free speech generally is Chapter 2 of John Stuart Mill's *On Liberty*. There Mill argues that the ability of people to express their views freely without fear of being censored can help us arrive at truths and create the atmosphere needed for geniuses to thrive. One reason persons should not be silenced is that we can never be sure that their opinions are false.[2] Truths are often partial, and we need contestation to get the whole truth.[3] Even if we are sure that what people say is false, we should not censor them, for if we never test what we

---

1   See Chapter 1, "Building a Framework."
2   J.S. Mill, "On Liberty," in *Collected Works* (Toronto: University of Toronto Press, 1963–), Vol. 18, pp. 229, 258.
3   Ibid., pp. 231, 252ff., 258.

DOI: 10.4324/9781315763132-4

presently accept as truths against competing viewpoints, they become dead dogma or superstition; if there are no opponents of important truths, Mill writes, we must imagine them, and "supply them with the strongest arguments which the most skilful devil's advocate can conjure up."[4] Even if most people do not avail themselves of the opportunity to test and challenge received truths, a society with the freedom of speech will enable the few people, "the salt of the earth," to do so; without such people, "human life would become a stagnant pool."[5] But, Mill notes, we need freedom of thought not just so "persons of genius" can thrive; it also enables "average human beings to attain the mental stature which they are capable of."[6]

Not all speech even pretends to contribute to truth. Mill recognizes that invective or sarcasm may be weapons aiming only to humiliate or degrade. Mill also recognizes that much speech, by many people, is cast unfairly or incompetently, or without good faith. Yet his position is that even this speech should be permitted.[7]

Many defenders of free speech, particularly in the United States, share Mill's reluctance to limit speech. They argue that while dysfunctional speech may serve no legitimate purpose and even be harmful, a policy of free speech is superior to a policy in which some speech can be censored. Once we begin to restrict some speech because we regard it as dysfunctional, it may be hard to draw the line and we may end up curtailing a good deal of valuable speech. This is the slippery slope argument, which resembles a rule-utilitarian argument that I will discuss in Chapter 5. The U.S. Supreme Court once employed this argument when striking down a law that prohibited the sale of pulp fiction devoted to stories of bloodshed, lust, and crime: if the state bans vulgar magazines today, tomorrow it may seek to ban the free expression of unpopular or subversive political views.[8] But it is precisely this reluctance to limit any speech that we need to critically examine. If we recognize that privacy has genuine value, we should not simply assume that restricting speech would never be worth the cost.

Speech has other beneficial functions besides facilitating the search for truth. It has a social function in conveying information that can be used to hold individuals or public actors accountable and enable the press to play its vital role as "public watchdog."[9] Sharing words or images that document animal abuse, human rights violations, questionable police tactics, or corruption can contribute to public debate on matters of legitimate public

---

4   Ibid., p. 245. At some point, Mill implies, we will not need a diversity of opinions: when we "have entered a stage of intellectual advancement which at present seems at an incalculable distance" (p. 252).
5   Ibid., p. 267: "Genius can only breathe freely in an atmosphere of freedom."
6   Ibid., pp. 242–243.
7   Ibid., pp. 258–259.
8   *Winters v. New York*, 333 U.S. 507, 518 (1948).
9   *Mosley v. the United Kingdom* [2011] ECHR 774, Par. 112, citing *Observer and Guardian v. the United Kingdom* [1991] ECHR 49, Par. 59.

interest and lead to positive reforms.[10] Speech can convey social criticism—this is no doubt part of what Mill had in mind in arguing that free speech enables geniuses to thrive: they will be free to express unpopular opinions and challenge existing customs. And having access to reliable information about individuals' past misdeeds can be valuable in deciding whether or how to do business with them.[11]

Free speech has another notable function. Freely expressing one's ideas in words or images is an important means of self-expression and self-realization.[12] Self-expressive speech can have social and aesthetic value when conveyed to others; it can also have value even when not outwardly expressed. Mill famously advocated the former sort of self-expression as it would promote "different experiments of living." "The worth of different modes of life should be proved practically," and one cannot do this by withdrawing into one's own protective shell.[13] Being able to convey and be exposed to different viewpoints will contribute to the "marketplace of ideas";[14] and is a necessary condition of political autonomy and democratic self-government.[15] But there are also reasons for valuing the other sort of self-expressive speech, the sort that is not shared with others. Though in *On Liberty* Mill focuses on the value of outward expression, there is value in expressing oneself privately in diaries or drafts that one keeps to oneself.

Self-expression is furthered not only when we express our thoughts visually or through language or music, whether we share them with others or not, but by having access to material that enables us to satisfy our intellectual and emotional needs. In *Stanley v. Georgia*, the Supreme Court defended a person's right to receive and consume information and ideas.[16] Stanley had been arrested for possessing obscene material in violation of a Georgia law. The Court held that when the police searched Stanley's home

---

10   See Chapter 1, "The democratization of the media"; and Seth Kreimer, "Pervasive Image Capture and the First Amendment," *University of Pennsylvania Law Review* 159(2):335–409 (2011), pp. 344–347.

11   Richard Posner, "The Economics of Privacy," *American Economic Review* 71(2):405–409 (1981).

12   See Jonathan Gilmore, "Expression as Realization: Speakers' Interests in Freedom of Speech," *Law and Philosophy* 30:517–539 (2011).

13   Mill, *On Liberty*, ch. 3, pp. 260–261.

14   For further discussion of this defense of speech see Frederick Schauer, *Free Speech: A Philosophical Enquiry* (Cambridge: Cambridge University Press, 1982); and Richard Smolla, *Free Speech in an Open Society* (New York: Alfred Knopf, 1992), pp. 6–8.

15   See Alexander Meiklejohn, *Political Freedom: The Constitutional Power of the People* (New York: Harper, 1990); Cass Sunstein, *Democracy and the Problem of Free Speech* (New York: The Free Press, 1993); Dawn Nunziato, *Virtual Freedom: Net Neutrality and Free Speech in the Internet Age* (Stanford: Stanford University Press, 2009) (arguing that the state should regulate private conduits of expression to facilitate democratic self-government); and Owen Fiss, *The Irony of Free Speech* (Cambridge: Harvard University Press, 1991).

16   394 U.S. 557 (1969).

with a warrant that authorized them to look only for evidence that Stanley was engaged in illegal gambling, and they happened to discover and seize pornographic films, they violated a right to privacy that in this case was anchored in the First Amendment and the value of individual autonomy; the First Amendment gives us the right to read books and view films as we please "regardless of their social worth."[17]

As *Stanley* indicates, free speech can contribute to individual autonomy by giving us access to materials that let us express ourselves. Access to information can also promote individual autonomy by letting each of us make informed decisions that may enable us to better obtain our goals. But privacy, too, promotes individual autonomy. Privacy shields people with unpopular views from harsh criticism or censure, and enables us to choose how we present ourselves to others. Sometimes one needs the anonymity afforded by privacy to feel free to communicate, or to participate in self-government.[18]

So far I have discussed some of the reasons for defending free speech. But free speech has its critics as well. Plato's Socrates, in *The Republic*, advocates censorship on the ground that there are some ideas that can corrupt us and to which we are better off not being exposed. The guardians of his ideal city would "control the story tellers." Children would not be told any tales "of gods warring and plotting and fighting against each other" or of "hating their friends," because citizens should be persuaded that it is impious to hate another; rather, they should be told stories that dispose them to virtue.[19] Plato's Socrates would exclude poetry because he thinks it does not tend to the betterment of the city.[20] He has a very different assessment from Mill of the consequences of allowing free speech. It may be that their dispute hinges on a disagreement about the values it is ultimately acceptable to pursue, or about the knowledge it is possible to have about how to live a good or virtuous life. A Millian or contemporary liberal might endorse value pluralism—the idea that there is no single correct conception of a good life or proper way of living—whereas Plato's Socrates apparently believes there is an identifiable and correct conception of the good which

17 394 U.S. 557, 564–566 (1969). Justice Stewart would have reversed Stanley's conviction by relying not on the First but on the Fourth Amendment; the police had a warrant to search Stanley's home for materials related to bookmaking; seizing the pornography went beyond the scope of the warrant (394 U.S. 557, 571–572).

18 See Rodney Smolla, *Free Speech in an Open Society*, pp. 119–20; Annabelle Lever, "Mill and the Secret Ballot," *Utilitas* 19(3):354–378 (2007); and David A.J. Richards, "Public and Private in the Discourse of the First Amendment," *Cardozo Studies in Law and Literature* 12(1):61–101 (2000), pp. 89–90: Privacy and free speech both protect, "in mutually complementary and supportive ways," underlying human rights to "live lives free of the unjust force of irrationalist stereotypes of gender and sexuality."

19 Plato, *Republic*, Bk II, 377c–378c.

20 Plato, *Republic*, BK X, 599c–e.

all citizens ought to pursue.[21] If there is no single correct way to live, it might be important to allow people critically to reflect on different possibilities unhampered by censors of speech. While I shall not address that debate, I do want to note that one can advocate restrictions on free speech without accepting Plato's Socrates' non-liberal political theory. By bringing unwanted attention to an individual, some forms of speech can undermine an individual's autonomy. A liberal can argue that such speech should be restricted in the name of the broader value of individuality that free speech ultimately promotes.[22]

Free speech and open access to information can be valuable in a number of ways: as a means of discovering truths, debating and reforming social policies, making informed decisions, and self-expression. But not all speech is alike or deserves the same protection. At least since Socrates, a distinction has been drawn between speech that is and is not constructive in serious discussion of matters of public importance. Socrates pursued the answers to questions such as what is justice, friendship, and courage by testing his own set of beliefs against those of his interlocutors; he assumed that if anyone held a false moral belief they will always have at the same time true beliefs that contradicted that false belief and would be forced to reevaluate their convictions.[23] But for this method of inquiry—the elenchus—to succeed, Socrates repeatedly notes, one must say what they sincerely believe—otherwise we will get nowhere.[24] In addressing the question of which speech does and does not deserve special protection, David Richards similarly recognizes that not all speech promotes constructive inquiry. He argues that the speech that deserves special protection is speech used in "critical discussion and rebuttal central to the conscientious formation, revision, and evaluation of values." Such speech should satisfy what Richards calls the demands of "rational autonomy."[25] Uttering statements known to be false would fail to satisfy one of these demands.[26] In his opinion against the owner of the website that posted defamatory comments about London solicitors, Justice Tugendhat took a similar position: "Freedom of expression can only advance the objective of truth if the participants in a debate aim at truth"; the benefits of free speech do not apply to defamation.[27] Richards argues also that we need not protect

---

21   For an account of value pluralism, see Isaiah Berlin, "John Stuart Mill and the Ends of Life," in *Four Essays on Liberty* (London: Oxford University Press, 1969). I discuss value pluralism also in Chapter 5.

22   Cf. Adam Moore, *Privacy Rights* (University Park: Pennsylvania State University Press, 2010), p. 142.

23   See Gregory Vlastos, "The Socratic Elenchus," *Oxford Studies in Ancient Philosophy* 1 (1983), p. 52.

24   Crito 49d; Laches 178b; Charmides 159a3–4; Gorgias 495a8–b2; Republic 350de.

25   Richards, p. 73.

26   Ibid., pp. 85–86.

27   *The Law Society v. Kordowski* [2011] EWHC 3185 (QB), Pars. 176–177.

statements that are true but further no compelling interest "from the perspective of the critical expression and discussion of general values."[28] He argues, for example, that "nothing in the reasonable purposes of free speech" requires that we disclose the names of rape victims.[29]

We need not take Richards' argument to imply that only thoughtful or sincere speech deserves legal protection. Speech can have social value even if it does not promote critical thinking; it can have value as a means of individual self-expression even if it does nothing to promote debate about public issues. Even speech that merely entertains has value. But when speech implicates legitimate privacy interests we must weigh the value of free speech against the value of privacy, and in doing so we need to recognize that not all speech deserves the same protection.

Should interests in free speech be put on a balancing scale? The E.U. vs. the U.S.

The thought that we must balance interests in speech and privacy will be obvious to anyone familiar with privacy law in the European Union. Article 8 of the European Convention on Human Rights (ECHR) provides that "[e]veryone has the right to respect for his private and family life" and that public authorities shall not interfere "with the exercise of this right except such as is in accordance with the law and is necessary in a democratic society … for the protection of the rights and freedoms of others." Article 10 provides that "[e]veryone has the right to freedom of expression" and that "the exercise of these freedoms, since it carries with it duties and responsibilities," may be subject to restrictions as are "necessary in a democratic society," restrictions that may include the need to respect the Article 8 right.[30] Neither right trumps the other—they must be balanced.[31] In addition, Directive 95/46/EC of the European Parliament, which imposes restrictions on the spread of personal data, provides for exemptions or derogations where restricting the flow of data would conflict with principles of free expression, and leaves it to the national courts to decide whether an exemption is warranted; in considering that question, regard is given to the values expressed in both Article 8 and Article 10 of the ECHR.[32]

Disagreement about the relative weight of Article 8 and Article 10 rights is not uncommon in the E.U.—not only among different Member States (as we shall see below), but among judges sitting on the same bench; but there

28 Richards, p. 74.
29 Ibid., p. 91.
30 http://conventions.coe.int/Treaty/en/Treaties/Html/005.htm.
31 See, e.g., *Douglas v. Hello! Ltd* [2001] QB 967, Par. 133; and *Campbell v. MGN Ltd* [2004] UKHL 22, Par. 111.
32 Text available at http://eur-lex.europa.eu; cf. Raymond Wacks, *Privacy and Media Freedom* (Oxford: Oxford University Press, 2013), pp. 172–179; and Rosemary Jay, *Data Protection Law and Practice*, 4th ed. (London: Sweet and Maxwell, 2012).

is consensus that free speech must be put on a balancing scale. In one of the leading U.K. cases, *Campbell v. MGN,* the House of Lords had to consider whether freedom of the press includes the freedom to report that supermodel Naomi Campbell had a drug problem and sought treatment. It ruled that *The Mirror* had the right to report the fact of the drug addiction and that she was receiving treatment because Ms. Campbell had publicly denied having a drug problem, and the press is entitled "to put the record straight."[33] But three of the five judges held that the newspaper violated privacy rights in publishing details of the treatment, the name of the facility, and a photograph of Ms. Campbell leaving the facility. Lord Nicholls, who would have allowed publication of details of the addiction and the photo, believed that non-publication would rob a legitimate news story of detail "which added colour and conviction."[34] Lord Hoffmann, also dissenting, agreed that publishing a humiliating photo would be improper, but believed there was nothing embarrassing about the picture, which was "an essential part of the story."[35] Lord Hope, reflecting the views of the three judges who opposed publication of the photo, explained that political expression has greater importance than commercial expression, and believed that publishing the photo of Ms. Campbell reflected a wish to attract interest in the newspaper rather than to promote political or democratic values.[36] Baroness Hale, who also opposed publication of the photo and details of the treatment, added that the speech in question here deserved less protection than political speech, which she characterized as "the free exchange of information and ideas on matters relevant to the organization of the economic, social, and political life of the country" that is "crucial to any democracy."[37] All five judges agreed, however, that the privacy interests at stake were less substantial than the public's interest in knowing that Ms. Campbell had lied.[38] It may be hard to see how knowing that a supermodel deceived the public about a medical condition that most people would expect to remain private contributes to democratic values; this suggests that even those judges who give special weight to speech that contributes to political life recognize that speech serves other values as

---

33 [2004] UKHL 22, Par. 129 (Lord Hope). See also *Rio Ferdinand v. MGN Ltd* [2011] EWHC 2454 (QB) (defending the *Sunday Mirror*'s Article 10 right to report on a soccer star's marital infidelities because of the public interest in correcting a false image that the athlete had conveyed).

34 [2004] UKHL 22, Par. 28.

35 [2004] UKHL 22, Pars. 76–77.

36 [2004] UKHL 22, Pars. 117, 120.

37 [2004] UKHL 22, Par. 148.

38 [2004] UKHL 22, Pars. 24 (Lord Nicholls), 36 (Lord Hoffmann), 82, 117 (Lord Hope), 151 (Baroness Hale), and 163 (Lord Carswell). Raymond Wacks has I think properly challenged the Court's position by noting that surely a celebrity with AIDS or cancer can deny he is a sufferer without the media having a right to "put the record straight," in *Privacy and Media Freedom,* pp. 149, 151–152.

well. But the point I want to emphasize is that all of the judges agreed that speech in principle can be limited if privacy interests are more substantial. They differed as to the importance of the speech in question but they all weighed the importance of the speech against the importance of Ms. Campbell's right to respect for her private life.

In the United States, in contrast, there has been some resistance to the very idea that we should put free speech on a scale of values. I want to be clear and avoid confusion: U.S. courts *do* balance interests in speech with other interests—though in the section below entitled "Deciding what is newsworthy" I will suggest that they seldom undertake this balancing test as seriously as it is undertaken in the U.K. My point is that in the U.S. the position that speech should simply not be put on a scale to be balanced is taken very seriously.

The primary source of protection for free speech in the U.S. is the First Amendment, which declares that Congress shall make no law "abridging the freedom of speech, or of the press." It limits not only Congress but states, having been incorporated into the Fourteenth Amendment's require-ment that no state shall deny any person life, liberty, or property without due process of law.[39] In 2011, the Supreme Court struck down a state law prohibiting the sale or rental of violent video games to minors over the objection that this category of speech was harmful and did not advance the goal traditionally associated with the First Amendment of protecting discourse on public matters. Justice Scalia was unconvinced by this objec-tion: "we have long recognized that it is difficult to distinguish politics from entertainment, and dangerous to try";[40] and he refused to create a new content-based category of unprotected speech "by applying a 'simple balancing test' that weighs the value of a particular category of speech against its social costs and then punishes that category of speech if it fails the test," calling that a "startling and dangerous" proposition.

Scalia's use of "long recognized" may be misleading. He cites but one prior case, *Winters v. New York* (1948), to which I referred earlier. In that case, a man was convicted for possessing a publication "principally made up of criminal news, police reports, or … stories of deeds of bloodshed, lust or crime," in violation of a state law. Such publications were outlawed by many states at the time out of concern that they may incite crime. In reversing the conviction, the Court did say that the distinction between speech that informs and speech that entertains is "too elusive" and that "[w]hat is one man's amusement teaches another's doctrine."[41] The law was struck down, though, not because a line between worthwhile and dysfunc-tional speech could not be drawn, but because the legislature drew the line

---

39   *Gitlow v. New York*, 268 U.S. 652 (1925).
40   *Brown v. Entertainment Merchants Assoc.*, 131 S.Ct. 2729, 2733 (2011), citing *Winters v. New York*, 333 U.S. 507, 510 (1948).
41   333 U.S. 507, 510.

without sufficient care: "the specification of publications, prohibited from distribution, [was] too uncertain and indefinite to justify the conviction." The Court added that "[t]o say that a state may not punish by such a vague statute carries no implication that it may not punish circulation of objectionable printed matter, assuming that it is not protected by the principles of the First Amendment, by the use of apt words to describe the prohibited publications."[42] Still, Scalia's line has been echoed by other judges who say that they should not be in the business of distinguishing worthwhile speech from speech that lacks social value.[43]

On its surface, the First Amendment may seem to impose an absolute bar to any state action abridging freedom of speech. But the Supreme Court has held that speech may be restricted for compelling reasons, and, in determining whether a restriction is justified, courts have recognized the need to determine whether speech has sufficient public value, despite Justice Scalia's suggestion to the contrary. As we will see shortly, the Court has ruled that speech promoting public debate about issues of legitimate public interest has more value than speech on private matters or speech that appeals to prurient interests, and deserves more protection. But in contrast with the European Union, in the U.S. some judges and First Amendment scholars express a reluctance even to attempt to decide which speech does or does not have sufficient public value—the same reluctance expressed by Mill—a reluctance to teeter on a slippery slope that could gravitate us to a society in which ideas are censored merely because they are unpopular or lack respectability. Because my position assumes that in addressing cases of unwanted attention in the age of social media we must balance privacy and free speech, it is particularly important to address this argument.

The slippery slope objection to protecting only some speech

Eugene Volokh argues that the law should not distinguish speech that is and is not of legitimate public interest or newsworthy. Appealing to a classic slippery slope argument, his position is that if you start restricting some speech that you do not regard as newsworthy, you will create a precedent for restricting other speech. Allowing a "private concern" exception would effectively let the government determine what one can say or listen to.[44] One case in which he thinks speech was wrongly restricted is *Diaz v. Oakland Tribune*.[45] A newspaper reported that the first woman student

42   333 U.S. 507, 519–520.
43   See *U.S. v. Stevens*, 559 U.S. 460, 471 (2010); *FCC v. Pacifica Foundation*, 438 U.S. 726, 763 (1978) (Brennan, dissenting); and the concurring opinion of Judge Smith in *J.S. v. Blue Mountain School District*, 650 F.3d 915, 939, 941 (2011), discussed below.
44   Eugene Volokh, "Freedom of Speech and Informational Privacy," *Stanford Law Review* 52(5):1049–1124 (2000), pp. 1088–1089.
45   188 Cal.Rptr. 762 (1983); discussed in Volokh, pp. 1089–1090.

body president of a community college was transsexual and she sued the paper for revealing a private fact. The Court held that a reasonable jury could find the speech not newsworthy and left it to an actual jury to decide. But on Volokh's view, "surely it is not for government agents—whether judges or jurors … to use the coercive force of law to keep others from informing them of things that they may consider relevant to [their political] choices."[46] Because of his concern for the consequences of allowing any exception to a rule permitting speech, Volokh seems willing to oppose restrictions even on speech that shows people in ridiculous, embarrassing, or demeaning contexts. He implies that we might even protect the printing of a picture of him on the toilet. His reason is not that this particular speech has value to society. Rather, he appeals to the slippery slope argument: "The danger is that the vague, subjective "public concern," "newsworthi-ness," or "legitimate public interest" test will flow far beyond this zone"; this risk "may be enough to abandon the test altogether."[47] This is the same objection that Justice Goldberg made in a leading case that I will discuss in the next section, *New York Times v. Sullivan*: if a jury could impose liabil-ity for malicious false statements criticizing official conduct, minority groups might be unable to publicize their views on public affairs.[48] Neither Goldberg nor Volokh trust judges or juries to make judgments about the worth of particular speech. Volokh concludes that a rule that allowed restrictions on speech that is not of legitimate public concern "deserves to be abandoned, even if it would yield the right results in a narrow subset of the cases in which it would be applied."[49]

This fear of teetering on slippery slopes is not as commonly found in the U.K. When Dame Elizabeth Butler-Sloss granted an injunction to prevent the reporting of the new identity of the murderers of James Bulger, she dismissed worries that granting the injunction in this case would open the door to restrictions on the media in other cases where anonymity would be desirable; she was confident that injunctions could be limited only to cases where restraints are "strictly necessary."[50] Her confidence was borne out when not long after, a Court of Appeal refused to issue an injunction to prohibit the reporting of the details of a case in which a mother allegedly killed her elder son and it was thought that identifying her in further news accounts would not be in the interest of the younger son, who might be bullied or suffer mental harm. The Court noted that the reasons Dame Elizabeth Butler-Sloss had for issuing her "novel" injunction did not apply in the case at hand.[51]

46 Volokh, p. 1090.
47 Volokh, p. 1094. Volokh appears to retreat somewhat from this position when he adds that if we do not abandon the test, we must at least clarify and narrow it.
48 376 U.S. 254, 299–300 (1964).
49 Volokh, p. 1095.
50 *Venables v. News Group Newspapers Ltd* [2001] 1 All ER 908 (D11).
51 *In re S* (A Child) [2003] EWCA Civ 963.

The problem with Volokh's view is that it assumes that free speech interests should always prevail over privacy concerns. While there is always a danger in giving discretion to judges or juries that they could apply a test for newsworthy speech in ways we would regard as misguided, if we recognize the importance of privacy we may be willing to accept that risk.[52]

Volokh rejects a newsworthy test not because he thinks free speech is an absolute right, but because he fears that adopting it would open the door to an incorrect balancing of interests. For example, a test to regulate speech on private concerns, he argues, could be mistakenly applied in ways that would restrict sexually themed speech. Judges or lawmakers might decide that such speech is not expressive and only serves to sexually arouse, does not contribute to the marketplace of ideas, and is not really speech.[53] One response to this concern is that it need not be too difficult to distinguish instances of sexually themed speech that do impinge on legitimate privacy interests and those that do not. Pornography placed online with the subject's informed consent raises no privacy concerns even though it may not be newsworthy. Speech that does not implicate privacy or other compelling interests would not be subject to a balancing test, and there would be no call to review its newsworthiness.

Because this point is so important, I want to emphasize it by drawing on another example. The case of *J.S. v. Blue Mountain School District* concerned a high school student who was suspended for posting a fake Myspace profile that demeaned her high school principal. J.S. created the profile on her home computer during the weekend, after she had been twice disciplined by the principal for dress code violations. She did not identify the principal by his real name, and indicated he was a principal in Alabama though J.S.'s school is in Pennsylvania; but she used his actual photo from a school district website. She portrayed the principal as a sex addict, using outrageous language that few people would take as truly portraying him.[54] The speech involved was not particularly valuable. But because it was so outlandish, and the record indicated that no one took it seriously, a majority of the Third Circuit Court of Appeals did not believe it implicated genuine reputational interests, and in a vote of 8-6, held that the school violated J.S.'s First Amendment rights in suspending her. The reason the decision was so close was that the dissent believed another compelling

---

52   There are of course other values besides those associated with privacy that can conflict with free speech: an interest in public safety may justify restrictions on threats; a concern that people not be wronged or subordinated might justify hate speech codes, see Andrew Altman, "Liberalism and Campus Hate Speech: A Philosophical Examination," *Ethics* 103:302–317 (1993).

53   Volokh, pp. 1099–1100.

54   650 F.3d 915 (3rd Cir. 2011). The profile lists the principal's interests as "detention, being a tight ass, riding the fraintrain [the principle's wife being named Ms. Frain], spending time with my child (who looks like a gorilla), baseball, my golden pen, fucking in my office, hitting on students and their parents" (p. 920).

interest was at stake: maintaining discipline and authority in the school. The dissent worried that allowing such assaultive speech might foster an attitude of disrespect towards teachers and staff and cause teachers to stop teaching altogether;[55] but the majority thought it unlikely that the speech would disrupt the school environment. Because privacy or other compelling interests were not at stake, it did not matter if the speech in question had little or no value.

Volokh might point to the closeness of the Court of Appeals' vote to support his view that we should not trust judges to determine when other interests outweigh interests in free speech—the decision nearly went the other way. But this leads us to a more fundamental problem with Volokh's argument. His defense of speech ultimately relies on a weighing of interests—on his view, for example, a world without sexually themed speech would have less utility than a world with it. But while he may be right in particular cases, he rigs the balance in favor of speech. That Volokh relies on a prejudged weighing of interests is apparent in his discussion of whether we should allow the publication of the names of rape victims. Volokh argues, "reluctantly," that we should allow their publication because of the dangers of restricting speech said not to be of legitimate public concern, a standard he finds too vague and broad. In defending this position he argues that the names of rape victims can often be quite relevant to public affairs: stating their names may be important in reassuring citizens that the right person has been accused, or that police are able to make arrests in rape cases; or reader attention might be better captured by giving the names of rape victims. He characterizes this as a "long, diverse" catalog of reasons why a rape victim's name is newsworthy.[56] But fear of the slippery slope should not deflect us from critically examining the catalog of reasons when legitimate privacy interests are at stake. It is difficult to envision why we would need to publish a victim's name in a newspaper to prompt new witnesses to appear who might be able to establish that the wrong person had been accused. What information could such a witness have that depended on their knowing the name of the victim, and why could this information not be elicited simply by informing the public that a rape took place at a particular time and place? Nor does Volokh explain how naming the victim is a sign that police are able to make arrests—that information could be conveyed simply by reporting that the police arrested the person who raped an unidentified victim at a particular time and place. Finally, while readers might be curious about the identity of a rape victim, Volokh never explains why it is valuable for people to have that information: will they remain unaware that the threat of rape looms in a particular community merely by reading that an unnamed person was raped, and take insufficient precautions? That, too, seems unlikely.

55   Dissent of Fisher, joined by five others, 650 F.3d 915, 945–946.
56   Volokh, p. 1116 and note 268.

By trying to establish that there is a public interest in publicizing names of rape victims Volokh appears to be conducting a balancing test; but the reasons he gives for valuing free speech in this case do not stand up to close scrutiny. Nor does he make a serious effort to assess the value of the rape victim's privacy interests. This casts doubt on the reliability of Volokh's balancing of interests in this particular instance. But we also have reason to be skeptical of his assessment of the relative importance of free speech and privacy generally. Volokh never shows that a world with unrestricted speech but little privacy is better than a world with privacy and reasonable restraints on speech. But, until that is established, we have no basis to join him in concluding that rules favoring free speech would generally yield the proper balancing of interests. While judges or juries might sometimes reach an undesirable outcome, or arrive at desirable outcomes only by the slimmest of margins, this is something we must live with when we must choose between competing values.

The speech that merits legal protection

If we reject the slippery slope argument and agree that we sometimes must balance speech and privacy interests, we must then ask in which kind of speech are interests more weighty. Despite the reluctance expressed by the likes of Justice Scalia to distinguish worthwhile speech from dysfunctional speech or mere entertainment, courts both in the U.S. and Europe have recognized that not all speech has the same value. We saw that several of the opinions in *Campbell v. MGN* distinguished political speech that is crucial to a democracy from other forms of expression; and the U.K.'s Data Protection Act 1998 as well as a number of media codes in England single out for protection speech that serves the "public interest."[57] The European Court of Human Rights (ECHR) has expressed its wariness of any limitations on freedom of expression when the press carries out its role in a democracy of "informing the public and imparting information and ideas on matters of public interest" but has indicated that "different considerations apply to press reports concentrating on sensational and, at times, lurid news, intended to titillate and entertain."[58] Another distinction well-known in Europe is between speech concerning public figures, in which the public has a greater interest, and speech about private citizens, though in Europe the concept of a "public figure" can extend beyond politicians to include their spouses, or to public role models who may never run for an elected office. In the U.K. it has been applied to soccer players;[59] and the ECHR

---

57 Data Protection Act 1998, section 32(1), online at www.legislation.gov.uk/ukpga/1998/29/section/32; and Julian Petley, "Public Interest or Shaming?," in Petley, ed., *Media and Public Shaming* (London: I.B. Tauris & Co., 2013), pp. 21–28.

58 *Mosley v. the United Kingdom*, [2011] ECHR 774, Pars. 112, 114.

59 See *A v. B plc* [2002] EWCA Civ 337; *Rio Ferdinand v. MGN Ltd* [2011] EWHC 2454.

held that the public has the right to be informed of the fact that the husband of a member of the Finnish Parliament was on trial for drunk and disorderly conduct even though the subject matter did not directly bear on political issues and even though one motive for reporting the event was to boost news sales.[60]

In this section I examine a line of cases in which the U.S. Supreme Court has drawn a number of distinctions to help identify speech that deserves special protection. I have two goals: to demonstrate that even in the U.S., where the slippery slope argument has its most zealous supporters, not all speech receives the same protection; and to argue that the distinctions the Court has drawn, while helpful, may not suffice for dealing with problems of unwanted attention in the age of social media.

Three of the four cases I shall focus on are a series of landmark decisions on libel law, the first being *New York Times v. Sullivan*.[61] L.B. Sullivan was a police commissioner in Montgomery, Alabama. The *New York Times* ran a full-page ad that did not mention Sullivan by name but did refer to "Southern violators of the Constitution" and "police" who tear-gassed student protestors, bombed the home of Martin Luther King, Jr., and padlocked a college dining hall to try to starve student protestors into submission. Sullivan claimed that the statement libeled him as he was known to be the head of the police. Some of the statements were not accurate; for example, there was no padlock on the dining hall. The state Supreme Court sustained an award of $500,000 against the *Times*.

The U.S. Supreme Court reversed that judgment and ruled in favor of the newspaper. The Court held that not all speech is alike: speech about the activity of public officials in their official capacity deserves greater protection than speech about private individuals. The First Amendment did not permit public officials to recover damages for a defamatory falsehood relating to their official conduct unless they prove that the statement was made with actual malice, or knowledge or reckless disregard of whether it was false.[62] Justice Brennan, representing the views of five of the nine Justices, wrote that the First Amendment protects speech on matters of the "highest public interest and concern"; its aim is to secure "the widest possible dissemination of information from diverse and antagonistic sources"; the Amendment reveals a "profound national commitment to the principle that debate on public issues should be uninhibited, robust, and wide-open."[63] Even false statements are protected when they are on matters of public interest because "erroneous statement is inevitable in free debate" and "must be protected if the freedoms of expression are to have the "breathing

60   *Karhuvaara and Iltalehti v. Finland* [2004] Case No. 53678/00, Pars. 44–46.
61   376 U.S. 254 (1964).
62   376 U.S. 254, 279–280.
63   376 U.S. 254, at 266, 270.

space" that they need ... to survive."[64] One may question what value false statements have in public debate, and Justice Brennan responds by drawing on what looks like the sort of rule-utilitarian argument that I will consider in more detail in Chapter 5: a specific utterance that is false may create disutility, but society receives greater overall utility when we adhere to a rule that protects even false statements, so long as they are not said with actual malice, because with this rule we avoid the "pall of fear and timidity" that would arise if people worried when voicing public criticism that they could be sued if they got some of the facts wrong.[65]

Times v. Sullivan left uncertain whether a publisher should be shielded when its article concerns a public issue but not a public figure, a question addressed in the next landmark case, *Gertz v. Robert Welch, Inc.*[66] Gertz was the attorney in a civil suit on behalf of the family of a man who was killed by a police officer. The Court regarded him as a private figure as he was not a public official, he had achieved "no general fame or notoriety in the community," and none of the prospective jurors had heard of him.[67] An article in a publication of the John Birch Society, *The American*, attacked Gertz as a Leninist conspirator out to frame the police. The publisher made no effort to verify these charges, and reprints of the article were distributed in Chicago, where Gertz lived. The editor denied actual malice, or knowledge that the statements were false, but the jury awarded $50,000 to Gertz on the ground that he was not a public official and therefore under the *Sullivan* rule the defamatory speech was not protected by the First Amendment. In a way, Gertz won, but in another way he did not. The Supreme Court ruled that being a private figure, Gertz does merit some protection against defaming speech that he would not merit were he a public official. Even though the published statements involved a matter of public interest, the Court decided that it is not speech about matters of public interest that is most strongly shielded by the First Amendment, but speech about public officials or public figures, and as Gertz was neither, liability for actual injury could be established on a less demanding showing than required by the *New York Times* standard of actual malice. However, the Court still protected publishers by not allowing liability absent a showing of negligence, or presumed or punitive damages absent a showing of knowledge of falsity or reckless disregard for the truth. This was a higher hurdle for plaintiffs than had existed in most states or at the common law. Justice Powell defended the distinction between speech about public and private figures by appealing to the importance of "private personality" and "the essential dignity and worth of every human being."[68] He also noted that private figures should

64   376 U.S. 254, 271–272, citing *NAACP v. Button*, 371 U.S. 415 (1963).
65   376 U.S. 254, 278.
66   418 U.S. 323 (1974).
67   418 U.S. 323, 351–352.
68   418 U.S. 323, 341, citing *Rosenblatt v. Baer*, 382 U.S. 75 (1966).

have a less demanding hurdle because they do not have the same access to channels of effective communication as public figures have and are therefore more vulnerable to defaming speech; in addition, public figures require greater scrutiny and invite more attention.[69]

Justice Brennan dissented, and his position is worth noting. He holds that speech on matters of public interest should receive special First Amendment protection even if the subject matter is a private individual. As citizens, he argues, we all have an obligation to be the subject of attention insofar as what we do concerns others: "Voluntarily or not, we are all 'public' men to some degree."[70] But Justice Brennan does not discuss what sorts of information about us are matters of legitimate public concern. On his view, the First Amendment should protect speech attacking Gertz because as an attorney he was weighing in on a debate of legitimate public concern. But consider the case of a man who is not a public figure who is arrested in a bar for an offense that it later turns out he did not commit: if a news station broadcasts the arrest but never indicates that the man was immediately released, should it be shielded from a false light tort claim on the ground that the arrest, though false, is a matter of legitimate public concern?[71] That Justice Brennan's account of this obligation could have troubling implications was recognized by Justice White, who agrees that the private citizen risks some exposure as a result of living in a civilized community, but does not think this leaves "society powerless to vindicate unfair injuries to his reputation."[72]

The last in the trio of landmark defamation rulings is *Dun & Bradstreet, Inc. v. Greenmoss Builders, Inc.*[73] Whereas *New York Times* involved alleged defamation of a public official in his official capacity, and *Gertz* involved defamation of a private citizen involved in a matter of public interest, in *Dun & Bradstreet* the plaintiff was a private figure and the defamatory speech was not a matter of public concern. Dun & Bradstreet is a credit reporting agency that sent a small group of subscribers a report that the petitioner had filed for bankruptcy—which was false. Unsatisfied with the firm's corrective notice, the plaintiff sued and was awarded $50,000 in presumed damages and $300,000 in punitive damages for the mistake of a 17-year-old student employee. The company was negligent in failing to verify the information it sent out, but there was no actual malice. The Court affirmed the award of damages on the ground that the *Gertz* standard does not apply to private speech. Justice Powell, writing for a 5-4 majority, again balances privacy against free speech interests. At stake is an individual's right to protect his private personality, and "the essential dignity and worth

69   418 U.S. 323, 344–345.
70   418 U.S. 323, 364.
71   Cf. *Penwell v. Taft Broadcasting*, 469 N.E.2d 1025 (1984), discussed in Chapter 6.
72   418 U.S. 323, 402.
73   472 U.S. 749 (1985).

of every human being"; on the other side of the privacy/free speech scale, speech that is not a matter of public concern does not merit much protection.[74] The plaintiff's credit report is not a matter of public interest; it is not speech that is needed "to ensure that debate on public issues will be uninhibited, robust, and wide-open."[75]

Finally, a more recent case identifies further dimensions to the problem raised in the earlier cases of deciding which speech is and is not deserving of special protection. *Snyder v. Phelps* concerned the activity of members of Westboro Baptist Church, who had picketed nearly 600 funerals to express their views on a variety of issues.[76] Phelps, the founder of the church, along with his children and grandchildren, picketed a funeral at a Catholic Church for Matthew Snyder, who had been killed in the Iraq War. Phelps' group stood on public land about 200–300 feet from where the funeral procession passed, carrying signs such as "God Hates the USA/Thank God for 9/11," "Thank God for Dead Soldiers," "Pope in Hell," "God Hates Fags," and "You're Going to Hell." Although Matthew's father testified that he could see the tops of the picket signs as he drove to the funeral, he did not see what was written on the signs until later that night when watching a news broadcast.[77] He objected to the group's false accusation that Matthew was gay, and sued for defamation, giving publicity to private facts, intentional infliction of emotional distress, and intrusion upon seclusion. A jury ruled for Snyder on the latter two torts and awarded substantial damages. The district court agreed that Snyder was wronged, although it reduced the punitive award from $8 million to $2.1 million. The Court of Appeals reversed these judgments on First Amendment grounds and the Supreme Court agreed.

The Supreme Court followed earlier libel cases in finding that public speech is entitled to greater First Amendment protection. Speech is public if it relates to any matter of political, social, or other concern to the community, or is a subject of legitimate public interest.[78] The Court cited as examples of speech that is *not* public the credit report at issue in *Dun and Bradstreet*, and the video of an employee engaging in sex acts that was at issue in another case, *San Diego v. Roe*.[79] Phelps' speech, according to the Court, clearly related to broad issues of interest to society. The Court identified the speech as public not merely because its content related to public issues; it was also important that the speech was expressed to others in a

74   472 U.S. 749, 757–759. See also the Restatement (Second) of Torts Sec. 580B, cmt. H (1977): "Informing the public as to a matter of public concern is an important interest in a democracy; spreading of mere gossip is of less importance"; cited in *Parnigoni v. St. Columba's Nursery School*, 681 F.Supp.2d 1, 16 (2010).
75   472 U.S. 749, 762, citing *New York Times v. Sullivan*.
76   131 S.Ct. 1207 (2011).
77   131 S.Ct. 1207, 1213–1214.
78   131 S.Ct. 1207, 1215–1216.
79   543 U.S. 77 (2004).

public place. Such speech receives special protection under the First Amendment. The Court added that the speech disturbed Snyder not because of its loudness but because of its content, and so regulating it would not be content-neutral.[80] But not all the Justices agreed that the speech was public. In his dissent, Justice Alito argued that the motive of Westboro—to raise awareness about public issues—does not turn its attack of a private figure into public speech. Matthew Snyder was not a public figure, and a personal attack on him for his religious affiliation, military status, and alleged sexual orientation is not speech that is of public concern. Alito argued that the context in which the speech occurred should be recognized for what it was—the mourning of a dead soldier—and not as a forum for public debate.[81]

These four cases point to a variety of different sorts of speech. There is speech spoken in private, which can be on public or private affairs, as distinct from speech spoken in public for public consumption; there is speech on public matters, as distinct from speech on private matters; there is speech spoken about public figures or officials as distinct from speech about those who are not; and there is speech spoken by the media as opposed to speech of ordinary citizens. The Justices found several of these differences in context relevant in evaluating the relative importance of speech as against privacy interests. In his concurring opinion in the case of *J.S. v. Blue Mountain School District* that was discussed earlier, Judge Smith invoked the slippery slope argument and suggested that the vulgar Myspace profile J.S. made of her principal is protected simply because it is speech: "there is no First Amendment exception for offensive speech or for speech that lacks a certain quantum of social value"; and he echoed Justice Scalia in adding that "courts have long disclaimed the ability to draw a principled distinction between 'worthless' and 'valuable' speech."[82] But the consideration of the four U.S. Supreme Court precedents has indicated that courts in the U.S. indeed take up the challenge Judge Smith says judges should not take up, of assessing the value of speech and its consequences to legitimate privacy interests.

The four cases distinguish public and private speech, with the former meriting more protection. Justices in *Snyder* appealed to two distinct criteria for designating speech as public—is it spoken in a public place or otherwise accessible to the public? Is it on an issue of public concern?—and these criteria may conflict. There can be private speech, not intended for the general public, about a public matter; and speech about private matters can be spoken in public—it is with this latter sort of speech that the

---

80   131 S.Ct. 1207, 1217–1219.
81   131 S.Ct. 1207, 1222, 1226–1228.
82   650 F.3d 915, 939, 941. Yet Judge Smith proceeded to infer a social value to J.S.'s speech: it is a "safety valve" that enables "citizens to vent their frustrations in nonviolent ways" (650 F.3d 915, 940, citing Smolla).

tort of publication of private facts is concerned. Drawing on the majority opinions in the four cases, and being attentive to the distinct ways of defining public speech that are apparent in *Snyder*, it might be tempting to extract a simple formula: speech that is accessible to the public about a public figure on a matter of legitimate public interest should get the most protection; speech that is publicly accessible about a private figure on a matter of legitimate public interest is also protected even when it impinges on legitimate privacy interests (such as the interest in keeping private one's sexual orientation), as suggested by *Snyder*, though based on *Gertz* it merits less protection than the first sort of speech; speech that is publicly accessible about a private matter that is not of legitimate public interest deserves the least protection, as does "private speech," defined as speech that is not made accessible to the public, no matter its subject matter.

While some of these distinctions can be helpful in many contexts, in others they may be less so, particularly in the age of social media. Speech may be accessible to the public merely by virtue of being spoken loudly or to a gossiper, and now with the ability to capture someone's image or record their conversation and share it on the Internet, or to forward an email to people who were not meant to receive it, the line between private and public speech may seem to be dissolving.[83] Referring again to *J.S. v. Blue Mountain School District*, when J.S. first created the fake profile of her principal she waited a day until limiting access to it, so for that first day it was accessible to the public, although it was unlikely anyone other than those J.S. notified would find it.[84] After that first day, the profile was directly accessible only to people J.S. designated as her friends on Myspace, and she probably did not intend for it to be made available to the principal. It was not readily accessible to the school community from within the school since the school prevented Myspace from being accessed on school computers.[85] Yet it was not as private as it would be if it were related to the student's friend in a private conversation; and it did become public when someone showed it to the principal.

The simple formula may be problematic also in assuming that speech that is accessible to the public deserves more protection; this ignores how such speech, by virtue of it having a wider audience, can also be more disruptive, invasive, or damaging to someone's legitimate privacy interests. Yet there are sometimes reasons for protecting public speech just because it is public even though it may pose more of a threat than private speech. There is no substantial public interest at stake that would justify restricting

---

83   This does not mean that the distinction is of no value; see Chapter 3, "Controlling the intended audience of one's message"; and the section below entitled "Newsworthy for a select group."

84   A decision the previous year, not mentioned by the court, held that whether one can expect privacy in what one posts on Facebook or Myspace depends on the privacy settings one selected, see *Crispin v. Audigier et.al.*, 717 F.Supp.2d 965 (2010).

85   650 F.3d 915, 921 (2011).

the speech of a student who tells another student in private that the assistant principal is "such a dick." In contrast, a student who tells the assistant principal to his face in a crowded hallway, "You are the biggest dick I know," may well act against the public interest by directly challenging the official's authority and potentially undermining discipline in the school.[86] But while only the public speech poses a threat, there is also a reason to protect it. The slope we travail when we repress speech that challenges authority is exactly the slope we want to avoid slipping down when we think of free speech protections as a check on tyranny and a vital tool of democratic self-governance.

We need a more nuanced guide than the simple formula provides on its own. The fact that speech is readily accessible to some members of the public does not mean it ought to be readily accessible to everyone for all time; and the interest the public has in newsworthy matters—whether they concern private or public figures—may sometimes be adequately promoted without identifying them or showing their image to the general public. In the rest of this chapter, I will discuss some additional principles we can draw on to determine if particular speech is newsworthy. But before doing so I want to address a lingering question regarding the scope of legal protections of free speech: do they apply only to the press?

Do legal protections of free speech apply only to professional journalists?

With new technologies that have allowed what in Chapter 1 I referred to as the democratization of the media, many people now have the ability to gather and disseminate information. Can bloggers, those who post to a Facebook wall, or producers of entertainment shows all don the cloak of the First Amendment or Article 10 of the European Convention on Human Rights (ECHR) to shield themselves from liability when they invade someone's privacy, or are these protections primarily intended for recognized members of the news media?

Article 10 of the ECHR says "*Everyone* has the right to freedom of expression" and so the right is not limited to professional journalists or the press. However, Directive 95/46/EC of the European Parliament imposes restrictions on the processing and movement of personal data, and Article 9 of that Directive requires Member States to "provide for exemptions or derogations ... for the processing of personal data carried out solely for journalistic purposes or the purpose of artistic or literary expression," if those exemptions are "necessary to reconcile the right to privacy with the

---

86   See *Posthumus v. Bd of Educ. of the Mona Shores Pub. Sch.*, 380 F.Supp.2d 891, 895 (W.D. Mich. 2005).

rules governing freedom of expression."[87] Whether an exemption is warranted is for the national court to decide, and there is no consensus as to how broadly exemptions for free speech should extend. Sweden and Denmark extend free speech exemptions to most anyone, whereas Eastern European countries provide few exemptions.[88] One individual in Sweden used a website to spread information about alleged malpractice in the Swedish banking system and to publish derogatory comments about particular individuals working at certain banks. Lower courts found that the defendant was not exempt as a journalist from restrictions on sharing personal data, but Sweden's Supreme Court reversed that judgment: since Article 10 accords rights to free expression to "everyone," the Court held, the Directive's Article 9 exemption for journalistic purposes could apply to non-professional journalists who share information about issues of social significance.[89]

In the United States, the First Amendment seeks to protect speech that informs and educates the public on issues of public concern, and the Supreme Court has held that the press does not have a monopoly on the ability to enlighten.[90] The "freedom of speech" clause surely protects anyone who produces such speech; it even protected J.S., though her speech did not enlighten. But why is the clause "or of the press" there? Does it offer protections not already provided by the free speech clause, and if so, do these protections extend to "citizen-journalists"?

Justice Burger explored the former question in a concurring opinion in *First National Bank of Boston v. Bellotti*. On his view, the history of the clause suggests it does not confer special privileges on the institutional press. The "press" referred to any man communicating to the public, and freedom of speech and freedom of press were used synonymously. Freedom of the press is a personal right not limited to newspapers and periodicals but encompasses the speech of "lecturers, political pollsters,

87   Text available at http://eur-lex.europa.eu/. A proposed revision includes a similar provision: Article 80 would oblige Member States "to adopt exemptions and derogations from specific provisions of the Regulation where necessary to reconcile the right to the protection of personal data with the right of freedom of expression" and is based on Article 9 of Directive 95/46/EC, "as interpreted by the Court of Justice of the EU"—COM/2012/011 final, available at the same website (accessed January 24, 2014).

88   According to David Erdos, Oxford Privacy Information Conference: "The 'Right to be Forgotten' and Beyond," June 12, 2012. Online at www.csls.ox.ac.uk/conferences/oxpilsconference2012; cf. Thomas Zerdick, in the same conference proceedings.

89   Lee Bygrave, "Balancing Data Protection and Freedom of Expression," *Privacy Law and Policy Reporter* 8:83–85 (2001), referring to Case B 293-00 decided June 12, 2001. Cf. the Finnish case *Tietosuojavaltuutettu v. Satamedia*, Case C-73/07 (2008), Pars. 61–62: derogations allowed for in Article 9 apply not only to traditional media but to those who use the Internet solely to disclose information, opinions, or ideas, as determined by the national court.

90   *First National Bank of Boston v. Bellotti*, 435 U.S. 765, 781–2 (1978).

novelists, academic researchers, and dramatists" as well as almost any author.[91] He suggests the press clause was probably included because of the threat the printing press had posed to governments and the desire to ensure the press would not be censored.[92] Justice Stewart, though, argues that the free press and free speech clauses are distinct.[93] What is provided in the free press clause that is not already contained in the free speech clause are privileges accorded to members of the Fourth Estate so that they can serve their function. An example might be immunity from libel suits, which individuals are not given on the basis of the free speech clause; or the right to refuse to tell a grand jury the identity of a source of information—though in one case the Supreme Court refused to shield a member of the press from a court order requiring him to reveal his source.[94]

Some have objected to the idea that the Fourth Estate should have special protections. Eric Barendt argues that disclosure of private information by the press can be "much more damaging than conversation between family and friends" and "media gossip" more damaging than "village gossip"; if anything the press should face more restrictions because it has amassed so much power.[95] Simon Dawes argues that we should not assume that a free press necessarily serves the public interest: the press is subject to market forces that can have a distorting effect on its conception of the public interest, and he notes how in many respects the press is now an "entertainment industry."[96] It would be troubling to give special protection to the news media when it does not act responsibly, and it does not always do so. In Chapter 1, I noted one striking example regarding Dateline NBC's program "To Catch a Predator," and there are others, an obvious one from England being the hacking by *News of the World* reporters of Milly Dowler's mobile phone, which led to the Leveson Inquiry.[97] Such examples cast doubt on the position, defended by some scholars, that we should leave journalists to police themselves and draw on their own professional judgment to avoid abuses of the exercise of free speech.[98] It is unlikely that

---

91   435 U.S. 765, 801–2, citing *Branzburg v. Hayes*, 408 U.S. 665, 704–705 (1972), which quotes *Lovell v. Griffin*, 303 U.S. 444, 450 (1938).

92   435 U.S. 765, 799–801.

93   Potter Stewart, "Or of the Press," *Hastings Law Journal* 26:631–637 (1975), pp. 633–635.

94   *Branzburg v. Hayes*, 408 U.S. 665 (1972).

95   Eric Barendt, "Privacy and Freedom of Speech," in Kenyon and Richardson, eds., *New Dimensions in Privacy Law* (Cambridge: Cambridge University Press, 2006), p. 23.

96   Simon Dawes, "Privacy and the Freedom of the Press," in Petley, ed., p. 50 (citing the work of James Curran).

97   See www.levesoninquiry.org.uk/; and Sarah Lyall and Eric Pfanner, "Scandal Grows over Hacking of Girl's Cell," *New York Times*, July 6, 2011, p. A1. For a fictional account of an irresponsible press see Heinrich Böll, *The Lost Honor of Katharina Blum or: How Violence Develops and Where It Can Lead*, tr. Leila Vennewitz (New York: McGraw Hill, 1975).

98   Amy Gajda, "Judging Journalism: The Turn Toward Privacy and Judicial Regulation of the Press," *California Law Review* 97:1039–1104 (2009).

self-regulation would ensure an adequate balancing of competing interests.[99]

Nor would self-regulation by professional journalists help address problems of unwanted attention created by "citizen-journalists." If the "free press" clause was to be extended to protect those who are not formally part of the news media, it might be possible to limit the protection it affords only to those who perform what Barry McDonald refers to as "legitimate and valuable information gathering and dissemination functions."[100] Courts in the U.S. are beginning to address how we might discern who is and is not performing these legitimate functions. Though the Supreme Court ruled that the First Amendment may not give journalists a right to refuse to name confidential sources when served with a court order, many states have enacted shield laws to give journalists that right. Courts are now dealing with the question of to whom this newsperson's privilege extends. In one decision in New Jersey, it was extended to the author of a book about a public figure, at least when that author was a staff writer for a newspaper and drew on material for his book that had also appeared in a newspaper, even where the book has a lighter tone than would a news article.[101] But another court held that the same New Jersey shield law does not extend to a self-described journalist who posts on an Internet message board, though in a later case the shield was extended to a blogger.[102] In Oregon, a blogger who apparently had a history of making defamatory allegations and seeking payoffs in exchange for a retraction relied on unnamed sources to accuse an individual and a company of fraud, money-laundering, and other illegal activities. A district court judge ruled that the blogger was not protected by Oregon's shield law. If the blogger was regarded as the "press" then according to the First Amendment and the *Sullivan* line of cases the plaintiffs would need to prove "actual malice" to recover presumed damages. But the judge refused to regard the blogger as "media": she had none of the attributes of a member of the media such as education in journalism, credentials of affiliation with the media, or proof of adherence to journalistic standards such as attempting to get both sides of a story, or keeping notes of interviews.[103] However the Ninth Circuit reversed that part of the district court ruling and decided that First Amendment defamation rules "apply equally to the institutional press and individual speakers" and "do not turn on whether the defendant was a trained journalist" or

99   See Anita Allen, "Why Journalists Can't Protect Privacy," in LaMay, ed., *Journalism and the Debate over Privacy* (Mahwah, NJ: Lawrence Erlbaum, 2003).
100 McDonald, "The First Amendment and the Free Flow of Information," *Ohio State Law Journal* 65:249–356 (2004), p. 257.
101 *Trump v. O'Brien*, 958 A.2d 85 (Sup. Ct. of New Jersey 2008).
102 *Too Much Media, LLC v. Hale*, 20 A.3d 364 (Sup. Ct. of New Jersey 2011); and *In re January 11, 2013 Subpoena by Grand Jury of Union County*, 75 A.3d 1260 (2013).
103 *Obsidian Finance Group v. Cox*, 2011 WL 5999334 (D. Or. 2011), p. 5.

"tried to get both sides of a story."[104] It cited the U.S. Supreme Court opinion of *Citizens United v. Federal Election Commission*, which noted that "with the advent of the Internet and the decline of print and broadcast media … the line between the media and others who wish to comment on political and social issues becomes far more blurred."[105] The Court apparently takes the descriptive fact that the media has become democratized as a normative argument for treating "citizen-journalists" the same as traditional media. This may not be a problem, but only if there are sufficient checks on both.

Deciding what is newsworthy

When we weigh the interest in speech against privacy interests, one of the considerations relevant in assessing the value of speech is whether it informs the public about topics of public interest. Such speech deserves to be given special weight. Justice Brennan, we saw, argues that we have an obligation to be the subject of attention insofar as what we do concerns others. But I now want to think about this point more critically. How do we determine which of the many things about us are matters that concern others and therefore may be the subject of speech that merits special protection?

At times, courts have construed the speech that serves the public interest or is newsworthy quite broadly. In the U.K. case of *A v. B plc*, Lord Woolf seemingly implies that the press may publish whatever the public is interested in reading. He set aside an injunction that would have prevented publication of the fact that a well-known soccer player slept with other women despite being married. It is difficult to see how this fact contributes to the goals of a democracy, but Lord Woolf argued that "the public have an understandable and so a legitimate interest in being told the information" especially as it concerned a sports figure who plays a role in public life.[106] But he also made what seems to be an argument to protect speech with no political relevance and that merely entertains: "if newspapers do not publish information which the public are interested in, there will be fewer newspapers published, which will not be in the public interest."[107]

But the position that we should protect speech so long as it may be interesting to people cannot be correct. Karen Sanders has suggested that this would sanction stripping and photographing someone in public who members of the public would be interested in seeing naked.[108] Her

---

104 *Obsidian Finance Group v. Cox*, 740 F.3d 1284, 1290–1 (9th Cir. 2014).
105 558 U.S. 310, 352 (2010). Cited in 740 F.3d 1284, 1291 (2014).
106 *A v. B plc* [2002] EWCA Civ 337, Par. 11 (xii): "certain facts relating to the private lives of public figures, particularly politicians, may indeed be of interest to citizens, and it may therefore be legitimate for readers, who are also voters, to be informed of those facts."
107 Ibid.
108 Karen Sanders, *Ethics and Journalism* (London: Sage, 2003), p. 90.

particular example ignores the great difference between sharing interesting gossip about your private life and forcibly stripping you, but the underlying point is sound. Before we give speech of public interest special protection, we need some account of which speech is a matter of *legitimate* public concern. Speech that impinges on legitimate expectations of privacy should have to meet some standard beyond merely being of interest to others.

Speech that does not would not need to meet a higher bar. This is a crucial point worth emphasizing again: if it does not intrude upon privacy or other compelling interests, there would be no need for entertainment such as video games or pulp fiction or expressive speech like J.S.'s fake Myspace profile to promote discussion of public issues. But, in cases where privacy is at stake, we might need to distinguish politically relevant or otherwise valuable speech from mere entertainment, though some judges say they are reluctant to try. Courts in the United States have attempted to draw this distinction by asking whether speech is "newsworthy," and courts in the European Union by asking whether speech serves the "public interest." I will treat these as identical questions.

In Chapter 2 I referred to a photo that appeared on the front page of a national edition of the *New York Times* of a couple passionately embracing on a beach in New York City on a balmy day in April. The photo caption, titled "Loving the Weather," included their names, presumably with the couple's consent. I then raised a different scenario to which I now want to return. Suppose that the photographer took their photo surreptitiously, and used facial recognition software to determine their names, and the paper published the photo and their names without their consent or prior knowledge. Suppose they would have objected: perhaps each was married to someone else and publishing the photo would reveal their infidelity and ruin their marriages.[109] Should the *New York Times* legally be able to publish the photo? Would it be ethical of them to do so? Answers to either question depend on how we weigh competing interests. If privacy were not implicated, there would be no need to ask if the *Times* had sufficient reason to publish the photo. But the argument put forth in Chapters 2 and 3 suggests that even though the couple is in a public place, they can still have a legitimate privacy interest in anonymity. Assuming we agree, we then need to consider the countervailing free speech interest, and in this case it is minimal. There is no need to publish the photo of and identify a non-consenting couple whose privacy would be implicated in order to achieve either of the two most likely purposes of the photo: to show that New York experienced a day in April that was so warm that a man could go shirtless and a woman

---

109 Compare *DeGregorio v. CBS*, 473 N.Y.S.2d 922 (N.Y. Sup. Ct. 1984), discussed in Chapter 1, in which a couple, each married to someone else, was filmed walking along a sidewalk hand in hand and the footage was used for a television news segment about romance in New York.

could wear a bikini at the beach; or to titillate the readers with an image of a passionate embrace. Those purposes could be achieved in other ways.

This conclusion is at odds with precedents, particularly in the U.S., in which courts have allowed publication of photos or videos taken in a public place over the objection of those who did not welcome the attention, on the ground that one cannot reasonably expect privacy in public places, and by relying on a very expansive conception of information that is newsworthy. In this section, I argue that we need to reevaluate our understanding of newsworthiness. Some private facts may be so newsworthy that they should be published. But some public facts may not be newsworthy and perhaps should not be published if they implicate significant privacy interests. Rodney Smolla also distinguishes private and non-private information that is and is not newsworthy. On his view, once we determine that information is newsworthy, "newsworthiness always wins, whether the plaintiff is a public figure or a private figure."[110] I will argue that matters are not so clear-cut: there can be non-newsworthy details of a newsworthy event, and information that is newsworthy for a certain group may not be newsworthy for the general public.

Courts have of course recognized that not all facts are newsworthy. Some courts in the U.S. have held that publicizing private facts about someone who is not a public figure can be a cause of legal action if the publication has no legitimate news value.[111] One court found that broadcasting a rapist's video of his assault may serve only prurient interests and be inessential to conveying the news that a rape took place.[112] Another court held that publishing gossip about an individual's love life, even if the information is true, violated privacy rights insofar as a person's romantic life "is not a matter of public concern."[113] Still another court found that the government violated a defendant's civil rights when, following a request from the media, it staged a "perp walk"—taking the defendant outside, handcuffing him, and having him walk back into the very precinct room he had been brought into two hours earlier—solely so that a local television news station could film his arrest. The Court held that this placed the defendant in a humiliating situation while serving no legitimate government interest, and constituted an unreasonable seizure.[114] In the U.K., Mr. Justice Eady ruled in

110 Smolla, *Free Speech in an Open Society*, p. 127, and ch. 5 generally.

111 Amy Gajda, "Judging Journalism," pp. 1066, 1081–1086, 1104; Smolla, *Free Speech in an Open Society*, ch. 5 (allowing that sexual behavior of a public figure may be newsworthy, p. 136, but arguing that we should treat private figures differently, p. 135).

112 *Doe v. Luster*, 2007 Cal.App. Unpub. Lexis 6042 (2007).

113 *Benz v. Washington Newspaper Publishing Co. and Bisney*, 34 Media L. Rep. 2368 (D.C. 2006).

114 *Lauro v. Charles*, 219 F.3d 202 (2nd Cir. 2000); distinguished from *Caldarola v. County of Westchester*, 343 F.3d 570 (2nd Cir. 2003) in which the court found no rights violation when government made a video of an actual rather than a reenacted perp walk. I return to these cases in Chapter 6.

the *Mosley* case that there is no public interest in seeing images of the depraved activity even of a public figure. While publicizing a sex orgy involving the leader of an international automobile association might serve a legitimate public interest if the orgy had a Nazi-theme, Mr. Justice Eady did not find persuasive evidence that it did: the purpose of publication was titillation for its own sake and not to contribute to "debate of general interest."[115] Video of the orgy no doubt interested the public, as indicated by the thousands of people who watched it;[116] but being of interest to the public does not make the video a matter of public interest.[117]

Yet while there are some significant exceptions, the rule in the U.S. has been that most anything is regarded by courts as newsworthy. Some courts have defined matters of legitimate public concern, or what is newsworthy, quite broadly to include any subject of public interest.[118] In *Sweenek v. Pathé News*, the plaintiff claimed her privacy rights were violated under a state civil rights law when a newsreel exhibited her and other women, without their consent, using new, specially designed gym equipment to lose weight. The Court rejected her claim for two reasons: first, she was in a public gym where she could not reasonably expect privacy; second, so long as "a large proportion of the female sex continues its concern for dieting," then "pictures of corpulent women using a new apparatus is news."[119] In *Penwell v. Taft Broadcasting*, a court dismissed the suit of a plaintiff who objected to the broadcasting of a video showing him being falsely arrested, not just because the arrest took place in a bar open to the public but also because the arrest was thought to be a matter "with which the public had a legitimate concern."[120] *Harper's Magazine* published a photo of a couple holding hands in a confectionary concession in Los Angeles' Farmer's Market for a story about everyday people in love. While the picture may seem to have no news value, the Court found no violation of privacy as the couple was in a public place and the publication served "the function of entertainment as a matter of legitimate interest."[121] And a newspaper was permitted to publish the name of a 12-year-old girl who married a 20-year-old man and

115 *Mosley v. News Group Newspapers Ltd* [2008] EWHC 1777, Pars 124, 128, 132, 114.
116 [2008] EWHC 1777, Par. 132; cf. Adrian Quinn, "John Leslie: The Naming and Shaming of an Innocent Man," in Petley, ed., p. 213, on how sales of *The Mail* and *The Express* increased by 300,000 copies following public disclosure that the unnamed rapist referred to in Ulrika Jonsson's book *Honest* may have been a television personality.
117 [2008] EWHC 1777, Par. 114.
118 *Messenger v. Gruner + Yahr Printing and Pub.*, 94 N.Y.2d 436, 442 (2000): "this Court has held that 'newsworthiness' is to be broadly construed. Newsworthiness includes not only descriptions of actual events [b]ut also articles concerning political happenings, social trends *or any subject of public interest*" (my emphasis).
119 16 F.Supp. 746, 747–748 (1936).
120 469 N.E.2d 1025, 1028 (1984).
121 *Gill v. Hearst Publishing Co.*, 253 P.2d 441, 444 (1953).

gave birth to his son, against their wishes, as this "biological occurrence" would "naturally excite public interest."[122]

Courts in some Member States of the European Union have at times characterized the speech protected by the right to freedom of expression quite broadly as well, to include "banal and trivial expression as well as matters of public interest," or "reports for entertainment purposes" which might play a role in the formation of opinions. But the same courts note that where the right to free expression has to be balanced against privacy rights, "the extent to which the content is of public interest or contributes to a debate of general interest assumes a much greater importance." The reader's interest in being entertained may carry "less weight than that of protecting privacy."[123] U.S. courts, having invoked a broad conception of newsworthiness, do not typically take this further step of seriously assessing the value of speech found to be newsworthy when weighing it against the value of privacy.

A seminal case is *Gates v. Discovery Communications*, which overturned *Briscoe v. Reader's Digest*, a case I discussed in earlier chapters. *Briscoe* concerned an article on hijacking published by the *Reader's Digest* in 1968 that referred to a crime Mr. Briscoe had committed in 1956 and for which he had already served prison time. Because of the article, Briscoe's daughter and friends found out about his past crime, which he had kept a secret, and left him.[124] The California Supreme Court refused to dismiss Mr. Briscoe's cause of action for invasion of his privacy. While recognizing the benefits of reporting current criminal activities, and that reports of some past crimes may sometimes prove educational, it concluded that identifying Mr. Briscoe's crime serves little public purpose: it will no longer help to "bring forth witnesses or obtain succor for victims." Publication also may undermine the state's interest in the rehabilitative process by making it harder for Mr. Briscoe to lead a normal and socially productive life.[125]

The *Briscoe* court *did* think carefully about whether the information in question was newsworthy. But in *Gates*, the Court overturned *Briscoe* and held that a television station may broadcast a documentary that refers to the plaintiff's past crime though he had completed his punishment about ten years earlier. After reviewing several U.S. Supreme Court cases issued since the *Briscoe* decision that held that the press may not be prevented from publishing truthful information contained in official court records open to

122 *Meetze v. A.P.*, 95 S.E.2d 606, 610 (1956). Cf. Tunick, "Reality Television and the Entrapment of Predators," in Robson and Silbey, eds., *Law and Justice on the Small Screen* (Oxford: Hart Publishing, 2012), pp. 298–299.
123 *Rio Ferdinand v. MGN Limited* [2011] EWHC 2454 (QB), Par. 62; and *Von Hannover v. Germany (no. 2)* [2012] ECHR 228, Pars. 31–33 (characterizing a decision by the German Federal Court of Justice).
124 *Briscoe v. Reader's Digest Assoc. Inc.*, 4 Cal.3d 529 (1971).
125 4 Cal.3d 529, 537–538.

public inspection, the *Gates* court ruled that while the plaintiff's interest in privacy might be highly significant, it is not of the highest order.[126] The Court was reluctant to forbid publication of public records because such a rule would "make it very difficult for the media to inform citizens about the public business" or publish information that "should be made available to the public."[127]

In Chapter 2 I discussed how one can have a reputational interest in privacy; people who committed crimes many years before have an interest in reinventing themselves so that they can forge new ties and relationships, as well as an interest in avoiding continual punishment that exceeds what they deserve. Here I focus on the "free speech" side of the scales. What interest does society have in being informed about Briscoe's or Gates's crimes, neither of which was notorious or of historical significance? Volokh suggests that this information might be important in deciding whether to leave your child in the men's care for the day, or to conduct business with them.[128] But the number of subscribers to *Reader's Digest* or viewers of the documentary on Gates's past crime is much larger than the pool of Gates's or Briscoe's potential employers or neighbors with children, and there are alternative means of giving that pool of people the information they would require to decide whether to do business with either, such as making records of past crimes available to those who submit an inquiry. The *Gates* court does not explain why information about such a long-past crime "should" be made available to the public. It claims to balance privacy interests against interests the public has in access to information but does not closely examine these interests in order to fairly assess their relative value.

In contrast, courts in the U.K. have taken the idea of a balancing test more seriously—though one might still disagree with how they apply the test in particular cases. As an example, consider the case of *R(L) v. Commissioner of Police of the Metropolis.*[129] The appellant sought to quash a police decision to disclose certain information about her and her son on an Enhanced Criminal Record Certificate (ECRC) that she had to submit for her job as a midday assistant at a secondary school. Among the relevant information that the Chief Police Officer included was that L failed to properly supervise her 13-year-old son; that the son was engaged in criminal activities, missed school, and assaulted a teacher; that L had allegedly refused to cooperate with social services; that the child was put on the child protection register due to neglect; and that her son received a custodial sentence for robbery.[130] She was soon fired, and sought judicial review. While Lord

---

126 The intervening Supreme Court decisions included *Cox Broadcasting Corp. v. Cohn*, 420 U.S. 469 (1975); *Oklahoma Pub. Co. v. District Court*, 430 U.S. 308 (1977); and *Florida Star v. B.J.F.*, 491 U.S. 524 (1989).

127 101 P.2d 552, 561 (2005).

128 Volokh, p. 1090–1092, n.172, referring to Briscoe.

129 [2009] UKSC 3.

130 [2009] UKSC 3, Par. 15.

Hope ultimately did not grant her relief, he did undertake a far more rigorous balancing test than was undertaken in *Gates*. At stake was L's Article 8 right to respect for her private life. Lord Hope rejected the government's argument that this right was not engaged merely because the information was in the public record. "Respect for private life comprises, to a certain degree, the right to establish and develop relationships with other human beings," and one is entitled to protect her good name and reputation; that one was excluded from employment is "likely to get about" and create a stigma.[131] While L had no prior convictions herself, Lord Hope noted that the fact that L was the mother of the person who was convicted is private information, as was information about the degree to which she supervised her son and her refusal to cooperate with social services.[132] To bolster his case that one can have privacy interests in records kept by the police, Lord Hope pointed to a number of precedents issued by the European Court of Human Rights in Strasbourg suggesting that information about past convictions can fall within the purview of Article 8; though it is public information, "the systematic storing of this information" means it is available for disclosure long after the event "when everyone other than the person concerned is likely to have forgotten about it. As it recedes into the past, it becomes a part of the person's private life which must be respected."[133]

Privacy having been implicated, Lord Hope then proceeds to suggest why it might not have been properly taken into account. A rating system is used to guide the Detective Chief Inspectors in deciding whether information should be included in an ECRC. Risks to human rights are graded as "none," "little," "moderate," or "severe"; risks of failing to disclose information to the vulnerable group are rated "little," "moderate," or "severe." Then one checks the intersecting cells on the table to indicate either "disclosure" or "carefully consider." But, Lord Hope notes, a "striking feature" is that a check appears indicating "disclose" whenever the risk of failure to disclose is moderate but the risk to human rights is also moderate; careful consideration is only required when the risk to human rights is severe but the risk of failure to disclose is moderate. In all cases except where the risk in both categories is "little," the human rights category is trumped by the equivalent risk category of failure to disclose.[134] Lord Hope says that this should be revised to give both categories equal weight: "It should indicate that careful consideration is required in all cases where the disruption to the private life of anyone is judged to be as great, or more so, as the risk of non-disclosure to the vulnerable group."[135] For all that, the Court held that

131 [2009] UKSC 3, Pars. 22, 24.
132 [2009] UKSC 3, Pars. 24–28.
133 [2009] UKSC 3, Par. 27. Cf. the more recent ECHR case of *M.M. v. the United Kingdom* [2013] 24029/07.
134 [2009] UKSC 3, Pars. 31–32.
135 [2009] UKSC 3, Par. 45.

in this case the information provided in the ECRC was relevant to the ability of L to perform her job. Despite the care it took to ensure that the grid used by the Detective Chief Inspectors allowed for a fair weighing of competing interests, the Court did not question why the fact that L has trouble raising her son, who was living with the father at the time and who spent much of his time at the home of his sister, who might have been a bad influence, makes her unfit to ensure children do not leave a schoolyard during lunchtime by climbing over the gate.[136]

The contrast in the extent to which the *Gates* court and Lord Hope take seriously the task of balancing interests is striking; but so too is the difference in weight accorded to interests in shedding a criminal past. Courts in the U.S. recognize that an individual has a legitimate privacy interest in *medical* facts, such as that a woman gave birth to a child with two heads, or has an eating disorder.[137] But the *Gates* court, following U.S. Supreme Court precedents, assumes that in contrast to medical facts, a past crime necessarily is a matter of concern to the public and therefore newsworthy.[138] This assumption needs to be challenged for at least two reasons. First, some of the same privacy interests that one has in medical facts one can also have in facts about one's criminal past. We respect the privacy of medical facts in recognition of the interests people with a medical condition have in their dignity, in avoiding economic setbacks or damage to their reputation, and in controlling how they present themselves to others. The latter two interests are also at stake when former criminals want to control access to information about their past crimes. A second reason to challenge the view that medical facts should be treated as fundamentally different from facts about one's past crimes is that medical conditions, just like crimes, can be a matter of public interest: that someone was born with two heads or that a 12-year-old gave birth is newsworthy; it informs us all about the human condition. But while the fact that a medical condition exists legitimately concerns the public, the identity of a person with that condition does not; it may be of legitimate interest only to people who know and interact with the person or to officials who need to ensure public safety by making sure a contagious disease does not spread. An exception is that celebrities may want to *voluntarily* reveal a medical condition as a means of encouraging others to seek treatment or to challenge societal norms that stigmatize those with the condition, and doing so can serve a legitimate public interest.[139]

---

136 [2009] UKSC 3, Par. 14. The role of the sister and father are indicated at Par. 12.

137 *Y.G. and L.G. v. Jewish Hospital of St. Louis*, 795 S.W.2d 488, 498–500 (1990).

138 This position was recently endorsed by Robert Larson, who contends that the First Amendment requires that rap sheets be made readily accessible, in "Forgetting the First Amendment," *Communication Law Policy* 18:91–120 (2013).

139 Two examples are the cyclist Lance Armstrong publicly discussing his battle with cancer, see Armstrong, *It's Not about the Bike: My Journey Back to Life* (New York: G.P. Putnam's Sons, 2000); and the actress Angelina Jolie discussing her preventive double mastectomy, see Jolie, "My Medical Choice," *New York Times*, op-ed of May 14, 2013.

Just as the fact that a person has a medical problem can be a matter of legitimate public concern while the person's particular identity is not, that a crime was committed over a decade ago may be newsworthy but the identity of the criminal may no longer be.

A respect for privacy requires us sometimes to question whether specific information, such as the names of the couple portrayed in the *New York Times* photograph, or the identity of the 12-year- old mother, or of Gates or Briscoe, is important for conveying the story or whether that detail could be safely omitted. According to the slippery slope objection, engaging in such an inquiry might lead us down the road to full-blown censorship. But there is a difference between a society governed by Platonic Guardian-Censors who decide whether it is in society's best interest to be exposed to a story at all, and a society in which out of respect for privacy some inessential details are omitted, or faces are blurred.

The major concern of those who invoke the slippery slope argument to oppose a newsworthy test is that such a test would be subjective and arbitrary and invite unreasonable censorship. However, there are several principles that can provide a non-arbitrary and reasonable basis for distinguishing information that is and is not newsworthy, and there are instances in which judges have applied such principles to restrict or allow liability for some speech without precipitating a regime of censorship.

Substitutability (Finger and Kim Phuc)

Joseph Siprut, whose economic approach to privacy I discussed in Chapter 2, suggests a test we might apply at least when deciding whether images are sufficiently newsworthy to be published without the subject's consent. Siprut argues that the current law in the U.S. is over-inclusive regarding which information it finds newsworthy, as a photo is regarded as newsworthy merely if it has a reasonable connection or rational relationship to an otherwise newsworthy article.[140] The problem with this "reasonable connection" test is that it would allow setbacks to privacy interests without providing a countervailing First Amendment benefit when the photograph lacks "uniqueness" or "added value."[141] Siprut takes as an example the case of *Finger v. Omni Publications International*, in which the defendant published a picture of a husband and wife and their six children, without their consent, to illustrate an article on caffeine-aided in vitro fertilization.[142] None of the plaintiffs' children were conceived through in vitro fertilization and the couple did not participate in a fertility project. Yet the Court ruled for the publisher because on its view the article was newsworthy and

---

140 Joseph Siprut, "Privacy through Anonymity: An Economic Argument for Expanding the Right of Privacy in Public Places," *Pepperdine Law Review* 33:311–334 (2006), p. 327.

141 Siprut, p. 332.

142 566 N.E.2d 141 (1990).

because the plaintiffs did have six children, which provided a real relationship between the photograph and the article. But Siprut disagrees with this decision: "there is absolutely nothing about using these particular photographs that adds any value at all." The article could just as easily have been illustrated using the photo of another family who consented to its use or were paid for the rights to the photos, with "absolutely no loss of value to the public."[143]

Siprut suggests we use what we might call a "substitutability" test. If a photo could easily be replaced by another that uses a consenting subject, with no loss of value to the public, and publication of the original photo would impinge on legitimate privacy interests, the subject of the photo should control the right to the image. This principle is suggested in a dissent in one of the cases mentioned earlier, *Gill v. Hearst Publishing*. Justice Carter argued that *Harper's Magazine* could have easily employed models for the purpose of showing a couple in love, and the public would never know the difference.[144] So long as there is nothing unique about the couple holding hands at Farmer's Market, or the couple embracing on a balmy April day in New York City, there is no good reason not to respect their privacy by either getting their consent or finding a substitute. The principle of substitutability is also suggested by Baroness Hale in *Campbell v. MGN* when she notes that "there is no shortage of photographs with which to illustrate and brighten up a story about Naomi Campbell"; there was no need to publish the photo of her leaving a drug rehabilitation clinic, especially as that photo implicated privacy interests by revealing the location of her treatment center and showing her in the company of others who might have also been seeking treatment.[145] The principle was also invoked by Canada's Supreme Court in an opinion discussed in Chapter 2, when it noted that in considering damages to a plaintiff whose photo was published in a magazine without her consent, one might look at the cost of what the magazine would have had to pay for a model.[146]

The case would be otherwise if the photograph conveyed something unique that could not be as effectively conveyed by a substitute. A classic example is the Pulitzer winning photograph of the young Vietnamese girl, Kim Phuc, that captured her overwhelming distress and grief when, completely naked and in tears, she fled her napalm-ravaged village during the Vietnam War.[147] Publishing this photo implicates privacy interests of the highest magnitude that involve Ms. Phuc's dignity. But the photo is

---

143 Siprut, pp. 329–330. Another basis for opposing the use of the photo is that it puts the plaintiffs in a false light.
144 253 P.2d 441, 446.
145 *Campbell v. MGN Ltd* [2004] UKHL 22, Pars. 156, 155.
146 *Aubry v. Editions Vice-Versa* [1998] S.C.J. No. 30, Par. 74.
147 Discussed in Moore, *Privacy Rights*, pp. 149–150. Moore implies he would have been reluctant to publish the photo.

undeniably newsworthy; arguably it helped to increase anti-war sentiment in the United States. In this case, staging the scene with paid models would not have the same effect; it would be deceitful and detract from the impact of the photograph. What made the photo so effective was that it portrayed what actually happened.

In addition to considering whether an image is substitutable, there are other principles to take into account in determining whether particular speech is newsworthy. Some information may be newsworthy but specific details may not be; and some information is relevant and newsworthy only to a particular circle of people but not to the general public.

Non-newsworthy details of a newsworthy event (Y.G. and L.G.)

In *Y.G. and L.G. v. Jewish Hospital of St. Louis*, a Missouri Court of Appeals considered a case in which a married couple sued a hospital and television station for invading their privacy. The wife bore triplets from *in vitro* fertilization at the hospital and the hospital planned a social function for couples who had participated in its *in vitro* program. While the hospital is said to have assured the plaintiffs that there would be no public exposure at the function, in fact a news crew was there.[148] The plaintiffs attended, declined to be interviewed, yet were shown for three seconds on the station's broadcast coverage of the event, though they were not identified other than as a couple who had triplets. The plaintiffs had told no one other than the wife's mother about their use of fertilization methods and claim that following the broadcast they received many embarrassing calls and the husband was ridiculed at work.

The Court held that there was a possible cause of action for giving publicity to a private fact if the matter publicized would be highly offensive to a reasonable person and is not of legitimate concern to the public. To explain what might count as a matter of legitimate public interest, the Court relied on some illustrative examples from prior precedents. Where the operation of laws or the police or other public bodies are involved, or information is in court records open to the public, the Supreme Court has dictated that the information is a matter of public interest. So a mistaken arrest is newsworthy; but an upskirt photo is not, nor is a photo of a man's injuries sustained on the job, nor someone's pictures before and after plastic surgery. In this case, the Court held that while the fact that there was an *in vitro* program is a matter of public interest, as is the fact that the celebratory event was well attended, the identity of the plaintiff is not newsworthy nor a matter of public record.[149] The plaintiffs did not waive their right to privacy by attending, the Court notes, because they were

148 795 S.W.2d 488, 492 (1990).
149 795 S.W.2d 488, 500.

assured only fellow *in vitro* couples would attend and that the event would not be open to the media; they chose to disclose their participation only to other *in vitro* couples.[150] Similarly, participants in a drug rehabilitation meeting voluntarily reveal their participation to others in attendance but this does not mean they willingly disclose it to the media or that their attendance is a matter of legitimate public interest.

The reason not to broadcast footage of the plaintiffs is not that their image is easily substitutable; in fact it may not be in the sense that using hired models would be a form of deceit. (Had the *New York Times* hired paid models to pose on the beach for a photo that was presented as a candid shot, it would be deceitful as well; the *Times* could avoid deceit by getting the consent of a couple who was photographed as they really were, even if it later paid them.) But what was newsworthy could be conveyed without including their image and being insensitive to their privacy preferences. Blurring their faces could have conveyed the wrong message by stigmatizing people who participated in the *in vitro* event. But the plaintiff's image could have been edited out without detracting from the story. That the hospital indicated to the plaintiffs that they would not be exposed by attending the event suggests it was aware that unlike many public events in which no legitimate privacy interests are implicated and for which no consent would be needed to photograph the participants as part of a group or crowd, here privacy was at stake.

Newsworthy for a select group, non-newsworthy for the general public (Parnigoni)

Y.G. and L.G. involves a case in which specific details such as a person's identity are not newsworthy even though the event in which they participate may be. Another case illustrates how information may be newsworthy to a specific circle of people but not to the general public. In *Parnigoni v. St. Columba's Nursery School,* the plaintiffs sued for defamation and public disclosure of private facts among other things.[151] Ms. Parnigoni taught at a nursery school in the District of Columbia. In 2004 her fiancé at the time was charged and later convicted of indecently exposing himself to a minor. She informed her school Director but the school took no action. Then they were married and in 2007 they enrolled their 3-year-old son at the school. In August 2007, the new Director met with Mrs. Parnigoni and requested information regarding her husband. After further meetings the Director said the school would disclose the information about the husband's conviction as it concerned a parent of a student. The Rector explained to the staff that the disclosure would be due to Mrs. Parnigoni's "poor judgment in

---

150 795 S.W.2d 488, 502.
151 681 F.Supp.2d 1 (D.C. 2010).

marrying [him]." In October of 2007, after Mrs. Parnigoni withdrew her child from the school, the Rector sent a letter to all members of the parish identifying Mr. Parnigoni as a registered sex offender and the husband of a teacher at the school. The letter noted that until recently the son had attended the school, and indicated that the purpose of the letter was to let parents make informed decisions about the care and supervision of their children and to help them ensure their children's safety. The letter went not just to parents of children attending the school, but to over 3,500 households in the D.C. area. The Court permitted an action to proceed with respect to Mrs. Parnigoni. Judge Walton ruled that even if the school acted with the good intention of protecting children at school, it could have sent the letters only to the parents of the school's students.

The principle I want to take from this opinion is that information may be of legitimate concern to some members of the public, who have a need to know, but not others. (I do not mean to imply, however, that there was in fact a legitimate reason to send the letter to the parents; the Court suggested that the school used public safety as a subterfuge for its real reason for disclosure: to chastise Mrs. Parnigoni.) In cases where legitimate privacy interests are at stake, including reputational interests, a fair balancing of interests may require that we ask whether the information was spread more broadly than needed.[152]

One might think it pointless to blame or punish someone who spreads information too broadly so that it reaches people beyond those with a need to know because, especially in the age of social media, once the information is out, there is no way to prevent any of the original recipients from spreading it to others. Why punish the school for conveying information to 3,500 people rather than just the 300 who might have a direct interest in it if it was likely that many of the 300 people would share the information with others until most of those 3,500 would eventually have found it out? An odd twist of the slippery slope argument, the objection is not that if you restrict some speech you open the door to full-blown censorship, but that there is no point restricting private speech in the age of social media given how prone to gossip people are. Just as once you squeeze toothpaste out of the tube you cannot put it back in, once a story is out, it is out forever.[153]

I think we need to reject this argument. While I might not be able reasonably to expect that some information about me remains private to people with a compelling need to know it, I can still have a legitimate privacy interest in retaining control of that information so other people with no need to know cannot readily access it. In Chapter 2 we discussed several

---

152 Cf. *R v. Metropolitan Police Commissioner* [2004] EWHC 2229, noting that "Anti-social Behaviour Orders" that result in distribution of leaflets "should be drawn no wider than is necessary" (Par. 21).

153 *Glee*, Season 2:19, "Rumours" (2011).

examples including the case of Oliver Sipple, who was willing to reveal his homosexuality to some members of the gay community but not to his family. If we agree there is this privacy interest, then we agree that there is an ethical reason not to share private information about someone with just anyone. Absent a sufficient countervailing interest, someone who knew that Sipple was gay would act badly and fail to show him respect if they revealed that information to Sipple's family, aware of Sipple's interest in privacy. This ethical reason not to spread private information indiscriminately does not simply vanish because in practice that information could be spread by people who are not sensitive to the needs individuals may have for privacy. To argue otherwise would be similar to arguing that because other people lie or break their promises, doing so is not wrong and we should not expect or encourage people to keep their promises or not lie. Machiavelli relied on that argument in advising princes not to keep all of their promises, but it is an argument that has been contested by a long line of moral philosophers, most notably by Kant.[154] For Kant, morality is a categorical imperative, concerned with the good of an action regardless of the consequences.[155] If reason dictates that we ought to keep our promises, we ought to even if doing so would yield no benefits or even if nobody else keeps theirs. The argument is not precisely the same: it is that I no longer ought to do x to avoid y if y will occur regardless of my doing x because doing x would be pointless. But Kant's defense of promise keeping is relevant in that for Kant moral obligations are categorical and are not contingent on the consequences of our actions—so whether x is pointless would not matter.

If the Kantian argument that one ought to do what is right even in a world where few people do what is right seems unpersuasive, another argument is available that appeals to a practical distinction between a society that takes seriously an ethical norm of not sharing sensitive information indiscriminately even if that information could spread anyway, and a society that does not and even encourages a policy of "Open Access to All." In the latter society, the very existence of the open access policy would send a strong signal that it is not wrong to spread such information, and the society is unlikely ever to develop strong informational privacy norms. Even though ethical norms may be difficult to enforce, the society with a norm against sharing sensitive information indiscriminately is more likely than the other society to respect privacy interests. The fact that it is possible that sensitive information may be shared indiscriminately, making it readily accessible to the general public, is not a reason not even to attempt to limit its access.

154 See Machiavelli, *The Prince*, Chapter 18; and for an opposing view, Kant, *Groundwork of the Metaphysic of Morals*, tr. H.J. Paton (New York: Harper Torchbooks, 1964).
155 Kant, *Groundwork*, pp. 83–84/416.

Conclusion

Defenders of the First Amendment sometimes suggest that all speech deserves protection. One might respond that they are getting it all wrong: protecting even vapid entertainment regardless of its ability to contribute to rational discussion would undermine the very value that the First Amendment promotes of preserving the quality of public discourse.[156] *That* argument might seem to imply that we should have Platonic Guardians review all speech to determine which is appropriate to expose to citizens; and that is not the position I think we should take.

Rather, my argument has been that some information is not everyone else's business and when important privacy interests are at stake, we should carefully consider what interest society has in having that information shared with the public at large. We need to recognize that not all speech has the same value, and also recognize the difference between silencing and merely limiting ready access to speech. The public has an interest in having information relevant to public issues disseminated as widely as possible and drawing on diverse and antagonistic sources.[157] It would be wrong to silence such speech. But there is no such interest in having Mr. Parnigoni's prior conviction widely disseminated. To restrict access to speech about that conviction so that it is readily accessible only to people with a need to know about it is not to silence but to limit speech. It is not to decide that we should expose citizens only to some conceptions of how to live but not others; it is not to stifle an antagonistic, unpopular view. As the majority in *Snyder v. Phelps* argued, silencing views with which you disagree would not be content-neutral and not serve the goal of contributing to the marketplace of ideas. Rather, it is to recognize that some private information does not contribute to that marketplace. In *Snyder*, a majority of Supreme Court Justices had a legitimate concern that repressing speech because of the message it conveyed would undermine the true purpose of the First Amendment. They did not regard the speech conveyed near Matthew Snyder's funeral as about him in particular.[158] However, restricting access to speech not because of its message but because it is not relevant to a matter of legitimate public concern, as the court in *Parnigoni* did, does not similarly undercut the purposes of that Amendment.

Not all public facts are newsworthy to the general public. Someone of no particular note might have committed a crime twenty years ago that they have long regretted; while they should not be able to conceal this fact from everyone, such as potential employers—at least when the crime would be an indication of one's suitability for a job—it may be inappropriate for a

---

156 Cf. Richards, p. 95.

157 *New York Times v. Sullivan*, 376 U.S. 254, 266.

158 131 S.Ct. 1207, 1217: Westboro's speech was not "intended to mask an attack on Snyder over a private matter."

news network to broadcast this fact as part of a story on reformed criminals without the person's consent. While there is value in seeing a photo
of a couple embracing on a New York City beach in April, or learning that
a 12-year-old gave birth, or that someone was raped, there is little value in
the general public knowing their identities. Those invoking the slippery
slope argument are worried about empowering someone to decide who
needs to know what information. But the proposal to limit some speech for
the sake of privacy is not a proposal to establish a general censor of all
speech. The proposal rests on the assumption that because privacy can be
very important we need to think on some occasions about whether sharing
information indiscriminately is really worth the price.

5 Balancing privacy and free speech

Utilitarianism, its limits, and tolerating the sensitive

Introduction

We all have an interest in being able to access and disseminate information freely. But sharing information about someone without their consent diminishes their control over how they present themselves to the world, and could implicate other interests associated with privacy. Rather than take an absolutist position that free speech (or privacy) is inviolable, we should ask which of these interests has greater weight when they conflict.

After reviewing a proposed framework for balancing privacy and free speech that the previous chapters point to, I discuss some of its philosophical assumptions. The approach of balancing competing interests is central to utilitarianism but the balancing we need to undertake involves a weighing of considerations and not a calculation of net utility. I then turn to a difficult issue that has received little attention in previous discussions of privacy. As I discussed in Chapter 2, not everyone values privacy to the same degree. Some people welcome attention and seem happy to expose every detail of their lives to public scrutiny. Given this fact, one might wonder why we should think it necessary to accommodate those people who do care about privacy. What if Louis Conradt or Tyler Clementi, each of whom responded to unwanted attention by taking his own life, were unusually sensitive? Should we cater to their preferences for privacy? Or should we have counseled them to "get over it" on the premise that "the law does not protect the overly sensitive"?[1] What reasons are there for a society in which most people may not care a good deal about privacy to appease a minority who do by adopting pro-privacy policies when these policies have real costs? What consideration is due to an individual whom the majority regards as supersensitive? To address these questions we will need to consider the place of toleration in a liberal society.

---

1   Y.G. and L.G. v. Jewish Hospital of St. Louis, 795 S.W.2d 488, 504 (1990) (Judge Gaertner, in dissent); cf. R (Wood) v. Metropolitan Police Commissioner [2008] EWHC 1105, Par. 79: "The provisions of the convention are not designed for the protection of the unduly sensitive."

DOI: 10.4324/9781315763132-5

The framework

When facing an ethical question such as whether a newspaper should publish the name of a rape victim or details about a crime someone committed a decade ago, or a television station should broadcast a recording of an accident victim confiding to a paramedic that she just wants to die, or an individual should upload to YouTube a video of someone behaving badly, we might have an immediate gut reaction, or intuition. But such intuitions may be unreliable. They are immediate in the sense that they are not the result of critical thought. I believe that we are better off putting our intuitions to the test by seeing whether they remain persuasive to us in the face of various considerations. The approach I think we should take to handle such questions relies not on a precise formula, but on what in Chapter 1 I referred to as a "framework" consisting of a set of questions we can ask to order our thoughts and test our intuitions.[2] I assume we will now agree that there are good reasons to value privacy but also good reasons to value the ability of people to collect, distribute, and access information, and that we should engage in a serious weighing of these competing values. Before undertaking this weighing, we must first establish that privacy is truly at stake. Someone may desire privacy but their desire may be misplaced; or they may have an interest in privacy but it is not a legitimate interest. You might want to keep private the fact that you have an embarrassing tattoo on your chest and even claim you have a right to keep this private, yet you cannot reasonably expect to keep your secret if you stand shirtless by an un-curtained window. In Chapter 3 I considered how we determine whether an interest in privacy is legitimate. I argued that even if I cannot reasonably expect to keep private certain facts about me that I knowingly expose to some circles of people, this need not mean that those facts may be memorialized and freely and indiscriminately disseminated to the general public. If I consent to being photographed by a friend, I cannot complain that they have violated my privacy by capturing my image. But if they then post the photo on Facebook and share it with people I do not know, who then distribute the photo to an even wider audience, my friend has given me more attention than I consented to provide and depending on what the photo depicts or how sensitive I am, might have acted badly.

If we do limit free speech in the name of privacy, we should do so only if a legitimate privacy interest is at stake. Once we have good reason to think that there is, we then need to decide whether that interest is important enough to be regarded as a right. As I noted in Chapter 3, the deliberative process may involve what John Rawls calls reflective equilibrium and not be simply sequential.

---

2   Here I am indebted to Adam Moore, *Privacy Rights* (University Park: Pennsylvania State University Press, 2010): Moore wants to ground our intuitions and recognizes the need for a framework, or set of considerations, in weighing privacy against free speech interests.

Interests and rights

Even if I personally do not care at all for privacy, I might still recognize that others have an interest in privacy. That interest may be important enough to warrant our sometimes saying that there is a right to privacy. While I will not engage extensively with the large literature on rights and their moral or legal status, some discussion about rights and interests is helpful in laying out the framework.

Interests can be distinguished both from rights and from desires. If I love someone I may well desire that they return my love; but I also may have an interest in their returning my love, an interest that is more substantial than merely having a desire fulfilled. To say I have an interest is to say my welfare is at stake. But having that interest does not give me a right to be loved;[3] so too, having a legitimate interest in privacy does not mean having a right to privacy. Interests are more than desires but they are not yet rights. A necessary though not sufficient condition for me to have a right to something is that my interest in it must be recognized as sufficiently weighty.

I want to address a possible difficulty some may have with the idea that we can have a right to something merely because there is such great value in our having it. When one says that I have a right to something—a right to property, or life, or privacy—we might think that what is meant is that I am entitled to it even if there is greater overall good in my not having it. Consider the hypothetical used in introductory ethics courses in which a doctor could successfully harvest the organs of a healthy adult to save the lives of five other people: two of the five each need a lung, two each need a kidney, and one needs a heart; without a healthy organ they will die. There might be greater social utility in killing the one person to save the other five, but still we might think we should not permit the harvesting, because to kill a blameless person would violate that person's right to their life. To say one has a right to one's life, here, is to say one is entitled to it regardless of the consequences.[4] One can certainly argue that people have a right to privacy in this sense and that privacy should be respected even if society would suffer as a result. Justice Scalia argued that the state of Maryland was wrong to take a buccal swab of the inner cheek of a man who had just been arrested in order to see if his DNA was a match with the DNA evidence in an unsolved rape case that occurred six years earlier. Scalia would have reversed the man's conviction for the rape because in searching his DNA without a warrant the state violated his Fourth

---

3   Joel Feinberg, *Harm to Others* (New York: Oxford University Press, 1984), p. 32; discussed in Chapter 2.

4   See Judith Jarvis Thomson, "The Trolley Problem," *Yale Law Journal* 94:1395–1415 (1985), p. 1404 ("rights trump utility"); the organ transplant case is taken from Thomson (p. 1396), who in turn draws on P. Foot, "The Problem of Abortion and the Doctrine of the Double Effect," in *Virtue and Vices and Other Essays in Moral Philosophy* (New York: Oxford University Press, 1978).

Amendment rights, and we should not violate those rights even if doing so would let us solve more crimes.[5]

But the argument that privacy is a right that must not be sacrificed for a greater good is likely to be unconvincing to many people. Utilitarians and "law and economics" proponents reject the idea that rights should be allocated in any other way than by appealing to a principle of utility or economic efficiency;[6] and the position that privacy must not be sacrificed for a greater good is unlikely to persuade advocates of free speech. Justice Scalia's judgment that Fourth Amendment rights should win out even if that means letting a guilty person go free did not prevail, as a majority of Justices decided that Fourth Amendment privacy rights are not absolute but are determined by a balancing of privacy and public safety interests and that in this case permitting relatively minimal privacy invasions was justified by the greater good of fighting crime.[7] Instead, when I refer to a right to privacy I refer to an interest in privacy that ought to be regarded as of sufficient importance that we should choose it over free speech in some cases where the two values conflict.

Someone who adheres to the political philosophy of John Rawls might argue that privacy is a primary good, or is essential to other primary goods, which is to say that every rational human being is presumed to want it.[8] Rawls speaks of the social bases of self-respect as a primary good;[9] and one might think that privacy is essential to self-respect. One might argue that on this basis alone there is a right to privacy. But we cannot rely on that argument, either, to establish that privacy must necessarily prevail over free speech. For free speech could also be regarded as one of the basic liberties that count as a primary good.[10] While I shall not adopt Rawls's approach, some of my discussion about privacy and free speech could be translated into a framework that refers to primary goods, although it is

5   *Maryland v. King*, 133 S.Ct. 1958 (2013).
6   See Jeremy Bentham, "Anarchical Fallacies," in *The Works of Jeremy Bentham*, vol. 2, ed. Bowing (Edinburgh: William Tait, 1843); Louis Kaplow and Steven Shavell, *Fairness vs. Welfare* (Cambridge, MA: Harvard University Press, 2002); and the discussion below.
7   Even Justice Scalia did not adopt the position that rights must be adhered to regardless of the costs: in *Maryland v. King* he reasoned that the privacy interests at stake are not minimal, and according to case precedents the only legitimate state interest for taking DNA samples of arrestees would be to identify them—not to solve past crimes—and DNA testing was not used in this case to identify the defendant.
8   John Rawls, *A Theory of Justice* (Cambridge, MA: Harvard University Press, 1971), pp. 62, 90–95. Examples of primary goods are health, intelligence, and "rights and liberties, powers and opportunities, income and wealth" (62). Anita Allen rests her argument that government should sometimes prohibit people from waiving their privacy rights on the view that privacy is a foundational good, in *Unpopular Privacy* (New York: Oxford University Press, 2011), pp. xii, 12.
9   Rawls, *Theory of Justice*, pp. 62, 178.
10   See Rawls, *Political Liberalism* (New York: Columbia University Press, 1993), pp. 340–347; and *Theory of Justice*, p. 225.

unclear how that framework would help us choose among competing primary goods without some weighing of values.

Balancing privacy against free speech (as opposed to public safety)

Before turning to the philosophical foundations of a balancing approach, I want to call attention to what exactly we are balancing in cases of unwanted attention. A balancing approach is frequently used by courts in criminal cases, where we need to weigh the value of living in a society where people can expect privacy against the value in enabling the police to fight crime. Cases of unwanted attention present a different conflict of interests. But in balancing privacy against free speech interests we cannot ignore discussions of how we are to balance privacy against the need to fight crime. Society's judgment of whether an expectation of privacy can be reasonable may be shaped by the thought that we need to give up some privacy for the sake of public safety. Yet it is important to keep the distinct balancing tests separate.

To see what I mean, consider the events that occurred following the bombing at the Boston Marathon in 2013. The suspects were captured after police gained access to photographs taken by surveillance cameras situated in public places right where the bombing took place. Without this evidence, they might have remained free long enough to commit further acts of violence. A New York Times/CBS News poll was taken a week after the attack, after it became known that the video-surveillance cameras were instrumental in capturing the terrorists. 78 percent of the respondents said surveillance cameras in public places were a good idea.[11] Such successful use of surveillance cameras will no doubt shape people's views on the extent to which they can reasonably expect privacy in public places. Using cameras to see what happens on a public sidewalk is likely to be regarded as a legitimate means of observing criminals;[12] but that does not mean that images with no law enforcement benefit taken by these same cameras may legitimately be distributed as part of a human interest story. When crime is rampant or there is a war on terror, people may be willing to sacrifice some privacy to promote public safety, and a balancing of privacy interests against the state's interest in public safety may tilt away from privacy. But the balance of privacy against free speech interests raises different considerations. The benefit of the balancing framework I am proposing is that it

11   Mark Landler and Dalia Sussman, "Poll Finds Strong Acceptance for Public Surveillance," *New York Times*, May 1, 2013.
12   But there are risks as well. A teenage boy was wrongly identified as a suspect in the Boston Marathon bombing and when his photo spread on the Internet, he was terrified. See *Mail online*, April 18, 2013: www.dailymail.co.uk/news/article-2311185/Boston-marathon-bombing-High-school-track-runner-forced-deny-involvement-Boston-Marathon-bombings-picture-widely-circulated.html.

lets us explain why it might be reasonable for the police to have access to public surveillance photos for some purposes, yet not be reasonable for someone to upload similar photos of an individual in a public place to the Internet without that individual's consent. We can say that people may have a legitimate privacy interest in not having their image disseminated even when it is captured when they are in a public place and even though they cannot expect not to be seen by others in that location; but we can conclude that this interest is outweighed by the state's compelling interest in capturing criminals or terrorists, whereas the interest in anonymity that an embracing couple or a nude sunbather has even when they are on a public beach may outweigh any competing free speech interest in publishing their photo without their consent.

The utilitarian approach

The idea that in deciding how to act we should balance competing interests and choose the path in which our interests most lie has roots in the philosophy of utilitarianism. Utilitarianism is a complex philosophy with many distinct variations that it will not be possible to explore here. But it will be helpful to discuss the utilitarian approach generally, two of its particular variants, and a few of its limitations.

Utilitarians have a particular approach to answering the question "what is right?" or "how ought we to act?" For example, a utilitarian has a distinct approach to answering the question "ought we to kill?" There are a variety of different approaches one might take to such a question. One can consult one's religion ("God commands that one shall not kill"); or shared social judgments rooted in customs ("it is not our way to kill"); or one's moral intuitions or feelings ("it just seems wrong to kill"); or a universal law such as Kant's categorical imperative ("it is wrong to kill insofar as we could not will a maxim that permitted me to kill to hold as a universal law");[13] or we could take a vote (by asking "who thinks we ought to kill?") and be guided by the majority's will, which is what might be called the democratic solution. The utilitarian's answer is distinct.

---

13   Kant illustrates his approach with the example of promises. Why ought I to keep my promise? Because there is a moral imperative, and not for prudential reasons. The moral imperative dictates that I ought never to act except in such a way that I can also will that my maxim should become a universal law. Kant argues that I cannot make a promise with the intent of not keeping it, for to make this maxim a universal law would annul itself. Another variation of the moral imperative that Kant gives is that I should act always in a way that treats humans as ends in themselves and not merely as a means; and to break a promise is to treat the promisee merely as a means. See Immanuel Kant, *Groundwork of the Metaphysics of Morals*, tr. H.J. Paton (New York: Harper Torchbooks, 1964), 403, 429–430.

The answer given by one of the leading classical utilitarians, Jeremy Bentham, is that we should approve or disapprove of every action whatsoever "according to the tendency which it appears to have to augment or diminish the happiness of the party whose interest is in question." This is the principle of utility, utility being defined as "that property in any object, whereby it tends to produce benefit, advantage, pleasure, good, or happiness."[14] For Bentham, the party whose interest is in question is "society," and I shall focus on versions of utilitarianism that decide upon policy alternatives based on which most augments overall social utility. On Bentham's view, there is no such thing as right except what increases pleasure and decreases pain, and so if it is wrong to kill it is because killing creates more pain than pleasure in society.[15] Bentham criticizes the view that "the right is prior to the good." That view holds that when we pursue the good life we are constrained in that we must first and foremost do what is right and avoid wrong, and we determine what is right and wrong independently of and prior to determining what promotes utility and is good. For example, it is wrong to punish the innocent, and we must not even if doing so would have greater overall utility for society. But for Bentham the right is not prior to the good; rather, it is defined as that which yields the good. Bentham suggests there are no constraints on our calculation of the good apart from a consideration of what promotes utility. For Bentham the idea that privacy or free speech should prevail by default because there is a natural right to it is "nonsense";[16] we decide whether there ought to be that right only by calculating the social utility or good of having that right established and enforced.

Consider the question of whether Dateline NBC ought to be permitted to broadcast its "To Catch a Predator" program, which I described in Chapter 1. On the utilitarian view just depicted, we would attempt to calculate the program's net utility to society. Broadcasting the show can have obvious disutility to the adult males whose risqué online chats with decoys presenting themselves as young teenagers are shared with a national audience and who are caught on film showing up at a house to meet the decoy. For Louis Conradt, the prospect of having his private online chat exchanges exposed was apparently so painful that he killed himself. People who knew and cared about him or others who are featured on the show may also suffer disutility. On the other hand, there is utility in broadcasting the show inasmuch as people simply enjoy watching it—it was one of Dateline NBC's highest rated programs;[17] and conceivably the show has some deterrent

---

14   Jeremy Bentham, *Principles of Morals and Legislation* (New York: Prometheus Books, 1988), 1:2 and 1:3.
15   Bentham, *Principles of Morals and Legislation*, 1:10.
16   Bentham, "Anarchical Fallacies," p. 501.
17   See Brian Stelter, "'To Catch a Predator' is Falling Prey to Advertisers' Sensibilities," *New York Times*, August 27, 2007.

effect on adult predators, and might spur parents to monitor their children's online activities more diligently.

There are some other potential factors to consider in undertaking a utilitarian calculation: if we were to censor the show, we might need to take into account the effect a policy of censorship would have. Society may suffer disutility in not having access not only to "To Catch a Predator" but to other programming that might not ever get off the ground for fear of being censored. Those making the slippery slope argument that we discussed in Chapter 4 emphasize precisely such indirect and long-term consequences in arguing that we should not limit free speech even in cases where the speech is deeply invasive of someone's privacy. How such indirect consequences should enter into our calculation is a question at the center of debates between act and rule utilitarians.

The act utilitarian considers the consequences in terms of social utility of the act being contemplated (such as permitting the broadcast of a television episode that brings someone unwanted attention). The rule utilitarian focuses instead on the consequences in terms of social utility of having a rule that would govern the sort of act we are contemplating. The rule utilitarian would ask which is best: a policy that allows censorship of some material, or a policy governed by a rule that prohibits censorship. If, on utilitarian grounds, we believed a policy that did not allow censorship was superior, then we would simply defer to the rule that defines that policy: no censorship. We would not be permitted to make exceptions to that rule even where a particular application of that rule creates net disutility. The rule utilitarian is content with adhering to rules that themselves are justified on utilitarian grounds. The act utilitarian, in contrast, is willing to make exceptions to rules in particular cases.

Act and rule utilitarians can arrive at very different conclusions, as is illustrated with another, well-known example. Suppose a white woman was raped in a southern town in the U.S. in the 1930s, and a large number of enraged, racist citizens are preparing to lynch every black man in the town, not knowing who the actual rapist is but overcome with irrational fear and hatred. To avoid that prospect, the sheriff selects a man who has no ties to anyone and would not be missed, announces that this man was the rapist, and hangs him in front of the townspeople with the aim of preventing the lynching of a dozen innocent people. The act utilitarian arguably would approve, since there appears to be greater utility in unjustly punishing this one innocent person than allowing a dozen others to be killed. But the rule utilitarian disapproves: there is more utility in having a practice of punishment, which is governed by the rule that we punish only the guilty, than in having some other practice that allows the state to inflict pain on people who are innocent; such a practice could not be called "punishment"—John Rawls, who provides one famous account of rule utilitarianism, suggests we give it some other name, like "telishment"; as utilitarians we adopt punishment not telishment, and once we do, we are no longer free to violate its rules.[18]

As an example of how an act- and rule-utilitarian might approach the question of whether one should have a right to privacy, consider the question of whether a publisher preparing an article on medical malpractice should have to get the consent of a doctor to refer to a case in which the doctor committed malpractice two decades ago. This fact about his past was accessible to a motivated and resourceful reporter but is not readily accessible to the general public unless the story is published. It may be that publishing this information would have greater disutility to the doctor and his family than utility to society. Suppose he is retired so that this information would not benefit future patients; and that none of his former patients have potential lawsuits against him which would be advanced by knowledge of his past mistake. He may worry that this information will hurt his reputation in the eyes of his children and grandchildren, and make their lives more difficult. On an act utilitarian account, publication might well require the doctor's consent. The rule utilitarian, however, would ask whether publishers in general should be required to get an individual's consent before revealing publicly accessible information about that individual. Some rule utilitarians might conclude that to require this would be so great a deterrent to speech that society is better off not requiring consent, even though in some cases publication of particular information will create significant disutility.

It might appear as if the slippery slope argument as used by free speech advocates, discussed in Chapter 4, is a straightforward application of rule utilitarianism. But I believe it is a misapplication. On their view, a policy governed by a rule that all speech is permitted has greater social utility than a policy that allows judges or juries to determine in particular cases if speech is sufficiently newsworthy to justify intrusions upon privacy. To make exceptions would lead us down a slippery slope to all-out censorship. But the slippery slope argument does not fulfill the requirements of a proper rule-utilitarian argument as Rawls presents it, for two distinct reasons. According to rule utilitarianism, we adopt one rule-governed practice or institution over others because it has greater social utility, and only once we make that determination are we justified in adhering to its rules. Rawls illustrates with the example of baseball: at some point an authoritative commission decided that a game with the rule that a batter is out after three strikes has greater utility than one with the rule that a batter is out after four strikes. That choice having already been made, an umpire is not free in the middle of a game

---

18 See John Rawls, "Two Concepts of Rules," *Philosophical Review* 64(1):3–32 (1955), pp. 10–12, drawing on a similar example that appeared in Carritt, *Ethical and Political Thinking* (Oxford: Clarendon Press, 1947), p. 65. A more perspicacious act-utilitarian might decide that there would be greater disutility in punishing the innocent person, even if dozens died as a result, if word ever got out and thereby undermined the entire criminal justice system; but still, the act-utilitarian differs from the rule-utilitarian in not feeling bound to rules of practices in particular cases.

to decide to give a batter an extra swing after he was thrown three strikes if he thinks doing so would be best on the whole; the umpire is bound by the rules already in place.[19] Rule utilitarianism appeals to what Rawls calls a practice conception of rules: one reason we must defer to rules of a practice is that failing to do so would no longer be to engage in the practice. If one is playing baseball, one cannot depart from the rules that constitute the game; at least one cannot do so and still be playing baseball. The practice conception of rules that underlies rule utilitarianism does not fit cases of unwanted attention because free speech is not a practice or institution with constitutive rules in the way that punishment or baseball is.

Even if it were, or if we did not think the practice conception of rules is a necessary feature of a convincing rule utilitarian argument, the slippery slope argument fails to satisfy another criterion of a successful rule utilitarian argument. Rule utilitarianism assumes that the rule-governed practices we adopt are justified by their social utility; but advocates of the slippery slope argument have not established that living according to a rule of "no censorship" has greater utility to society than living under a regime that allows exceptions in cases where privacy is at stake. Free speech advocates suggest that a policy that allows for censoring speech has net disutility because it can have a long-term chilling effect; but they have not taken into account the similarly chilling effects if people cannot expect privacy in public places. The plaintiffs in *Y.G. and L.G. v. Jewish Hospital of St. Louis*, discussed in Chapter 4, sued because they were shown on a local news program attending a social function for participants of the hospital's *in vitro* program without their consent and though they were originally assured there would be no public exposure at the event. They were upset because they had not told family members about their use of fertilization methods, and now word was out.[20] While ruling in their favor may burden the news media, ruling against them would send the message that attending such events might land someone on television or YouTube. This might prompt some people to avoid such events. The chilling effect of a lack of privacy is not speculative. China has experienced a rise in blackmailers who take incriminating photos or videos of government officials and then email them to the official with a threat: "pay up, or become the next online viral sensation." In one case an official received a blackmail threat when an incriminating photo showed him at a public function wearing a luxury watch that he could hardly afford just on his official salary. Not long after, as his son prepared to get married, the official decided against a lavish wedding as this "would have been too public."[21] While in some cases publication may serve the public interest by deterring illicit activity such as

19   Rawls, "Two Concepts of Rules," pp. 25–26.
20   795 S.W.2d 488 (1990).
21   Dan Levin and Amy Qin, "True or Faked, Dirt on Chinese Fuels Blackmail," *New York Times*, June 18, 2013.

corruption, in many other cases it may deter legitimate and valuable activity. Censorship of speech has long-term chilling effects, but the prospect of receiving unwanted attention has chilling effects as well. Proponents of the slippery slope argument have not weighed these effects, or other negative consequences of unwanted attention, and so they have not established that there is greater social utility in adhering to rules that favor speech over privacy.[22]

Some theorists who adopt an economic approach to privacy and free speech suggest a similar criticism of the slippery slope argument. Richard Murphy adopts an economic approach but insists that "one ought to be careful to get the utility calculus correct" by not ignoring the psychic value of privacy. Rather than assume there is more utility in having a rule that allows all speech, he would permit disclosure only if the value of disclosing exceeds the value of the pure privacy preference of the individual about whom information is disclosed.[23] Steve Penney, also taking an economic approach, recognizes that privacy allows people to conceal information such as fraudulent or criminal activity; but also that some concealment can be beneficial. Rather than defer to a rule that assumes that more information is always better for society, he argues that if privacy conceals harmful conduct, its legal protection should be weak, but if privacy encourages efficient behavior, its legal protection should be strong.[24] Privacy can promote efficient behavior by reducing the costs of avoiding disclosure. Privacy protections against eavesdropping, for example, can free people to talk more candidly without having to expend resources to create soundproof rooms; and privacy protections against some use of video-surveillance may encourage people to participate in beneficial activities they otherwise would not engage in, such as using needle exchanges or going to an AIDS clinic.[25]

Limits of a utilitarian approach

The utilitarian aims for policies that increase the overall happiness of society. While it might seem hard to argue with a philosophy that hopes to make us better off, there are a few concerns about utilitarianism that I think push us toward an alternate method of balancing free speech and privacy interests.

---

22 Cf. Chapter 4, "The Slippery Slope Objection."
23 Murphy, "Property Rights in Personal Information: An Economic Defense of Privacy," *Georgetown Law Journal* 84:2381–2417 (July, 1996), pp. 2387, 2400.
24 Steve Penney, "Reasonable Expectations of Privacy and Novel Search Technologies: An Economic Approach," *Journal of Criminal Law and Criminology* 97(2):477–529 (2007), pp. 491–492.
25 Penney, pp. 492–494.

Feasibility problems

The utilitarian who proposes to calculate what action will most augment social utility assumes that people have utility functions that map their subjective preferences. For example, a small piece of delicious mocha cheesecake gives me less utility than a larger piece and one piece gives me only half the utility that two pieces give me; but my utility would not double again if I had four pieces rather than two, since so much cheesecake would make me sick. The goal of utilitarians is to map people's preferences in this way so that we can estimate how much utility they would experience under various scenarios and then calculate the aggregate net utility based on the preferences of everyone in society. One problem with a utilitarian approach to cases of unwanted attention is that we simply do not have the empirical data to let us make the calculation.[26] Recall the example of whether NBC should be permitted to broadcast "To Catch a Predator." To calculate the social utility of allowing the broadcast, we would need to quantify the value of airing the show; while the show's high ratings indicate that it was popular, and we can estimate how many people watched it, we could only guess at the utility the show brought to each viewer. But it would be misleading to enter that data even if the estimate were reliable. What really matters is the incremental difference in utility that would be experienced if certain privacy protecting measures were taken such as blurring the faces of the men the show exposes, and not providing their names. The best means of determining that might be to observe what would happen to the viewership of the show after it were to implement such measures—something NBC was never willing to do. (A rabbi caught on camera requested that NBC obscure his face and not mention his occupation; but NBC's reporter Chris Hansen writes: "these were obviously conditions we couldn't comply with.[27]) Other data crucial to assessing the utility of the broadcast—the extent to which the unexpurgated show, as opposed to a version that blurred faces, incrementally increased the deterrent effect on those who would potentially prey on children online, or incrementally increased the motivation of parents to supervise their children in their online activities—is also necessarily speculative and perhaps impossible to assess accurately. Nor is there an obvious way to calculate the disutility suffered by those receiving unwanted attention from the show.

---

26 There are versions of utilitarianism that rely on "rules of thumb" and other shortcuts, but relying on rules of thumb would be justified only by a calculation of their net utility, which we would need to make before putting them to use.

27 Hansen, *To Catch a Predator* (New York: Penguin, 2008), p. 27 n.4; discussed in Mark Tunick, "Reality TV and the Entrapment of Predators," in Robson and Silbey, eds., *Law and Justice on the Small Screen* (Oxford: Hart Publishing, 2012), p. 292.

The respect and dignity problem

Another difficulty in applying the utilitarian theory concerns not the feasibility of making the calculation it requires, but rather a moral objection. Utilitarianism is sometimes criticized as a moral theory for being crass and hollow; it focuses on pleasures when, according to this criticism, a meaningful life involves more than just material satisfaction.[28] I want to focus on a more specific concern regarding the adequacy of utilitarianism as a moral or ethical theory: that by treating privacy as a subjective preference the theory fails to take into account the importance of treating people with respect and dignity.

Consider the following case. In the summer of 1963, rangers in Yosemite National Park received complaints about lewd homosexual behavior in the public restrooms at Camp Curry. This prompted Ranger Twight to cut holes in the ceilings over the toilet stalls, holes that he disguised as air vents, enabling him to covertly observe dozens of people doing their business in the stalls without their knowledge.[29] The ranger's behavior seems clearly wrong since there are other ways to deter misconduct that are not so intrusive. But can a utilitarian account for why Ranger Twight acted badly given that the innocent people whose privacy was intruded upon were never aware of the intrusion and therefore did not experience any frustration of their subjective preferences for privacy? A utilitarian might argue that if we were to condone what the ranger did, and word got out, others might undertake similar secret observations as well. While the utilitarian would not yet have a reason to regard that as wrong so long as the observations were undetected, if those further observations were made by people who were not as discreet and whose targets discover that they are being observed, and if people in that society who discovered they were observed would generally experience significant disutility given their privacy preferences, a utilitarian might conclude that society is better off prohibiting such observations. But secret observations of the sort Ranger Twight made seem wrong apart from the possibility that they will create disutility if they are ever discovered. The wrong involved does not seem to depend on whether a person experiences a frustration of a subjective privacy preference. If we agree that Ranger Twight acted badly, as I think we should, then utilitarianism would be deficient as a theory of privacy ethics.

---

28 See the sources cited in Hanna Pitkin, "Slippery Bentham," *Political Theory* 18(1):104–131 (1990), p. 104; and Amy Peikoff, "The Right to Privacy: Contemporary Reductionists and their Critics," *Virginia Journal of Social Policy and Law* 13:474–551 (2006).

29 *Smayda v. U.S.*, 352 F.2d 251 (9th Cir. 1965). Two of three judges decided to permit the search without a warrant as they believed the observations were in plain view given that the stall doors lacked locks and had an open space of 18 inches from the floor to the stall door's bottom and the top of the door had a height of just three feet.

Let us think about this example some more. How could I be wronged when someone secretly observes me if I am never aware of the observation? Why should we not conclude instead that what I don't know can't hurt me? Of course if in observing me without my knowledge someone is able to gather information that they can then use to my detriment, a utilitarian could explain why that would be wrong. Someone who watches me in secret to learn my daily routine in order to determine the best time to rob my home causes me to suffer disutility by robbing me. But a utilitarian could not account for why it would be wrong for someone, like Ranger Twight, merely to observe me secretly without making me vulnerable to some further wrong.

Stanley Benn addresses why it may be wrong in an article I briefly mentioned in Chapter 2 and now want to return to.[30] Benn defends a "general moral principle" that one is presumptively entitled to feel resentful if one is watched without leave, though this "presumptive immunity" can be outweighed by other considerations.[31] The reason Benn gives is that observing someone without leave can treat them without respect, insult them, or be impertinent.[32] Benn gives the example of A listening in on C's conversation with D without C's permission. If C knows that A is listening, A's intrusion "alters C's consciousness of himself"; knowing that A is listening, C may want to adjust what he says in order to avoid A's disapproval. Even if C is not self-conscious, his conversation may be changed by A's presence. The uninvited intrusion is impertinent because A "treats it as of no consequence that he may have effected an alteration in C's perception of himself."[33] A ignores C's wishes in a way that shows a lack of respect. Benn then proceeds to defend the claim that it is presumptively wrong to observe C without his consent even if in being observed C suffers no obvious damage, as when C is observed secretly. Secretly observing C is objectionable "because it deliberately deceives a person about his world, thwarting, for reasons that cannot be his reasons, his attempts to make a rational choice." Though C is unaware of being observed, "the significance to him of his enterprise, assumed unobserved, is deliberately falsified by A. He may be in a fool's paradise or a fool's hell; either way, A is making a fool of him" and shows disrespect for C as a chooser.[34]

Benn's argument is essentially Kantian. Kant argues that all human beings, as rational agents, are entitled to equal respect as persons and that

---

30 Stanley Benn, "Privacy, Freedom, and Respect for Persons," in Schoeman, ed., *Philosophical Dimensions of Privacy* (New York: Cambridge University Press, 1984).

31 Benn, pp. 231, 234; cf. p. 225, defending a prima facie claim that B should not observe and report on A unless A agrees to it, a prima facie claim being a claim that can be overridden with sufficient justification.

32 Benn, pp. 228–229.

33 Benn, pp. 229–230.

34 Benn, p. 230.

it would be wrong to treat them as mere means to your own ends rather than treating them as ends in themselves.[35] Wronging someone on this view does not require that you actually frustrate their subjective privacy preferences. However, and here I depart from Kant but not Benn, that an action fails to respect someone as a human being by violating their privacy may depend on the existence of cultural norms that dictate that certain activities in certain locations are private.[36] Without those norms, which themselves can be the basis for subjective privacy preferences, the observation might not be regarded as failing to show respect for persons. In California in the 1960s, just as today, evacuation is regarded as a private matter. Instead of respecting the reasonable privacy expectations and dignity of the dozens of people he observed, Ranger Twight treated them as casualties in his quest to uncover crime, and on the Kantian view that is wrong even if these people were unaware they were being disrespected.

To find this criticism of the utilitarian account of privacy ethics plausible we need not agree with all aspects of Kant's moral philosophy; it may suffice merely to agree that secret observations of the sort that Ranger Twight conducted are wrong, and to recognize that the utilitarian philosophy cannot convincingly explain why. Nor need we agree with Benn's "general moral principle" that there is a prima facie claim not to be observed without leave. But we do need to recognize certain behavior as failing to show respect. Someone sitting on a park bench who casually observes people walking their dogs or playing near a lake does not necessarily treat those people with disrespect or act badly. But someone who stares at a particular person may, in some contexts. One might stare at someone discreetly because one admires their beauty—that is not disrespectful. Using video surveillance in an office stockroom to see if employees are stealing might not risk affronting their dignity or fail to show them respect, if stockrooms are not customarily regarded as areas in which one could expect privacy and particularly if there is notice and general acceptance of the use of surveillance cameras in such places to deter stealing. But there are contexts, such as the one surrounding events in Yosemite Park in the summer of 1963, in which observing you without your leave disrespects and wrongs you even if you are not aware you were observed.

Another way to express this criticism of utilitarianism as a theory of privacy ethics is that privacy should not be regarded merely as a subjective preference with a price tag. On the "law and economics" version of utilitarianism, discussed in Chapter 2, whether a person should have a right to control who may publish a picture of them taken in a public place depends

---

35   Kant, *Groundwork*, 429–430.

36   Benn, pp. 224, 234 (recognizing the role of cultural norms). Kant, however, takes the view that morality should not depend on the existence of shared social practices; for discussion of his view, see Mark Tunick, *Practices and Principles* (Princeton, NJ: Princeton University Press, 1998), ch. 2.

on whether assigning them the right would promote social utility.[37] If individuals did not control the right, the nude sunbather on a public beach might have to pay to avoid having her photo taken and published, and negotiate not only with one photographer but potentially many. The law and economics argument is that making her pay would be inefficient. But rather than think the reason individuals should control the right is because that is the solution recommended by a calculation of net utilities, we might think that individuals should not have to negotiate or pay a price in order to be treated with respect and dignity.[38] Privacy can be regarded as a demand and not a mere preference or taste.

On the economic approach that is rooted in utilitarian philosophy, justice, fairness, and privacy are regarded as tastes that can be assigned a value in terms of utiles.[39] With regard to privacy, that premise may not seem unreasonable given the fact that people vary in the extent to which they value privacy; and if privacy were merely a taste, it might be appropriate to weigh its strength against the strength of other tastes to determine which policies provide the greatest pleasure to the greatest number. But, I have argued, privacy has value as a means of showing respect or of preserving one's dignity, a value that is not readily measured and therefore hard to take into account in a utilitarian calculation. If Benn is right, privacy can also have value even to someone who is unaware that their privacy is being intruded upon. That it may be hard to put a price on the value of being treated with dignity and respect does not mean these values are mysterious or unintelligible, though this may explain why they are rarely taken seriously within a law and economics framework. It means we should seek an approach that will let us weigh a variety of reasons and considerations without being limited only to the tools available to the economist.[40]

Before turning to that approach, it is important to address a problem raised by the fact that preferences for privacy do vary. One could imagine a society in which most people did not care much about privacy, and got used to being observed, so that even if they were aware of Ranger Twight looking at them in a restroom stall they might not be upset. I do not live in such a society; but it is not beyond the realm of possibility, and might

---

37   Joseph Siprut, "Privacy through Anonymity," *Pepperdine Law Review* 33:311–334 (2006), pp. 324–325, discussed in Chapter 2. Cf. Robert Cooter, *The Strategic Constitution* (Princeton, NJ: Princeton University Press, 2002), p. 287.

38   See Mark Tunick, "Efficiency, Practices, and the Moral Point of View," in Mark White, ed., *Theoretical Foundations of Law and Economics* (New York: Cambridge University Press, 2009), pp. 91–92.

39   See e.g. Kaplow and Shavell, *Fairness versus Welfare*; and Edward Glaeser and Bruce Sacerdote, "Sentencing in Homicide Cases and the Role of Vengeance," *Journal of Legal Studies* 32:363–381 (2003) (treating retribution as a taste).

40   See Tunick, "Efficiency, Practices, and the Moral Point of View," p. 90.

even be cast as an ideal by some defenders of "radical transparency."[41] The utilitarian's calculation of the overall social utility of permitting such observations would obviously produce a different result in that society. Should a society expend resources to provide privacy for some individuals with unusually strong subjective preferences for privacy that most people in society might regard as idiosyncratic? The force of the argument based on respect and dignity may also be affected. For if very few people would be disturbed by such observations, could we say that Ranger Twight failed to show them respect or affronted their dignity?

Toleration and respect for persons

Privacy can be a primary good, something that has value to all rational beings, even if not every person values it in the same way. But when society must make choices about policy, it may matter what the relative proportion of people is who care about privacy. Consider again the question of who should own the right to one's image in a public place. If we assign the right to the public so that it is within anyone's right to take and publish my photo without my consent, then devious photographers could identify individuals with strong privacy preferences, take their photo, and agree not to disseminate the image only if they are given a sizeable payment. This would not technically be blackmail; the photographer simply offers to refrain from doing something that he has a right to do. If instead we assign the right to the individual, the photographer would be guilty of blackmail because he threatens to do something that he would have no right to do. What is the desired public policy? The answer may depend on the distribution of privacy preferences within the society. Suppose in a society of a million people that only 1,000 would object to having images of them in a public place published. Only these 1,000 people would be subject to blackmail.[42] We might think that it would be more efficient to require those 1,000 people to be careful when going out in public or even to wear disguises, rather than shift presumptive rights from the public to individuals. Why, after all, should policy for a million be determined by a

41   See David Brin, *The Transparent Society* (Reading, MA: Addison-Wesley, 1998); and David Kirkpatrick, *The Facebook Effect* (New York: Simon and Schuster, 2011), p. 200 (on "radical transparency" as an ideal to which Facebook wants us to aspire).

42   This arbitrary figure may in many societies wildly underestimate the number of people who would desire privacy in this context. In *Gill v. Hearst*, 40 Cal.2d 224 (1953), the majority held that an ordinary person should not be offended by having a photograph of them shown in a magazine. Justice Carter, in dissent, wrote that "courts should consider the effect of such publication upon the sensibility of the ordinary private citizen, and not upon the sensibility of those persons who seek and enjoy publicity and notoriety" and estimated that 90 percent of our population remain private citizens who desire to be left alone (234). But his figure may be just as arbitrary. For discussion of American responses to privacy surveys up to the early 1990s, see Priscilla Regan, *Legislating Privacy* (Chapel Hill: University of North Carolina Press, 1995), ch. 3.

minority of .1 percent? On the other hand, if most people come not to care about having their image published, does this mean we all must not care?

The issue is the same as the one I raised in Chapter 3 with the example of the "Carefree" and "Careful" societies. In "Carefree Society," the vast majority of people do not mind when other people look into their homes using pocket telescopes—a practice called homeviewing. Not only do they not expect privacy, they do not even care for it. But what if there are a small number of people who resent this practice? In Chapter 3, I conceded for the time being that in Carefree Society one cannot reasonably expect privacy against homeviewing. In "Careful Society," in contrast, a significant number of people are unhappy when they are homeviewed, and take measures to avoid being observed such as covering their windows. They resignedly accept the practice of homeviewing with great reluctance. Despite prevailing practices, in Careful Society one can still have a legitimate interest in and even a right to privacy in one's home against homeviewers. A utilitarian could support this conclusion by reasoning that pro-privacy policies might augment the total utility within society given the substantial number of people for whom the practice creates disutility; a Kantian such as Benn might support this conclusion by arguing that homeviewing in Careful Society fails to give due respect to each human being. But now let us return to the case of Carefree Society. Should we so readily concede that homeviewing there is legitimate because it is so widely accepted, or should a liberal society accommodate the needs of even a very small minority who object to the practice? To address this question I must step back and discuss the role of toleration in a liberal society.

Among the defining features of a liberal society are that people are regarded as free and equal, and the fact of pluralism is accepted. The fact of pluralism is that people hold diverse conceptions or "comprehensive doctrines" as to the meaning, value, and ends of life. Accepting this fact, a liberal society addresses conflicts by seeking what John Rawls has called an "overlapping consensus" that does not favor one particular comprehensive doctrine such as a particular religious or philosophical world view, because no such view would be acceptable to all members of society; to impose one comprehensive doctrine would require the oppressive use of state power.[43] On one account, individuals in a liberal society should be free to do as they please and act on their own conception of what life is worth pursuing so long as they leave a similar freedom to others. Kant expressed this ideal by saying that people ought to be free to act in such a way that the free use of their will is compatible with the freedom of everyone according to a universal law.[44] In a liberal society, we tolerate others, up to

43   John Rawls, "The Idea of an Overlapping Consensus," *Oxford Journal of Legal Studies* 7(1):1–25 (1987), pp. 3–4.
44   Immanuel Kant, *Metaphysics of Morals*, tr. Gregor (Cambridge: Cambridge University Press, 1991), p. 63.

a point, in recognition that all of us are free and equal persons capable of making choices about how to live and are entitled to invoke our own comprehensive doctrines or conception of the life worth living in selecting the ends we choose to pursue.[45]

Liberal political theory clearly does not permit others to harm us to the point where we would be incapable of pursuing our own conception of a good life, for that would violate the condition that we should all be free to do as we please so long as our freedom is compatible with others having a similar freedom. We should not tolerate others whose conception of a good life includes randomly killing other people. But there are harder cases. Suppose your conception of a good life includes beating horses and using drugs, but my conception of a good life involves living in a community in which animals do not suffer and peoples' minds are not clouded by artificial chemicals. Must I tolerate your behavior? Or rather should you tolerate me by respecting my desires even if this requires you to stop being cruel to animals and to give up drugs? Liberal theorists differ in how they answer this question. John Stuart Mill argues that you should be free to do as you please so long as you do not harm others.[46] (While Mill does not discuss at length whether animals count as "others" when applying the harm principle, in one passage he suggests they do.[47]) The freedom we are accorded on that view depends on our understanding of what it means to harm others. But as I discussed in Chapter 2, there are cases of unwanted attention in which someone might not be harmed yet still has an interest that it may be reasonable to respect and be sensitive to.

Jeremy Waldron offers an account of how a liberal society should deal with conflicts that goes beyond Mill's "harm principle"; and while he does not think his account satisfactorily resolves some of the most difficult examples of conflict, I think it is helpful in addressing many cases of unwanted attention. Waldron characterizes the liberal ideal as securing order in a way that is fair to the aims and activities of all.[48] A liberal society should permit a range of actions that is adequate for each individual to pursue their ends at least as long as these actions do not conflict with one another. Working with one of his examples, suppose I participate in a funeral procession that follows a particular route that a group of noisy bikers wants to ride along at the same time. There is no physical incompatibility between the two activities since the procession could still proceed despite the bikers'

45 Cf. David Heyd, "Education to Toleration: Some Philosophical Obstacles and Their Resolution," in McKinnon and Castiglione, eds., *Culture of Toleration in Diverse Societies* (Manchester University Press, 2003), p. 205; and Martha Nussbaum, "Perfectionist Liberalism and Political Liberalism," *Philosophy and Public Affairs* 39(1):3–45 (2011), grounding toleration in the Kantian idea of treating humanity as an end and people as equal, which is linked to the idea of dignity.

46 Mill, "On Liberty," in *Collected Works*, vol. 18, ch. 1, par. 9.

47 J.S. Mill, "Whewell on Moral Philosophy," in *Collected Works*, vol. 10, pp. 185–187.

48 Jeremy Waldron, "Toleration and Reasonableness," in McKinnon and Castiglione, p. 14.

presence; and we probably cannot say that the bikers harm me or my fellow mourners. But the bikers keep us from adequately achieving our ends; their noisy, disruptive behavior utterly spoils the somber atmosphere we require to show our respect for the dead.[49] Waldron considers two possible sets of constraints that a society might adopt to guide us when we face conflicts such as this. The first possibility is that society should simply leave people free to pursue their ends as best they can so long as they do not engage in activity that prevents others from pursuing their ends; the second alternative is that it should adopt a set of constraints that requires all of us to be accommodating so that each of us may *adequately* pursue our ends. According to the first policy, so long as no regulations preclude us from having our funeral procession, society has done all that is required. The problem here is that this is not enough for me to pursue my ends adequately; that can happen only if the bikers can be forced to be sensitive to my aims. The second policy allows for that, and Waldron thinks that this is the policy a liberal society should adopt.[50]

The second policy, unlike the first, requires people to be sensitive to the aims of others.[51] Waldron distinguishes protestant aims, which are aims I can pursue myself without requiring the participation of anyone else, from communal aims, which can be pursued only if others are involved. A liberal society would not require someone to participate in the communal aims of others. "Sensitive aims" lie in between protestant and communal aims. The mourners' aim is not communal since they do not require other people to participate in the procession; but neither is it protestant, for they do require forbearance and respect. They require sensitivity.[52]

Waldron's point is that sometimes I cannot pursue my ends adequately unless others accommodate me, and a liberal society may require us to adjust our actions so that we are sensitive to the aims of others and help them adequately achieve those aims. Everyone should have a "fair shot" at pursuing their ends as long as the pursuit of those ends is compatible with the ability of others adequately to pursue their ends.[53] It is possible for the bikers to bike and the mourners to mourn, even at the same time and place,

---

49   Waldron, "Toleration," pp. 15–16.
50   Waldron, "Toleration," p. 16: if we reject this second option, "our concern for adequacy would be in danger." Waldron lays out the two options as follows: (1) "For each individual P subject to C [a set of constraints on conduct], the range of actions *permitted to P* by C is adequate for the pursuit of P's ends"; and (2) "For each individual P subject to C, the range of actions *permitted to anyone* by C is such that action within C is adequate for the pursuit of P's ends" (my emphasis).
51   The approach suggested here differs from the paternalistic approach that Anita Allen discusses in *Unpopular Privacy*: her point of emphasis is not that the government can force me to be sensitive to the aims of others, but that it can coerce me to not waive my own privacy rights; these may not be mutually exclusive approaches.
52   Waldron, pp. 25–27.
53   Waldron, p. 17.

but unless one side gives in at least one group will be unable adequately to pursue their ends. If it is the case that the mourners have special reason to be at that particular place at that time but the bikers do not, then the solution suggested by Waldron's approach is for the bikers to accommodate and be sensitive to the needs of the mourners so the mourners can adequately pursue their ends. This imposes a greater burden on the bikers than Mill's harm principle would; but presumably the bikers themselves will benefit by living in a society which requires other people sometimes to be sensitive to their own aims.

More difficult cases arise when being sensitive to the aims of others would mean that you could no longer adequately pursue your own aims. Some Muslims take their faith to require not that others practice the Muslim faith—that would be a communal aim—but that others not engage in blasphemy or insult. Their demand for others to be sensitive may conflict with people's ability to adequately pursue their own aims. One of the examples on which Waldron focuses involves Salman Rushdie, the cosmopolitan writer who cannot live the life he wants to lead unless he can mock his Islamic religious heritage. Rushdie takes advantage of the freedom of speech to challenge core beliefs of some Muslims. His opponents cannot live the life they want to lead unless they can vindicate the name of the Prophet, which Rushdie mocks. They issued a fatwa calling for Rushdie's death. Waldron takes it to be the case that "[e]ach is demanding something that would make life intolerable for the other."[54] If we demand that Rushdie be sensitive to the aims of Muslims by censoring himself, he would be unable adequately to pursue his own aims, unlike the bikers who, without making undue sacrifices, could find another time or place to ride, thereby permitting the funeral procession to proceed undisturbed. Yet by mocking the Prophet, Rushdie makes life intolerable for the Muslims. While the Muslims may be unable to provide reasons for why life is intolerable when the Prophet is mocked that would be acceptable to people who do not share their faith—in other words, they may be unable to express their sensitivities in "publicly accessible terms"—Waldron argues that a liberal society should not impose "externally stated adequacy conditions"; it should respect the internal point of view of religion.[55] In other words, a commitment to pluralism requires that we not inquire into the legitimacy of the Muslim's conception of the purposes of life and the means they require adequately to achieve those purposes or, for that matter, into Rushdie's conception according to which a life that does not permit expression of religious criticism would not be worth living. Such cases pose a dilemma Waldron leaves unresolved.[56]

54 Waldron, p. 30.
55 Waldron, p. 23.
56 Cf. Waldron, p. 33.

But cases involving unwanted attention need not be as intractable. Respecting the right of each person to adopt their own conception of a good or meaningful life need not require that we completely defer to their assessment of the means required to adequately pursue that life. Suppose the bikers asserted that they needed to ride the precise route used by the mourners at that exact time or else they could not adequately pursue their ends. We need not accept that claim without any inquiry. A liberal society must not impose one comprehensive doctrine on those who hold different ones. If the bikers point to a text that is holy to them that dictates that they ride their bikes at that precise place and time, then by adopting the liberal ideal we would accept that as a legitimate reason without inquiring into the validity of their holy text.[57] We would then face a dilemma similar to the dilemma presented by the conflict between Rushdie and the Muslim faithful. But if the bikers simply asserted that they needed to ride then and there, and after we ask for more of a reason they say "just because," we need not accept that response as sufficient to give their claim as much weight as the claim of the mourners. Cases of unwanted attention are more readily resolved with the help of Waldron's approach if we are willing to subject competing claims to free speech and privacy to some test of non-arbitrariness or rational scrutiny, which we may be able to do while still recognizing the fact of pluralism.

The conflict between Rushdie's free speech rights and Muslims' religious faith differs from the conflict between the free speech interest of the person who used social media to share a photograph of the Korean woman who refused to pick up the mess her dog left on a subway, and her interest in not receiving unwanted attention and being forever known as "Dog Poop Girl."[58] To require her unwelcome publicizer to be sensitive to her privacy interests probably would not be an obstacle to his adequately pursuing his ends, whereas to ask Rushdie to refrain from engaging in social criticism and mocking the Prophet would. If the publicizer did claim that publishing the photo was necessary for him adequately to pursue his aims, we may be able to evaluate his claim as well as the Korean woman's without calling into question the comprehensive doctrines of either.

To summarize the argument: a liberal society requires that we respect persons as free and equal and be sensitive to their aims. This might require being sensitive to the aims of individuals who want to share information as well as of those who do not welcome the attention. Where aims conflict, we might need to assess the claims of each party in the conflict regarding

---

57 In *U.S. v. Ballard*, 322 U.S. 78, 86 (1944), the U.S. Supreme Court held that the First Amendment precludes courts from inquiring into the truth of a defendant's religious beliefs. A more difficult question which I shall not address is whether a liberal society can properly inquire into the sincerity of one's religious beliefs when those beliefs are the basis for claiming that an activity is needed adequately to pursue one's ends.

58 See Chapter 1.

their ability adequately to pursue their respective ends, which we may be able to do without sacrificing a commitment to pluralism.

A good number of cases of unwanted attention may not involve interests in pursuing one's life goals or aims; interests, which involve matters affecting one's welfare, in some cases may have little weight; or they may not be at stake at all, merely desires. Still, in a liberal society we might reasonably be expected to be sensitive to such interests or desires if doing so would avoid conflict and would not prevent us from adequately pursuing our own. Consider the following example that is probably not uncommon in the age of social media.[59] An old friend with whom you went to elementary school finds a photo of you in fourth grade and scans and uploads it to Facebook. You dread the picture: you were chubby and had a mullet haircut. It is not a picture you want anyone else to see. But your friend tags you in the picture, and other people comment on it and it soon gets viewed by most of your Facebook friends. You are horrified. You could not expect privacy in your appearance back in fourth grade because that is how you showed yourself to the world for anyone to see, and the photo was evidently accessible to others. But it was not *readily* accessible until your friend made it so. Your friend took away your ability to control access to your past self. Perhaps the vast majority of people would not be bothered if they were in your place. But it bothers you. So you ask your friend to take the photo down and he refuses. Conceivably you have an interest in concealing the photo, an interest in controlling how you present yourself to others. You may think that by taking this control away from you your (now former) friend fails to show you respect. But if your reputation is not threatened, or the photo would not affect your ability to maintain your intimate relationships, or hurt you economically, or inspire people to shame, humiliate, or punish you, then one might think that your welfare is not at stake, only your desire, a desire that conflicts with your friend's desire to share the image. If interests with any weight are not at stake, we might be unable to say that one of you is preventing the other from adequately pursuing their aims. But we could still ask whether your friend should have been sensitive to your desires, or rather you should be sensitive to your friend's. In doing so, I think we find an asymmetry. Your demand that the photo not be shared is not arbitrary; there are legitimate reasons people have for controlling information about themselves. Even if your demand reflects a preference that does not rise to the level of an interest with any real weight, it is one to which your friend is being insensitive. But I think we can say that you, on the other hand, are not showing insensitivity to your friend by making your request or by expecting that he would not have uploaded the photo in the first place without your consent. A liberal society may decide that it should not use the law to coerce your friend to be sensitive merely to your desires, since desires unfulfilled do not prevent people

---

59 I thank Rachel Luria for suggesting this example.

from adequately achieving their ends. But that your friend is being insensitive in this case may be sufficient cause to judge them to be acting badly.

We can now return to the problem that originally motivated the discussion of toleration in a liberal society: should a society accommodate the demands for privacy of a very small minority whose preferences for privacy are regarded by the majority as idiosyncratic? What I hope to have established is that so long as those in this minority have a non-arbitrary reason for claiming that without privacy they cannot adequately pursue their ends, or so long as there is no non-arbitrary reason for giving them unwanted attention, then the fact that others regard them as supersensitive does not in itself undermine the minority's claim. Respecting them as free and equal human beings requires that we be sensitive to their aims.

If even just a small minority of people in Carefree Society have non-arbitrary reasons for claiming they cannot adequately achieve their ends because of the practice of homeviewing, and no one in the society needs to homeview in order adequately to pursue their ends, a liberal society should restrict homeviewing. There would be no need to completely ban it. If the small number of people with strong privacy preferences were able—without facing ridicule—to signal their sensitivity to the practice so that others were aware of it—perhaps by shading their windows or putting signs outside their homes—then people could refrain from homeviewing them while still engaging in the practice. Homeviewing them might be akin to forcibly removing the veil of a Muslim woman in a society in which women rarely wear veils; regardless of how uncommon her privacy preference is among women in that society, the Muslim woman's preference is not arbitrary and failing to respect it, without a sufficient reason, would be to fail to show her respect; it would also affront her dignity.[60]

However, one could imagine scenarios in which the issue may not be so simple. Suppose that people come to rely on homeviewing. For some people, *being* homeviewed may give them a sense of security, or is a means of self-validation, though they could not reasonably demand that others homeview them, as a liberal society should not require individuals to participate in the communal aims of others. But now imagine a "Carefree and Anxious Society" in which not being able to homeview one's neighbors would create overwhelming anxiety in a majority of people and in this respect they regard homeviewing as essential to adequately pursuing their ends. The majority might even seek to enact laws requiring people to forego the use of window coverings. Here we might need to look more carefully into the extent to which both homeviewing one's neighbors and not being homeviewed are really necessary for achieving one's aims. If the

60 Homeviewing an unwilling subject or forcibly removing a woman's veil affronts one's dignity and is not merely a failure to show respect because someone's body is observed against their will. But there may be other criteria for defining an indignity as well; see Chapter 2, "Dignity and respect for persons."

loss of privacy the minority experience meant only that they needed occasionally to retreat to a windowless room for moments of intimacy, we might
conclude that although they are inconvenienced, they still have adequate
means to pursue their aims. One might object that they should not have to
retreat, but in Carefree and Anxious Society we might be led to conclude
that this is just how things are. The conflict would be harder to resolve if
the loss of privacy had a more substantial impact on the minority's ability
to pursue their ends.

There might be practical difficulties in granting legal remedies to those
who most people would regard as supersensitive; a legal system that did so
might be subject to abuse by those who are not really sensitive but see an
opportunity for profit. For example, someone who is not really bothered by
having their picture published in a magazine might pretend to be in order
to reach a settlement with a publisher. Criminals in "Carefree Society" might
not really be sensitive to being homeviewed per se, but would benefit by
not having their criminal activities exposed. But while we would need to
work out some difficulties regarding appropriate remedies, as a matter of
principle ethical norms should take into account the privacy preferences of
the supersensitive and not simply dismiss them as idiosyncratic, if the
burden of doing so is not too great.

Respecting the privacy of those who do not welcome attention is one
way a liberal society can practice toleration. By respecting their privacy, we
are sensitive to their aims. There is another, distinct way of practicing toleration, besides respecting privacy. In a society in which people were not
shamed or humiliated for their misdeeds, or simply for being different,
there may be less of a need for privacy. Tyler Clementi might not have felt
the need to take his own life if society was more accepting of homosexuality. Louis Conradt, Marvin Briscoe, or Dog Poop Girl, too, might need less
privacy in a tolerant society that was less judgmental and more forgiving of
one's mistakes. While forgiveness is not what is called for in cases where
someone has not done anything blameworthy, it might be a meaningful
remedy for many people. But it can be more difficult to forgive an act if
you are constantly reminded of it.[61]

Weighing reasons and considerations without making a utilitarian calculation

I have argued that there are limitations to the utilitarian philosophy: actually making the sort of calculation that the theory envisions is not feasible;
and regarding privacy merely as a preference or taste ignores the dignity
interests associated with privacy, the weight of which cannot easily be

---

61 Meg Ambrose *et al.*, "Seeking Digital Redemption," *Santa Clara Computer and High
Technology Law Journal* 29:99–162 (2012–2013) (defending the view that privacy is
needed to promote forgiveness).

measured in terms of utiles. Some theorists prefer an approach that makes it easy to weigh competing interests by focusing on those that can be assessed in the same "currency." Boudewijn de Bruin emphasizes the importance of privacy in helping us avoid expenditures to protect against identity theft, and claims as an advantage of his way of understanding privacy's value, as against other approaches, that it is easier to weigh this liberty interest against competing liberty interests in free speech than it is to weigh free speech interests against the value of dignity or friendship. We can use the same "currency" of liberty, although he recognizes that "the actual weighing of interests is going to be a difficult task."[62] I agree with the general thrust of de Bruin's project, which is to show that privacy is a liberal value that in some cases outweighs the value of free speech;[63] but I do not think we should restrict our understanding of the value of privacy to avoid inconveniences. Dealing with values like respect and dignity is difficult for the utilitarian who seeks to calculate net aggregate utility; but we should adopt a method that lets us weigh all relevant considerations and not limit our considerations only to those that our instruments for balancing can easily take into account.

Utilitarianism is undeniably an attractive theory. It is reasonable when faced with conflict to conduct a balancing of interests, and in doing so we should take into account the consequences to society of the alternatives we are considering. But the approach I think we are led to, given the impracticality of conducting an actual calculation of utilities, and given the importance of considerations such as respect and dignity that cannot readily be assigned a value in terms of utiles, is one that weighs considerations by a different process than a calculation.

One promising model for the deliberative process we can invoke is the one used by the U.S. Supreme Court when it scrutinizes laws that infringe on liberty interests or fundamental rights. Where a law implicates liberty interests, the Court uses at least a rational basis test that demands that the law not be arbitrary; where those interests are so weighty that they are regarded as fundamental rights, the Court uses a more rigorous strict scrutiny test that demands not merely that the law is non-arbitrary or rational, but that it serves an important purpose and be narrowly tailored to achieve that purpose—or put another way, that there are no alternatives that could have achieved the important purpose without violating the fundamental right.[64] A similar strict scrutiny test has been used implicitly by the European Court of Human Rights when fundamental rights are at stake. The Strasbourg Court found that the Article 8 right to respect for private and

---

62 De Bruin, "The Liberal Value of Privacy," *Law and Philosophy* 29:505–534 (2010), pp. 519–520, 534.

63 De Bruin, p. 527.

64 See, e.g., *Nebbia v. New York*, 291 U.S. 502 (1934) (rational basis test); *Griswold v. Connecticut*, 381 U.S. 479, 485 (1965) (stricter scrutiny test).

family life was at stake when people living near London's Heathrow Airport were deprived of sleep because of loud airplane noise at night. The Court was not content to allow the night time flight traffic to continue merely because the flights have significant economic value; rather, it held that "[s]tates are required to minimize, as far as possible, the interference with these rights, by trying to find alternate solutions and by generally seeking to achieve their aims in the least onerous way as regards human rights."[65] The framework I am proposing has us first ask whether a legitimate privacy interest may be at stake when speech gives someone unwanted attention. If so, we scrutinize the reasons for the speech. If the speech advances a legitimate public interest, but the privacy interest it implicates is substantial, we would ask whether the interest the speech advances could be advanced in ways that are less intrusive to privacy.

Unwanted attention can implicate privacy interests and make it difficult for individuals adequately to pursue their aims by exposing someone to unjust punishment or other reputational harms or causing an economic setback. It can fail to show them respect and affront their dignity. These all would be non-arbitrary reasons to respect privacy. In the previous chapters, we encountered many examples of individuals for whom exposure was a significant setback, including Conradt, Clementi, Sipple, Briscoe, Dog Poop Girl, B.J.F., Ms. Shulman, the mother identified as "L" who lost her job as a school attendant, individuals who were falsely arrested, and individuals who were defamed. Courts could easily decide that speech that sets back such weighty interests is not justified merely if it entertains but serves no other legitimate purpose. As Mr. Justice Eady noted in an opinion discussed in Chapter 3, "[i]t will rarely be the case that the privacy rights of an individual or of his family will have to yield in priority to another's right to publish what has been described in the House of Lords as 'tittle-tattle about the activities of footballers' wives and girlfriends'."[66] In some cases, the weight of the privacy interest may seem less substantial, as in the Canadian case of the 17-year-old girl who was upset when a photo of her sitting on the front steps of a public building was published in a magazine that sold just 772 copies; her complaint was simply that people at school laughed at her.[67] But even in her case, given that there are non-arbitrary reasons to let her control how she presents herself to the world, there should be a countervailing reason for publishing her photo without her consent, though in cases like this we might be less demanding when scrutinizing the case for publication. If there is no appreciable purpose other than mere entertainment or avoiding the inconvenience of finding a consenting subject for the photo, the balancing of interests could favor privacy.

65 *Hatton v. U.K.* [2001] 34 EHRR 1, Par. 97.
66 *CTB v. News Groups Ltd* [2011] EWHC 1232 (QB), Par. 33 (citing *Jameel v. Wall Street Journal Europe* SPRL [2007] 1 AC 359, Par. 147).
67 *Aubry v. Editions Vice-Versa* [1998] S.C.J. No. 30, Par. 29.

Free speech advocates may scream foul and complain of censorship. But a liberal society requires us to be sensitive to the aims of others. If gratuitous use of a couple's image impedes them from adequately achieving their aims, and if the publisher could have used a consenting couple or even paid models to make its point without hampering anyone's ability to achieve their objectives, then respect for privacy may be the best outcome. In many cases, a substitute would not do. The photograph of the naked young Vietnamese girl fleeing her napalm-ravaged village during the Vietnam War is not substitutable; that photo could not have been staged using a consenting model and have the same effect.

Providing newsworthy information is not the only valid purpose of free speech. Many people may need access to entertainment to adequately pursue their ends. But when legitimate privacy interests are at stake we need to ask similar sorts of questions: was it necessary to expose a particular person to unwanted attention in order to entertain, or could that objective have been obtained in other, less intrusive ways. The interest individuals have in being informed about the threat posed by adults preying on underage teens on the Internet could adequately be met if NBC blurred the faces and did not reveal the identities of the sting targets it exposed on "To Catch a Predator." The thrill and excitement that NBC's viewers apparently experienced in seeing a rabbi or district attorney caught red-handed could have been attained by countless other forms of entertainment that are not insensitive to the aims of other human beings with legitimate privacy interests.

6 Cases

When I want to share information about you and you do not want the attention, we have a conflict. The framework I have proposed has us resolve the conflict by first asking whether your privacy really is at stake. That will depend on what information about you I am trying to share. The color of your hair? That is a public fact in which you cannot expect privacy, unless you are careful always to conceal it in public. The color of your hair twenty years ago? That may now be a private fact. If we can conclude that it is information in which you may have a legitimate privacy interest, we then must weigh this interest against the competing free speech interest. In doing so, we may need to ask whether it is information the recipients have a legitimate interest in knowing.

In previous chapters, I articulated some principles that are intended to guide us as we ask the above questions. While normally one cannot legitimately expect privacy in information that is in plain view, in determining whether something is in plain view and therefore a public fact we should ask not simply whether it is accessible to others by the use of legitimate means of inquiry; we should ask whether it is readily accessible. A court proceeding in the early 1990s for a person charged with driving under the influence might have been open to the public, but a layperson today may be hard-pressed to find out the name of the accused unless the clerk of that court made archived court proceedings accessible on the Internet. I also defended the use of two principles to qualify the plain view principle and identify circumstances in which one might still have a legitimate privacy interest even in public facts. The first principle holds that one may reasonably expect privacy in details about a public fact if those details implicate one's dignity. Even if the desperate words of an accident victim were accessible to others in a public place, she still has a legitimate interest in keeping that moment private.[1] The second principle holds that one can have a legitimate privacy interest that some information about oneself that is accessible and perhaps even readily accessible to others by

---

1   *Shulman v. Group W Productions*, 18 Cal.4th 100 (1998).

DOI: 10.4324/9781315763132-6

legitimate means of observation not be widely disseminated, as can occur when one memorializes it in the form of a photo or video and uploads it to the Internet where it can be found by a search engine and persist for a lifetime.

If we have decided that privacy may indeed be implicated, then we need to weigh the interest in privacy against free speech interests. If the privacy interest is substantial, we would strictly scrutinize the reasons for permitting the speech and ask whether the intrusion upon privacy is necessary to convey newsworthy information. We could begin by asking whether the speech concerns a matter of legitimate public interest or merely has entertainment value. While it is important that we have access to entertainment, perhaps even essential to a life worth living, speech that merely entertains may deserve less protection than speech that contributes to debate about matters of public interest. One reason for this distinction is that entertainers have a nearly infinite number of ways to achieve their objective besides infringing upon legitimate privacy interests; providers of important news do not. In closely scrutinizing the case for allowing speech there are some additional considerations we should take into account. Could we avoid implicating privacy interests by providing a substitute image to illustrate whatever we want to convey, or by omitting certain details, without impinging on society's interest in having access to newsworthy information? Is the information newsworthy to the entire audience to whom it is made readily accessible, or could it have been shared more selectively? The suggestion that we "omit details" or restrict access to some speech will worry free speech advocates. But the ideals of a liberal society require us to be sensitive to the aims of others when doing so does not keep us from adequately achieving our own aims. When privacy is at stake, this may require us to limit some speech. This need not lead us down a slippery slope to full-blown censorship.

In this chapter I turn to a variety of cases of unwanted attention to illustrate the sort of deliberative process I am suggesting we use. The discussion will reinforce the points I developed earlier but also provide the opportunity to think about some of their ambiguities or difficulties. Because circumstances matter in assessing the relative weight of privacy and free speech interests, I have arranged the cases into different categories based on features they share. Some cases involve private facts in private places that are not newsworthy; some involve private facts that are newsworthy, or that are observed in a public place; and some involve public facts. As we will see, the line between public and private facts can sometimes be blurry, and so while I think these categories can be helpful, we should not be worried if it is sometimes not entirely clear whether a particular fact pattern should be put into one category rather than another.

Publicizing private facts

*Private facts in private places (*Rear Window, Lake v. Wal-Mart*)*

Most of us will agree that it is wrong to intrude into a private place; even courts in the United States which have generally been unsympathetic to concerns about privacy have had no difficulty recognizing this. The First Amendment may include a right to gather information but it does not entitle Peeping Toms or detectives to videotape the inside of my home through the slats of my window blinds.[2] It certainly would not warrant a Peeping Tom to share that video with others. I can reasonably expect privacy in certain places even if others control access to those places. The fact that a landlord owns the property I rent does not make it legitimate for him to install a listening device in my apartment.[3] The High Court in New Zealand ruled that the fact that a woman is a guest in a man's home does not permit him to videotape her showering in his home without her knowledge or consent.[4]

These cases are straightforward. Yet suppose the Peeping Tom uncovers a crime? In Alfred Hitchcock's film *Rear Window*, based on a Cornell Woolrich short story, L.B. Jefferies looks through his neighbors' windows simply because he is bored while waiting for his broken leg to heal.[5] His nurse and his friends remind him that he has no business intruding into other people's private lives; but he cannot resist. He observes that the invalid wife of the man who lives across the courtyard, Lars Thorwald, is suddenly gone; using binoculars, he sees Mr. Thorwald tie up a large trunk and have it shipped; using a high-powered telescopic lens, he observes Thorwald cleaning a large butcher's knife; and his girlfriend Lisa finds the missing wife's wedding ring by stealing into Thorwald's home while he was out (having been led on a wild goose chase by a phone call from Jefferies). He puts this all together to conclude that Thorwald killed his wife. There are lots of innocent explanations for these observations. But if Jefferies was right, and Thorwald killed his wife and a murderer was caught, then using a balancing test could we still say that the Peeping Tom acted badly?

2   See *Alderson v. Bonner*, 132 P.3d 1261 (2006); *Souder v. Pendleton Detectives*, 88 So.2d 716 (1956); and Anita Allen, *Unpopular Privacy* (New York: Oxford University Press, 2011), p. 3.
3   See *Roach v. Harper*, 105 S.E.2d 564 (1958); and *Hamberger v. Eastman*, 206 A.2d 239 (1964).
4   *C v. Holland* [2012] NZHC 2155. See also *In re Marriage of Tigges and Tigges*, 758 N.W.2d 824 (2008) (a husband violated his wife's privacy by covertly videotaping their marital bedroom); *Clayton v. Richards*, 47 S.W.3d 149 (2001) (a wife violated her husband's privacy when she hired a detective to install a video camera in their bedroom); and *Lewis v. Legrow*, 670 N.W.2d 675 (2003) (defendant violated the privacy of his girlfriends by secretly videotaping his sexual encounters with them in his bedroom, even though the tapes were not shown to others).
5   Alfred Hitchcock, *Rear Window* (1954); Cornell Woolrich, "It Had to be Murder" (1942).

Rear Window presents us with a moral ambivalence: while Jefferies invades people's privacy, he may uncover valuable information. Jefferies at first did not have what Woolrich describes as the "fevered concentration of a Peeping Tom" in observing his neighbors. Only when he became suspicious of Thorwald did his means of observing become more intrusive, and at that point his motives were noble. And he has the defense that his neighbors could have drawn their shades if they really wanted privacy, as did one newlywed couple. Yet Hitchcock also conveys how intrusive Peeping Toms can be. Jefferies looks in on "Miss Lonelyhearts" and sees her conjure up out of her imagination a romantic dinner with an invisible beau; while we feel sad for Miss Lonelyhearts, we also feel that we had no business viewing her unfulfilled fantasy. Even here Hitchcock leaves us ambivalent about the morality of spying. Later, Jefferies' nurse Stella uses binoculars to observe Miss Lonelyhearts about to take enough sleeping pills to kill herself and is prepared to call for an ambulance; the Peeping Tom could have saved Miss Lonelyhearts' life.

Before we conclude that the Peeping Tom does not act badly, we must remember how improbable it is to discover that one's neighbor is a murderer. In any case, the moral ambivalence *Rear Window* explores concerns conflicts between privacy and public safety: it is not as if Jefferies filmed his neighbors and uploaded the video to YouTube.

Thorwald's privacy interest primarily involved informational privacy and a concern with his reputation. But private facts in private places often concern intimate activity and implicate other interests as well including dignity interests. In *Lake v. Wal-Mart Stores*, two young women, aged 19 and 20, were photographed naked in the shower by the sister of one of the women. The film was brought to a Wal-Mart store for processing. The women were told one or more photos were not processed due to their explicit nature. It became clear several months later that the photograph in question was not only processed but shared with others, after an acquaintance asked one of the women about her sexual orientation and a friend revealed that a Wal-Mart employee showed her a copy.[6] The women never consented to Wal-Mart employees looking at the photo except if needed to determine that it was properly developed; they surely did not consent to the employees sharing the photo with anyone else. Even if the women had shown the photo to a friend, it would be wrong of the friend to digitally scan and then share it on Facebook. While the photo might have entertainment value and be of interest to the general public, it depicts a private fact; sharing the photo implicates interests associated with privacy including dignity and reputational interests. The photo depicts a private fact not merely because it was taken in a private residence, for privacy would be at

---

6   *Lake v. Wal-Mart Stores*, 582 N.W.2d 231 (1998), permitting an intrusion upon seclusion tort claim to proceed.

stake even if it were taken in a public shower facility.[7] Facts about one's own intimate and sexual activity are perhaps as private as facts can be. Yet there are limits to the privacy one can expect even in such facts. A balancing test might have yielded the opposite result in *Lake v. Wal-Mart* if the photo depicted child pornography.[8] But no legitimate public interest was advanced in sharing the photo of the two adults showering.

Private facts can refer to what takes place in an area regarded as private, such as a bedroom or shower in one's home. Such facts implicate what Beate Rössler calls "local privacy."[9] Private facts might also refer to information that is not just anybody's business, such as the fact that an individual has a drug addiction, or frequents a brothel, or that a soccer player committed adultery. A plaintiff who was an editor at CNN successfully sued for defamation and invasion of privacy after personal information about her appeared in a newspaper's gossip column and on various websites. The material published on websites, written by her former colleague and ex-boyfriend, claimed that she was dating numerous people and once "hooked up" with a leading producer of X-rated videos, and implied that she dated power figures to advance her career. A federal district court rejected the defendant's argument that the information could be published because it was true.[10] The plaintiff had a case for defamation as well since the articles made some claims that were not true. In another case, a court sided with plaintiffs who sought damages for the broadcast of a documentary called "Hilary in Hiding" that includes a scene in which Hilary purportedly shows, using a doll, how her father allegedly sexually abused her. The Court reasoned that while sexual abuse of children is an issue worthy of public attention, "the specific facts about the alleged abuse of this one particular child" are not.[11]

If we were to define private facts, which often will be facts that occur in a private place but need not be, as facts that implicate legitimate privacy interests and which the general public has no legitimate interest in knowing, then by any plausible application of a balancing test they should not be shared without a person's consent because by definition there will be no offsetting public interest in making them known. But as we have seen with the example of the Peeping Tom in *Rear Window*, there can be a legitimate interest in sharing some private facts. In *Rear Window*, the countervailing interest is in public health and safety, which is the countervailing interest also in cases involving sexual abuse of children or spousal

---

7   See *State v. Dennison*, 2012 WL 1580610 (Ohio App. 6th Dist. 2012), discussed below.
8   However, see the film "Snap Decision" (2001), in which a single mother's best friend takes innocent photos of the mother's young children frolicking at home without clothes, and the photo lab reports this to the police as a case of child pornography.
9   Rössler, *The Value of Privacy*, tr. Glasgow (Malden, MA: Polity Press, 2005), p. 9.
10 *Benz v. Washington News Publications and Bisney*, 34 Media L. Rep. 2368 (2006).
11 777 F.Supp. 47 (D.C. 1991).

abuse. In other cases which I shall explore soon, the countervailing interest is in free speech. But in the examples above involving an eavesdropping landlord, creepy photo lab technician, and jilted ex-boyfriend, there was no legitimate public interest in having access to the very personal information that was exposed.

Private facts that are newsworthy (**Alvarado, Kaysen**)

Some private facts, though, *are* newsworthy. Under what circumstances might free speech interests be so compelling that they would justify exposure of private facts?

Suppose undercover officers are accused of misconduct. There is a legitimate public interest in knowing that such allegations are taken seriously. Yet the officers have a compelling privacy interest in not having their name and face broadcast to the community—that would blow their cover and could subject them and their families to life-threatening danger. In *Alvarado v. KOB-TV*, two officers were accused of committing sexual assault while undercover but were not yet charged, when a television station learned of the situation. The station broadcast a story about the allegations, using film its reporters took of the men each answering the door of their homes, and mentioning their names. The station broadcast the story at 6pm and 10pm but the court opinion indicates that the station announced that they learned that the officers were undercover agents only on its 10pm broadcast and implies that the faces were blurred only for that latter broadcast.[12] The officers sued the station for intruding upon their privacy and for intentional infliction of emotional distress. A federal appellate court ruled against them because, it argued, the public has a legitimate interest in stories about allegations of police misconduct and because there was no intrusion into a private place. The misconduct charges were dropped a few days later when the accuser recanted, one of the accused was vindicated by DNA evidence, and the other established that when the misconduct was alleged to have taken place he was out of the state.[13]

While the outcome the Court reached might have been reasonable assuming the officers' faces indeed were blurred beyond recognition, the Court's rationale was not clear or convincing. It found no significant privacy interests at stake on the grounds that news cameras did not enter the plaintiffs' homes, and that officers cannot expect privacy in their name, address, and appearance; in reaching this conclusion the Court effectively ignored the distinct interest one might have in not having one's image memorialized and shared with a broad audience—an interest in remaining anonymous. While the Court did understand that the officers were claiming a right to privacy in their status as undercover officers, it rejected that claim

---

12 *Alvarado v. KOB-TV*, 493 F.3d 1210, 1213–1214 (2007).
13 493 F.3d 1210, 1214.

because of the public's legitimate interest in learning about accusations of police misconduct.[14] But the Court did not even attempt to explain why the public has an interest in knowing the names and identities of the accused before they are indicted or convicted, as opposed to being told that unnamed officers were accused. It may be important for someone who was previously assaulted by one of the accused officers to be made aware of the accusations so that they could come forward with information that may be relevant to the investigation. If the allegations of misconduct were of the officers acting in their official capacity, the interest in bringing forth potential witnesses might be furthered by broadcasting their names without showing their faces and thereby destroying their cover. If the alleged misconduct was by the officers when acting undercover, it would be more difficult to bring forth potential witnesses while preserving the officers' undercover status, but alternatives could have been explored. Instead of scrutinizing the reasons for exposing a private fact, the Court simply assumes that one cannot expect privacy in one's name or appearance and that free speech interests must prevail.

Another case in which someone publicizes a private fact that gives someone unwanted attention but that may be newsworthy concerned the publication in 2001 of Susanna Kaysen's book *The Camera My Mother Gave Me*.[15] The book concerns the impact her chronic pain had on her personal relations. In one section, she describes how her former boyfriend pleaded with her to have sex despite her protestations that having sex causes her vaginal pain. She describes his impatience with her and how at one point he was physically forceful. Kaysen did not use the man's name or provide detailed descriptions that could easily identify him, but conveyed enough information that his friends and business clients could recognize him if they knew he had been her boyfriend. The man's interest in not receiving unwanted attention, which includes an interest in controlling how he is presented to others and a reputational interest in avoiding perpetual punishment, conflicts with Kaysen's free speech interest. The Court ruled that while the man does have a legitimate and legally cognizable interest against disclosure of details of his private life, Kaysen has an interest in publishing her autobiography, and the latter interest must prevail when the publicity involves "information to which the public is entitled." The Court suggested that Kaysen might not have prevailed had the purpose of her book been "a morbid and sensational prying into private lives for its own sake."[16] But the details she disclosed were central to one of the book's themes: when does undesired intimacy become non-consensual sex? Exploring that question clearly serves a legitimate public interest.

We should distinguish the free speech interest at stake in this case from

14   493 F.3d 1210, 1217–1220.
15   32 Media L. Rep. 1520 (2004), not reported.
16   32 Media L. Rep. 1520 (2004), at p. 5 of Westlaw edition.

a public safety interest. If Kaysen was raped by her boyfriend, she should not be deterred from telling the police out of a concern for his privacy. But the question the case poses is whether she was right to give him widespread attention in a book for the general public. That question is made more difficult because exposing intimate details of a relationship has consequences for our ability to enter relationships of trust. If it becomes acceptable to expose any and all details about our former intimate relationships, regardless of our motive, by publishing them in books or through social media, people might become more cautious and guarded when entering relationships.

The question of who should prevail is easy if we simply assume free speech must win out over privacy interests. But I do not think it is so easy. When important privacy interests are implicated, there should be sufficient justification for the speech. That Kaysen took measures to preserve her former boyfriend's privacy by not using his name suggests her motive for writing was not to be vindictive, but to explore an important social issue regarding rape. That is surely relevant in deciding whether Kaysen acted badly. But perhaps of even greater importance is whether the exposure of private information substantially advanced a legitimate public interest. In this case it did. Kaysen conceivably could have explored this issue without drawing on her own experiences, by writing a work cast as fiction. Doing so still might have implicated the former boyfriend's privacy interest seeing as how authors may not be able to disguise autobiographical aspects of fictional accounts from readers who know the author well. But Kaysen wrote an autobiography, and that makes a difference in our weighing of the competing interests. There is value in writing an autobiography—not just the value of self-expression, but the value of making concerns about unwanted intimacy concrete and real. Being able to say "this happened to me" is a powerful means of engaging the reader and getting them to empathize.

It is not always wrong to expose private facts. Whether it is will depend on the weight of the privacy interests that are implicated: revealing someone's former hair color is not likely to be as invasive as showing a photo of a showering couple. It also will depend on what interests are served in exposing the information. Where important privacy interests are implicated, we should set a higher bar when asking whether the exposure is justified. As an ethical standard, this higher bar requires potential authors and publishers to give pause and consider whether they are being sensitive to the need others may have for privacy, and have sufficient reasons for making private facts readily available to the general public. Kaysen apparently did give pause and had sufficient reasons. KOB-TV may not have had sufficient reason to show the unblurred faces of suspects who they knew to be undercover officers.

Private facts in public places (Upskirt videos, Dennison, Turnbull)

I now consider cases involving what we might regard as private facts in public places. Before doing so, I want to clarify the distinction between a public and private fact.[17]

There is no standard definition of "public fact." One might plausibly use the term to describe only information that is known or readily accessible to the general public through legitimate means; a public fact, so defined, would not be one in which you could reasonably expect privacy. One might object by arguing that if someone steals social security numbers and posts them online, the information is now descriptively a public fact since it is now readily accessible even though it was not made accessible by legitimate means, it being wrong to acquire and share such sensitive information. But normatively the information is not a public fact—it should still be regarded as private. As I discussed in Chapter 3, whether a means of acquiring or sharing information is legitimate can depend on numerous factors including existing norms and practices, laws, architecture, technology, as well as our assessment of the value of privacy. Even if certain practices of observation or of disseminating information are accepted in a society, one might argue that they are not legitimate if they undermine important values.

One problem with this definition is that we do sometimes speak of what one does in front of just a few strangers—such as the fact that someone is sunbathing on a public beach, or walking down a public street—as a public fact even if it is not made known to the general public.[18] To reflect this usage we can define a public fact as information that is readily accessible to the public through legitimate means, where "the public" refers not to the general public but to one or more persons who could come to the information through legitimate means and could not be expected or trusted to keep it private. Family members, for example, may expose what they do to each other, but this need not make what they do a public fact. This definition, which I shall use from here on unless I indicate otherwise, is less restrictive because *much* more information is readily accessible to just one or a few strangers than is readily accessible to the general public. Apart from the qualification that the information must be readily accessible and not merely accessible, this is a definition U.S. courts implicitly rely on in adopting the plain view doctrine that I discussed in Chapter 3. There we saw that the U.S. Supreme Court has ruled repeatedly that one cannot reasonably expect privacy in information that is in plain view *of anyone* using legitimate means of observation.[19] This is an assumption I have

---

17 The next few paragraphs draw and expand on Mark Tunick, "Privacy and Punishment," *Social Theory and Practice* 39(4):643–668 (2013), pp. 655–656.

18 See Restatement (Second) of Torts, §652D cmt.b (1977).

19 See e.g. *U.S. v. Knotts*, 460 U.S. 276 (1983); *California v. Greenwood*, 486 U.S. 35 (1988).

challenged. I have argued that one can have a legitimate privacy interest even in information that is readily accessible to a particular circle of people if that information implicates dignity interests, or if it is not legitimate for them to make that information readily accessible to the general public given the privacy interests at stake.

There is also no standard definition of a "private fact." One possible definition is that private facts are facts that are not public facts in the less restrictive sense. In other words, private facts are facts not readily accessible to one or more persons by legitimate means. But one might use the term, rather, to refer to all facts that are not public facts in the more restrictive sense, that is, to facts that are not readily accessible to the general public by legitimate means. This may be what an appellate court in New Zealand had in mind in characterizing a private fact as a fact that "may be known to some people, but not to the world at large."[20] Or one might use "private fact" to refer to information that is not just anybody's business. Some information can be a public fact, readily accessible to one or more people through legitimate means, yet also a private fact in the sense that it is not readily accessible to the general public by legitimate means or is nobody else's business: indiscriminately sharing such information with others may not be ethical even though that information might be characterized as a public fact. The point in working through the different ways one might define a public and a private fact is to help us recognize that while information might be plausibly regarded as a public fact for some purposes, it may still be reasonable to characterize it as a private fact for other purposes.

I now want to distinguish different kinds of circumstances in which one can legitimately expect privacy in information that might nevertheless be thought of as "public." Individuals can have a legitimate privacy interest in information about themselves, even if they are in a public place, if the information is not in plain view of even one or a few persons because it can only be seen by illegitimate means of observation (upskirt videos, *Dennison*); in this sort of case information about me is not a public but a private fact even though I am in a public place. In other cases, information might be in plain view of one or a few others, but not of the general public, and it would not be legitimate for them to make the information readily accessible to the general public. In these cases, the information is a public fact, but it is information in which one still has a legitimate privacy interest (*Turnbull*). There is yet another sort of case, in which information is in plain view of one or a few others but it is not legitimate even for this limited audience to associate what they see with the doings of a person that they identify or that they enable others to identify. This is a trickier sort of case to think about, and I will leave it to its own section at the borders (*Riley, Vazquez, Wood*).

20   *Hoskings v. Runting* [2004] NZCA 34, Par. 119.

Upskirt photos or videos are images taken by discreetly placing a camera at the rear and by the feet of women so that the lens is aimed to get a view under their dress. Though the women are in public places, such as on an escalator in a shopping mall, or in a supermarket, what is exposed is not in plain view. Because courts in the U.S. tend to assume one cannot reasonably expect privacy in public places, they have sometimes been reluctant to find a legal cause of action against those who capture these images. A state appellate court in Virginia found, in *C'Debaca v. Commonwealth*, that there was no violation of state law when the defendant took an upskirt video of a woman at a fairground. While the Court found the defendant's conduct "reprehensible," it ruled that state law prohibits such videotaping only if the person is totally nude or undressing or was in a place where they could reasonably expect privacy, and one could not reasonably expect privacy at a public fairground.[21]

Legal remedies are available in some other countries. Canada has a voyeurism statute that prohibits surreptitiously observing or recording "a person who is in circumstances that give rise to a reasonable expectation of privacy, if ... the observation or recording is done for a sexual purpose."[22] As in Virginia, the recipient of the unwanted attention must have a reasonable expectation of privacy; but unlike the *C'Debaca* court, Canadian courts recognize that one can expect privacy in public places.[23] In one case, an airport employee was arrested after he crouched behind a woman near the luggage pick-up and took an upskirt photo with his cellphone. The Court upheld his conviction, though it did not find the offense to be particularly serious.[24] In England voyeurism was not a criminal offense prior to 2003. A Home Office report of 2000 noted that "[r]ather like flashing, our traditional attitude to such activity has been to regard it as unpleasant but a nuisance rather than criminal."[25] But it now is. Section 67 of the Sexual Offences Act 2003 prohibits a person from observing another person doing a private act, or recording another person doing such an act, for the purpose of obtaining sexual gratification, and knowing the person being observed does not consent. It is unclear whether upskirt videos fall within the scope of Section 67.[26] But, even prior to 2003, a person could be

21   *C'Debaca v. Commonwealth*, 1999 WL 1129851 (1999). See also *State of Washington v. Glas*, 147 Wash.2d 410 (2002) (while finding defendant's behavior "disgusting" and "reprehensible," the state Supreme Court ruled that the state's voyeurism statute does not apply to actions taken in public places).

22   Criminal Code of Canada, S. 162 (1)(c), full text online at http://laws-lois.justice.gc.ca/eng/acts/c-46/page-77.html#docCont.

23   *Aubry v. Editions Vice-Versa*, [1998] S.C.J. No. 30; and *R v. Rudiger*, [2011] B.C.J. No. 1947, discussed below.

24   *R v. Rocha*, [2012] A.J. No. 163 (Alberta Provincial Court).

25   "Setting the Boundaries," para. 8.3; cited in *R v. Hamilton* [2007] EWCA Crim 2062, Par 28.

26   See The Law Commission, "Public Nuisance and Outraging Public Decency," *Consultation Paper No. 193* (2010), Sec. 4.40, online at http://lawcommission.justice.gov.uk/docs/cp193_Simplification_Public_Nuisance_Consultation.pdf.

convicted for taking upskirt videos in public places, not because doing so violated a right to privacy, but on the theory that doing so is a common law offense of "outraging public decency." So long as at least two persons *could* have seen the act of videotaping, and members of the public would have been outraged at someone filming up a woman's skirt, then even if no one in fact observed the filming there would be an offense. On this basis, a practicing barrister in Sussex was convicted for making upskirt videos of adults and a 14-year-old girl in a supermarket.[27]

In thinking about *C'Debaca*, it will be helpful to compare it with a few other cases. At issue in *State v. Frost* was an Ohio law that declares that no person "for the purpose of sexually arousing [h]imself, shall commit trespass or otherwise surreptitiously invade the privacy of another." Frost was in a parked vehicle at a public beach using binoculars to observe two bikini-clad females at the beach; while doing this for nearly half an hour he also masturbated. A state park official saw this and arrested him. Like the Court in *C'Debaca*, this Court found no infringement of a privacy interest. Why? Because there was no trespass, and "the young ladies had no right of privacy at a public beach, and they probably expected to be observed in their bikini bathing suits."[28] Another Ohio case, *State v. Dennison*, involved a man who surreptitiously used his cell-phone camera on at least three occasions to take nude photographs of men while they were showering at a YMCA gym. The Court affirmed the man's conviction for voyeurism. It reasoned that the men could reasonably expect not to be photographed nude. There were no security cameras in the locker room, and signs were posted that prohibited cell-phone usage there. The Court rejected the argument presented by the defendant that because the men knowingly disrobed in front of him they could not expect privacy.[29] Leaving aside the question of how much if any legal punishment voyeurs should receive, I believe the judgment as to whether a right to privacy was violated was correct in *Frost* and *Dennison* but not in *C'Debaca*.

The Court in *Dennison* properly recognized that one can have a legitimate privacy interest even in a public place: "The practical necessity that members of the same sex may share locker rooms [o]r use common showers [d]oes not remove all expectations of privacy in use of such facilities."[30] The Court rested on the position that even though the shower facility was public, one could reasonably expect not to be photographed in the nude.[31] It might have argued that, according to social norms, it is inappropriate not only to photograph but even to stare at others in a public shower: invoking even the less restrictive definition of public fact I laid out above, how

27   *R v. Hamilton* [2007] EWCA Crim 2062.
28   92 Ohio App.3d 106 (1994).
29   2012 WL 1580610 (6th District of Ohio, 2012), Pars. 10, 16.
30   2012 WL 1580610, Par. 22.
31   2012 WL 1580610, Par. 22.

one's naked body appears in this location is not a public fact because it is not readily accessible to one or more persons by legitimate means, because one ought to avert one's eyes.

This latter reasoning is suggested in dicta from a Canadian case. In *R v. Rudiger*, a man hiding in his van videotaped young children who were at a public park on the other side of a chain link fence as the children were playing and being bathed by their caretakers. After someone called the police, the man showed the officers his video camera, and they found footage of children including a close-up of the genitals of a female child. He was arrested for violating Canada's voyeurism statute, cited above, and for possessing child pornography. He appealed his conviction on the ground that people cannot reasonably expect privacy in a public park. The Court denied his appeal, arguing that while any member of the public at the park could see the caretakers bathe or dress the children, this does not mean there was no reasonable expectation of privacy. Such observations, the Court noted, "will be fleeting in nature."[32] But the video taken by the man in the van, using a zoom lens, "focuses in on the genital area and the buttocks of young girls."[33] While the expectation of privacy is lower in a park than in a home, "it nevertheless exists and can be violated."[34] In this case it was violated by affronting the children's' "dignity, integrity and autonomy."[35] Even though the children were in plain view, they had a reasonable expectation of privacy not to have their private parts stared at or filmed with a zoom lens. So too, the Court added, "[a] woman who lies on a blanket in a park does not anticipate a person can, with a telephoto lens, peer up her skirt."[36]

The *Dennison* court distinguished *C'Debaca* and *Frost*, both cases in which voyeurism was permitted, by arguing that one could not reasonably expect privacy in public places such as a state fair (*C'Debaca*) or public beach (*Frost*), but could expect privacy in a public shower.[37] But that reasoning does not quite work. A gym shower is in a sense a public place just like a state fair, shopping mall, or public park or beach: strangers are present who have a right to be there and who can legitimately see you. If instead the *Dennison* court recognized that there can be private facts in public places which are not legitimate to observe, it could have rejected *C'Debaca* on the ground that it is not legitimate to look up a woman's skirt without her consent, just as it is not legitimate to stare at or film a naked person in a public shower without their consent or to focus steadily through a zoom lens on the private parts of a child who is being bathed in

---

32   *R v Rudiger*, [2011] B.C.J. No. 1947, Par. 107.
33   [2011] B.C.J. No. 1947, Pars. 76–77.
34   [2011] B.C.J. No. 1947, Par. 92.
35   [2011] B.C.J. No. 1947, Par. 102.
36   [2011] B.C.J. No. 1947, Par. 91.
37   2012 WL 1580610, at p. 4 of Westlaw edition.

a public park. The woman at the state fair can still have a legitimate privacy interest in the fact of what she wears beneath her dress even though she is in a public place.

Frost differs from *C'Debaca* and *Dennison* in an important way. Assuming the beach was not secluded, the two bikini-clad women knowingly exposed themselves to others. Perhaps they normally go around with more modest dress and only on rare occasions such as beach trips do they reveal so much of themselves; if so, they might reasonably expect that their appearance in a bikini is known only to other beachgoers within their sight, and not to the people they normally present themselves to in a more modest form; they could rightly object if someone photographed them at the beach and shared the picture with the two women's friends or colleagues. But there are no social norms against gazing at adults sunbathing at a beach, while there are norms against staring at individuals showering in gyms or at children being bathed in a public park, and so their appearance was not a private fact. Had Frost photographed the women at the beach and shared the photos with others, the outcome might have needed to be different because, I have argued, one can have a legitimate privacy interest in not having some public facts memorialized and shared. But the *Frost* court left no basis for making this distinction because it did not quite get the reasoning right either: it is not that the young women could not expect privacy at the public beach; but that they could not expect not to be seen.

In Chapter 5 I argued that Ranger Twight affronted the dignity of the people he secretly observed in a toilet stall even though they were unaware of being watched. One might think we should say the bikini-clad women suffered an indignity when Frost observed them for his own sexual gratification even though they were not aware of the fact. But if they did suffer an indignity (and I am not claiming that they did), it would not be an indignity involving privacy, since they expected others to see them. It would be the indignity of being used without one's consent for someone else's sexual gratification. If this indeed were an indignity, it would be one that could be suffered merely by being observed and not recorded. If Rudiger had used binoculars merely to observe rather than a zoom lens to film the female children being bathed in a park, he still would have violated reasonable expectations of privacy and Canada's voyeurism statute.

Some people might not agree that there is a norm requiring one to avert one's eyes in a public shower. In a case from the U.K., Lord Justice Hughes suggested that there are circumstances in which one cannot reasonably expect privacy in a public shower even against being videotaped. In *R v Bassett*, a man had taken a small video camera hidden in a bag with a hole in it into the men's changing room at a public swimming pool and was seen filming or intending to film a man in swimming trunks who was showering. In considering whether to affirm a conviction for voyeurism, Lord Justice Hughes noted that while the showers that stood in a row along the side of the large changing room were probably separated by some kind of panel, the stalls had no doors and were open to the general space of the changing room. Perhaps not convinced that there is a social norm forbidding one to gaze at as opposed to catch a passing glance of someone in a changing room shower, he argues that while the men in the showers could have a reasonable expectation of privacy against being spied on by "someone outside who drilled a hole in the wall," they might not have one against being looked at by anybody passing through the room or using it, even if the observer intended to look for sexual gratification.[38] But the decisive reason Lord Justice Hughes quashed the conviction was that the statute at issue defined a "private act" that it is wrong to observe as one in which the person's "breasts" are exposed, and he held that the lawmakers meant to refer only to female breasts and not to the male chest.[39] He therefore had no cause to consider the relevance of the distinction between observing and recording someone.

If I am wrong about there being a norm that one should avert one's eyes in a public shower, then in *Dennison* the men's appearance in the shower would be a public fact given that the shower stalls are not curtained off from each other. But even so, the men still can have a legitimate privacy interest in their appearance while showering because it is not readily accessible to the general public by legitimate means. So there are two approaches one can take in *Dennison*. One might think that there is a societal expectation that people avert their gaze when in a public shower facility. If so, then even using the less restrictive definition of a public fact we can say that the appearance of one's naked body when showering in a public facility is not a public fact though the body is in plain view of others who have a right to be where they are, because it is not readily accessible to them by legitimate means, it not being legitimate to fixedly observe let alone photograph or film someone in this situation. Alternatively, we can concede that the fact that someone is showering in a public facility where no doors separate the shower stalls is a public fact, but hold that one can still have a legitimate privacy interest in that fact because memorializing it and sharing it with others could affront one's dignity. If we adopted the latter approach, we are left with the question of whether it would be wrong of Dennison to take the photos of the naked men if he never shared them with anyone. The Court did not address this question because the law Dennison violated prohibited merely the photographing of a person in a state of nudity regardless of whether the photos were distributed.[40] The answer might depend on whether the photos conveyed more than Dennison could recall in his mind without the aid of the camera. Or we might think, rather, that the very possibility that a photograph could be

38   *R v. Bassett* [2009] 1 WLR 1032, Pars. 7, 10, 12.
39   [2009] 1 WLR 1032, Pars. 13–14.
40   R.C. 2907.08 (B); cited in 2012 WL 1580610, Par. 7.

shared with others in the future makes it wrong to photograph the naked men rather than merely look at them fixedly. We avoid this question if we adopt the former approach.

An example of how one can have a legitimate privacy interest in not having a public fact shared with the general public is presented in *Turnbull v. ABC*. In *Turnbull*, an investigative reporter for ABC's news program 20/20 used hidden cameras to secretly film the plaintiffs for a segment on how budding actors and actresses use "casting workshops" to pay their way into a role in Hollywood, a practice which violates California law.[41] ABC's undercover journalist posed as an actress looking for a role, and secretly filmed conversations overheard from across a room. One plaintiff was shown on national television pretending to squawk like a chicken. Another was recorded making an offensive, overtly sexual comment. ABC claimed the workshops were in a public space and were advertised in newspapers and so they should be regarded as a public fact.

In a prior case, *Sanders v. ABC*, a court found a privacy violation when a hidden camera was used to film conversations in a tele-psychic's office.[42] The *Turnbull* court relied on the rule established in *Sanders* that workers may retain a reasonable expectation of privacy against covert media video-taping even if their interactions are witnessed by coworkers: "The mere fact that a person can be seen by someone ... does not automatically mean that he or she can legally be forced to be subject to being seen by everyone."[43] What happens at the casting workshop is a public fact in the sense that other people are there; but it is also private in the sense that even though anyone from the general public might have participated since the workshop was advertised in a newspaper, once the participants were selected and the workshop began, not just anyone could observe. If other people in the workshop could be expected or trusted not to disclose details about what transpired, then the event would not be a public fact as I have defined that term. But if they could not be trusted, and we regarded what transpired as a public fact, there would still be a legitimate privacy interest in not having what took place memorialized and widely shared. In this respect, the circumstances are not unlike those in *Y.G. and L.G. v. Jewish Hospital of St. Louis and KSDK Inc.*, discussed in Chapter 4. While the topic of the news segments in both cases was a matter of legitimate public interest, in neither case was that public interest advanced by impinging on the privacy interest. Seeing a budding actor squawk like a chicken may be entertaining; but one needs a more compelling reason to justify publicly humiliating someone who could reasonably expect that he was not being viewed by the general public.

---

41   32 Media L Rep 2442, 2004 WL 2924590 (C.D. Cal. 2004).
42   978 P.2d 67 (1999).
43   2004 WL 2924590, p. 12.

The notion that there can be a private fact in a public place, or indeed that one and the same subject can involve both a private fact and a public fact may seem paradoxical. Courts in the United States for the most part have been unable to see their way through the apparent paradox. But there really is nothing puzzling in the thought that a woman cannot expect privacy in the fact that she is at a county fair but still can expect the fact of what color underwear she is wearing at the fair to remain private; or that a couple speaking quietly at a corner table in a restaurant and who stops talking whenever the waiter or anyone else gets within earshot can expect privacy in their conversation even though they could not expect privacy in the fact that they are at the restaurant, it being a public place. One can preserve something as private even in a public place.

Cases at the border (*Riley*, *Vazquez*, and *Wood*)

Children being bathed in a public park or a man showering in a public facility may be in plain view of others but that does not mean they have no legitimate privacy interest against being stared at or photographed. I now want to extend this argument: nor does the fact that they are in a public place mean it is legitimate to *identify* them.

In *Florida v. Riley*, police identified marijuana in a greenhouse behind Riley's mobile home by observing from a helicopter flying 400 feet overhead—which they could do as the greenhouse had openings in the roof and sides. The U.S. Supreme Court upheld that warrantless search.[44] Justice White, writing for a plurality of four Justices, noted that more than 10,000 helicopters are registered in the United States and "[a]ny member of the public could legally have been flying over Riley's property in a helicopter at the altitude of 400 feet and could have observed Riley's greenhouse."[45] But it is one thing to take a passing glance at one's surroundings; it is another to undertake the concentrated effort that is required to identify an activity as well as the particular address where it occurs.[46] Such exposure from the skies, while possible, may not be legitimate without a warrant when it is intended to uncover information about an identifiable person who might expect to keep that information private. Attentiveness to this distinction between observations that are technically legal and those that are legitimate will be particularly important if governments become tempted to use drones to conduct warrantless surveillance.[47]

---

44 *Florida v. Riley*, 488 U.S. 445 (1989).
45 488 U.S. 445, 450–451 and note 2.
46 Tunick, *Practices and Principles* (Princeton, NJ: Princeton University Press, 1998), p. 181. For a similar case involving police use of a plane to see marijuana plants in a person's fenced-in backyard, see *California v. Ciraolo*, 476 U.S. 207 (1986), discussed in Chapter 3.
47 See Carol Cratty, "FBI uses drones for surveillance in U.S.," www.cnn.com/2013/06/19/politics/fbi-drones/ (June 20, 2013).

When I enter a building from a public street, I knowingly expose that fact to whoever might happen to see me; but that I am visible to the accidental glances of strangers does not mean that it is legitimate for them to determine that what they see me do are the doings of a specific person they identify, unless I am a public figure or celebrity who they recognize. In *U.S. v. Vazquez*, a federal district court addressed a case in which a woman videotaped people as they entered a Women's Center in Connecticut that provided abortions. She was charged with violating a federal law against blocking the access to abortion clinic entrances and was found not guilty. She claimed that she made the videotape to show that she was not preventing anyone from entering the clinic in violation of the federal law. A court order sealed the record so that the video would not be available to the public, and she appealed. The Court ruled that the people entering the clinic had no legitimate interest in privacy that would justify a court order to keep the videotape evidence sealed, because the video merely showed activities in a public forum; moreover, the Court found a legitimate public interest in having access to the video: public access to evidence in a trial lets us assess whether the judiciary is doing an effective job.[48]

If there is a legitimate and substantial privacy interest at stake, we should employ stricter scrutiny of the reasons for exposing the information. We would need to ask why the public must access the video as opposed to a summary of its content in order to assess the fairness of the trial. If the credibility of a summary account might be doubted, why not show the video but blur the faces of the people in it, as the government requested? But the Court did not reach these questions because it assumed no privacy interest was at stake. It reasoned that because "[a]ny images filmed by the video camera could also be viewed by members of the general public who were standing or walking in the vicinity of the clinic ... no one walking in this area could have a legitimate expectation of privacy."[49]

While one cannot expect not to be seen in a public place, one can sometimes expect not to be identified. In *Frost*, it was not wrong to look at bikini-clad women tanning on the beach; but it might have been wrong to identify them using Google Glass with face recognition. The *Vazquez* court did not believe the videotape was recorded for the purpose of identifying prospective patients.[50] But by permitting the release of the video, it facilitated its potential broadcast; and broadcasting Vazquez's video to the general public would be the functional equivalent of using Google Glass with face recognition, because if the video is available to a large audience, it is more likely that someone will be able to identify each individual in it. When one is videotaped, and the video can be shown to the general public, one loses the protection of anonymity which people who are not celebrities

48   31 F.Supp.2d 85 (1998).
49   31 F.Supp.2d 85, 90–91.
50   31 F.Supp.2d 85, 90.

or public figures can rely on when walking on a public street populated only by strangers. (As was discussed in earlier chapters, in the European Union even celebrities or public figures may have a right to respect for their privacy in public places, a right not to anonymity, but to not having their photograph taken and published, so long as they are not participating in a newsworthy event.[51])

The people shown in Vazquez's video may have a reason for keeping their identity anonymous: if they are identified entering the clinic, someone might infer that they are having an abortion, and whether they are is not just anybody's business. A person's *identity* in this context can be regarded as a private fact, as is what a woman at a county fair wears under her skirt; and the weight of their privacy interest might be substantial. The *Vazquez* court did not get to the point of strictly scrutinizing whether there was sufficient reason to permit the release of the video because it found no countervailing privacy interest. In contrast, the Court of Appeal of England and Wales, in *Wood v. Commissioner of Police for the Metropolis*, was willing to critically assess the claim that there was a public interest in retaining a photo of a person taken in a public place. In this case the conflict was between privacy and the government's interest in security. The police took and retained a photo of a man attending an annual meeting of a firm with connections to the arms industry for the purpose of identifying those who may possibly disrupt this and future meetings; they had no intention to publish the photo so there was no concern about the man being put before the public in an unfavorable light. The photo was taken while the man was standing on a public street outside the hotel where the meeting took place. Even so, the Court found that privacy interests protected by Article 8 of the European Convention on Human Rights (ECHR) were implicated. Against the dissent of Lord Justice Laws, Lord Justices Collins and Dyson then held that while it was legitimate to take the photo to see if anyone who in fact disrupts the annual meeting could be identified, once it has been determined that there was no disruption, the police had no cause to keep the photo.[52]

Depending on what we mean by the terms public fact and private fact, we could plausibly say that even though, when a woman enters a clinic, she is in plain view of others, her entering is a private fact because it is just not anybody's business to know this information. We could also say that how one's naked body appears is a private fact even in a public place like a gym shower. One could also plausibly regard both as public facts, but I have argued that they would be public facts in which one retains a legitimate privacy interest. Such cases are hard to categorize because one might define "public" and "private" in different ways. One's medical condition or

---

51   *Campbell v. MGN* [2004] UKHL 22; *von Hannover v. Germany (no. 2)* [2012] ECHR 228.
52   [2010] 1 WLR 123.

choices about whether to have an abortion can be regarded as private in that they are the business of me and my loved ones but nobody else's. A private fact might also refer to what is not legitimately observable by others; the fact that a person enters a clinic or attends an annual meeting seems not to be a private fact in this sense. But using Google Glass with face recognition or a camera in order to identify people entering the Center or attending the meeting may not be legitimate; when they enter or leave the premises, their identity can be a private fact, at least if they take care to avoid being seen by anyone who knows them.

Publicizing public facts

Vazquez is a case at the margins: it might be thought to involve a private fact like the one involved in *C'Debaca*; or it might be put with a category of cases to which I will now turn, that involve a public fact, as in *Frost* or *Turnbull*, in which privacy is still implicated. One may still expect privacy even in such public facts if their publication would implicate one's dignity; or one can have a legitimate interest in not having these facts memorialized and widely spread.

Public facts that are not newsworthy (the baseball fan)

In the previous chapters, I discussed cases in which information is accessible to others, perhaps even readily accessible, yet privacy is still at stake. A balancing test might require that we recognize the privacy interest as more compelling if the information is not newsworthy. Several examples involved potentially embarrassing public facts: the behavior of the portly baseball fan; that a student athlete's genitalia were exposed while he raised his leg during a soccer game; that a woman was using new gym equipment to try and lose weight.[53] Others involved potentially shameful public facts: that Mr. DeGregorio was holding hands on a public street with a woman who was not his wife; that someone was arrested for driving while intoxicated or had a prior conviction for hijacking; that a celebrity was leaving a drug rehabilitation clinic.[54] But experiencing embarrassment or shame is not a prerequisite for having a privacy interest in public facts. The couple photographed while holding hands in the Farmer's Market had nothing to be embarrassed or ashamed about.[55] Nor did the accident victim who was

---

53   See Chapter 1 (on the baseball fan who was caught on camera eating a salad as a Fox announcer commented: "Salad won't be enough for this guy!"); *McNamara v. Freedom Newspapers*, 802 S.W.2d 901 (1991) (student athlete); *Sweenek v. Pathe News*, 16 F.Supp 746 (1936) (woman using gym equipment).

54   *DeGregorio v. CBS*, 473 N.Y.S.2d 922 (1984); *Briscoe v. Readers Digest Assn.*, 4 Cal.3d 529 (1971)(hijacker); *Campbell v. MGN Ltd* [2004] UKHL 22 (celebrity).

55   *Gill v. Hearst Publishing Co.*, 253 P.2d 441 (1953)

recorded in a half-conscious state saying "I just want to die";[56] her interest is a dignity interest in not being exposed when she is so vulnerable. Mr. Arrington had nothing to be ashamed of when the *New York Times* published his photo as part of a cover story about the black middle class; he disagreed with the article, which claimed that the black middle class were growing more removed from less fortunate blacks, and did not want to be associated with it.[57] His privacy interest involved an autonomy interest in controlling how he presents himself to others. According to the framework I have proposed, once we recognize a legitimate privacy interest, we must weigh it against the value of disseminating the information. In several if not all of the examples above, there is no legitimate public interest served by seeing images of the individuals or identifying them: this information could have been omitted, or in some cases a substitute image of someone who would have consented to the attention would have been easy to obtain.

The case of the baseball fan is not so straightforward. Hundreds of other fans could have casually gotten a good look at him; but, unless Fox Sports Network cameras focus on him, he is not visible to the general public and he is anonymous to anyone who can see him who does not already know him. When Fox Sports Network showed him in close-up on television, they made him visible to tens of thousands of people and greatly increased the probability that he could be identified. He now risks no longer being anonymous, just as he is not anonymous if he is observed by someone using Google Glass with face recognition. He could have a reputation interest in not having his close-up image televised; or he might not want his wife or his boss to know he is at the game; or he could simply have a preference not to appear on television. On the other hand, while there is nothing newsworthy about the baseball fan there is a countervailing public interest in broadcasting scenes of the crowd to convey the experience and excitement of attending the game.

The baseball fan's privacy interest might be contrasted with the interest that Mr. DeGregorio had in not being featured on the CBS news segment concerning romance in New York City—and with the interest people had in not being filmed by Ms. Vazquez as they enter a medical center. The interest of the latter group seems weightier since people entering an abortion clinic are more likely to have secrets they do not want exposed, though as it turns out, Mr. DeGregorio also had a secret. One important distinction between the first two cases is that it would not have been very difficult for CBS to have gotten DeGregorio's consent prior to using his image; but it would have been impossible for Fox Sports Network to get consent to take a candid close-up of a fan during a live broadcast. One might argue that

---

56 *Shulman v. Group W Productions*, 18 Cal.4th 100 (1998).
57 *Arrington v. New York Times*, 449 N.Y.S.2d 941 (1982).

every fan tacitly consents to such close-ups by attending the game; but that consent does not seem genuine since one has no choice but to consent if one wants to attend.

If we recognize that a legitimate privacy interest in anonymity can be at stake, then according to the framework we should look more closely at the reasons for and against allowing the publicity. Some people might be deterred from attending public events if attending meant they could appear on television or the Internet. Of course, people who care deeply about their anonymity have the option of disguising themselves, perhaps by wearing caps and dark sunglasses, which may not be an undue burden. Yet Fox Sports Network also has alternatives. Certain areas of the stadium could be designated for candid shots, allowing people to decide whether to expose themselves when they purchase tickets, just as anyone sitting directly behind home plate at a baseball game chooses to sit there knowing they will be in the television camera's frame. The New York Knicks, in fact, provide courtside seats to celebrities who agree to be filmed for broadcast on the GardenVision screen during games.[58] Or Fox cameras could focus at first on a large group that singles out no one in particular, and zoom in on a particular individual only if they impliedly consent by waving to the camera. But focusing in on someone who does not consent to being made a public spectacle can implicate a legitimate interest in anonymity; and making a joke at his expense implicates his interest in being treated with respect. While these interests might not rise to the level that would warrant a legal remedy, they may suffice to conclude that Fox Sports Network acted badly, given that it had other options that are not unduly burdensome.

Publicizing newsworthy public facts (public meetings and lectures, police conduct, arrests)

A number of public facts are clearly newsworthy and reporting about them does not implicate legitimate privacy interests. For example, reports about a city council meeting or a university lecture that is open to the public promote a core interest protected by the First Amendment and Article 10 of the European Convention on Human Rights: the interest in informing citizens about matters of legitimate public concern and furthering debate about public issues. But even here, one might distinguish a right to attend and report about such an event, and a right to film it.

Even though a meeting or debate is open to the public, participants might not want to be filmed. Justice Scalia objects to videotaping the U.S. Supreme Court's oral arguments, which are open to the public, because he

---

58   Sarah Lyall, "Knicks Have a Star Magnet: Courtside Seats," *New York Times*, January 22, 2014.

fears being misrepresented by inadequate and misleading snippets.[59] There would be obvious objections to videotaping the Justice's private deliberations because even though they are about matters that very much affect the public, publicizing them might deter Justices from expressing their views. There are similar objections to Mill's proposal for open, non-secretive voting: though voting determines policies affecting the lives of all citizens, to force people to publicly reveal and defend their votes might have a chilling effect.[60] But apart from Justice Scalia's concern, why should an event open to the public that concerns matters of public interest not be memorialized and made readily accessible to whoever cares to view it, with or without the consent of the participants? Courts in some jurisdictions in the U.S. have found a common law right to videotape city council meetings free of unreasonable restrictions.[61] But courts in other jurisdictions have held that there is no such right if doing so is not essential to providing the right to public access.[62] In the U.K., members of various local councils have objected to bloggers or other citizens filming their committee meetings, and one blogger was arrested and detained for two hours for using her smartphone to film such a meeting.[63] But guidelines were issued in 2013 noting that filming is permitted and encouraging councils to have a clear policy on how members of the public who do not wish to be filmed can opt out.[64]

Using our framework, we would approach the question by first considering whether someone can have a legitimate privacy interest at such an event. The event is open to the public and what takes place may even be a matter of public record. However, I have argued, one can have a legitimate privacy interest that a public fact not be memorialized and shared. Suppose an individual who is not a public figure rises at a meeting and in the heat of the moment makes an offensive comment that he later regrets. Uploading a video of the incident to YouTube would expose the person to unwanted attention that could damage his reputation and effect his relationships and ability to form new ties. Even if individuals do or say nothing they would come to regret, it can be reasonable of them to want to be heard at a public meeting without being a spectacle for others on the evening news or YouTube.

---

59 For the views of Scalia and other Justices see http://series.c-span.org/The-Courts/Cameras-in-The-Court/, accessed February 14, 2014; for criticism see e.g. Todd Piccus, "Demystifying the Least Understood Branch: Opening the Supreme Court to Broadcast Media," *Texas Law Review* 71:1053–1098 (1992–1993).

60 See Annabelle Lever, "Mill and the Secret Ballot," *Utilitas* 19(3):354–378 (2007), and *On Privacy* (New York: Routledge, 2012), ch. 1.

61 *Tarus v. Borough of Pine Hill*, 916 A.2d 1036 (2007).

62 *Whiteland Woods LOP v. Township of West Whiteland*, 193 F.3d 177 (1999).

63 David Allen Green, "Arrested for Filming a Public Council Meeting," *New Statesman*, June 13, 2011.

64 Matt Warman, "Public Wins Right to Film All Council Meetings," www.telegraph.co.uk/technology/news/10119059/Public-wins-right-to-film-all-council-meetings.html, June 14, 2013; and www.gov.uk/government/news/eric-pickles-opens- up-planning-appeals-and-lays-down-challenge, August 22, 2013.

On the other hand, knowing that such videos may be uploaded might encourage people to act civilly at public events; or the videos might provide useful information to the general public. For example, suppose someone disrupts a public lecture at a university with loud and unintelligible rantings and appears to be on the verge of becoming violent. Using my smartphone to record the incident and share it on YouTube might deter future misconduct (assuming this person or those like him could be deterred) and also possibly inform people of threats to public safety. In addition, I might simply want to share what I experienced with friends. But given the legitimate privacy interests that may be at stake, we should further scrutinize these reasons. If the person presented an immediate danger, public safety would be most effectively promoted by calling the police. Prospective students deciding whether this campus provides a safe learning environment might be better served by having access to aggregate crime statistics. Mere words might not let me convey to my friends what I experienced as vividly as images; but my interest in showing friends visual evidence of an event I found memorable can be served by showing the image just to them without making it readily accessible to the general public. I might, for example, share it via Snapchat, so that it is automatically deleted after a certain period of time.[65] In unusual cases, the interest in free speech may outweigh privacy interests. If someone risks their life to restrain an individual who becomes violent during a public lecture, there would be an interest in showing the heroic act to the public. But even here the proper balance is not so obvious: a television network could advance that interest while blurring the face of the person creating the threat and leaving it to the state to determine what if any punishment that person deserves; so too, a reporter can legitimately write a news article that mentions that *an* individual made an off-color remark during a council meeting, but unless the person were a public figure there would be no purpose in identifying them to the general public without their consent. The situation is different with a public figure. For example, the NFL athlete Riley Cooper was recorded saying an offensive racial epithet in a public place—but he should expect the attention.[66]

In the 1950s and 1960s a popular television show in the United States would air footage of people who were secretly filmed in a public place such as a sidewalk, restaurant, or elevator in comical, embarrassing or stressful situations created by the show's director. When the time came to let them in on the secret, they were told to "Smile! You're on *Candid Camera!*" Today, with the prevalence of smartphones, we are all susceptible to being caught

---

65   See www.snapchat.com/.

66   Jeré Longman, "Eagles Receiver Who Used Slur Takes Leave Amid Uproar," *New York Times*, August 3, 2013. On the "very natural" distinction between public and private figures, see Rodney Smolla, *Free Speech in an Open Society* (New York: Alfred Knopf, 1992), pp. 134–137.

on camera. The producers of *Candid Camera*, though, would not broadcast video of someone without the person's consent.[67] I am arguing that in a liberal society that values toleration we should be sensitive to the aims of others, and this means that absent a sufficient reason we should not upload video that focuses in on a person without their consent to sites such as YouTube, even if the video is taken at a public event, if doing so could implicate legitimate privacy interests.

Consent would indicate that the attention one receives is not unwanted. Being a public official or candidate for political office implies that one consents to presenting oneself to the public in debates or council meetings. Being a member of the audience need not. It may not be an undue burden for town councils to set up multiple locations in an auditorium where citizens can stand up to speak, with only some of these locations in view of cameras, so that one can choose the extent to which one exposes oneself. Professors obviously consent to sharing lecture materials with their students; but they may not consent to having their lectures videotaped and shared. The German philosopher Georg Wilhelm Friedrich Hegel, for example, chose not to publish some of the liberal political views that he willingly expressed in his public lectures.[68] That someone agrees to share information with a large group of students does not mean one consents to having one's words memorialized.

There are two other sorts of cases concerning public facts I want to consider. I have argued in earlier chapters that the fact that Dog Poop Girl behaved badly in public, or that Mr. Briscoe committed a crime in the past, are facts in which they could have a legitimate privacy interest. This information is not newsworthy for the general public and exposes them to disproportionate or undeserved punishment. In some cases, that punishment can be severe: one individual took it upon himself to punish a released sex offender who he learned about on a sex registry website, by killing him.[69] I now turn to cases in which the police are videotaped while they stop citizens or make arrests, and cases involving the publication of the fact that a person has been arrested but not yet convicted.

A number of cases have arisen over the last decade or so in the U.S. in which citizens make audio or video recordings of the police, giving them unwanted attention, and the police seek redress. As I discussed in Chapter 4, the protections of the First Amendment apply not just to the press but to all citizens, although the press clause may provide journalists special

---

67   See Bradley Clissold, "Candid Camera and the Origins of Reality TV," in Holmes and Jeryn, eds. *Understanding Reality Television* (London: Routledge, 2004), pp. 40–42.

68   See Mark Tunick, *Hegel's Political Philosophy* (Princeton, NJ: Princeton University Press, 1992), ch. 1. Some student lecture notes were published after Hegel's death as "additions" in later editions of Hegel's work.

69   Blinder, "Double Murder Seen as Part of Man's Quest to Kill Sex Offenders," *New York Times*, July 27, 2013.

protections such as immunity from libel suits. Courts have approached these cases without regarding citizen journalists as any less entitled than the press to the protection of the First Amendment.[70] In some cases the police prevailed. A Massachusetts court upheld the conviction of a man who secretly recorded a traffic stop in violation of a state law prohibiting one from secretly recording an oral communication. The state law did not require that the conversation be one in which a person could reasonably expect privacy, and the court felt bound to enforce the law even if no legitimate privacy interest was implicated.[71] But in many cases, the citizen prevailed. One defendant in Maryland was held not to violate the state's law against unlawfully intercepting an oral communication when he video-taped a traffic stop and posted the video on YouTube, as the state law defined oral communication as a "private conversation" and the court did not regard the conversation as private.[72] For its report on racial profiling, ABC PrimeTime Live used "testers" to determine if police treated blacks differently during traffic stops. Police officers sued ABC for filming and broadcasting the traffic stops without their consent. The court ruled for ABC, noting that New Jersey anti-eavesdropping statutes, unlike those in Massachusetts, required that the intercepted conversation be one in which there is a reasonable expectation of privacy, and concluded that there is no reasonable expectation of privacy in a police stop.[73]

The public interest in knowing how the police conduct themselves when on-duty is weighty: exposure could deter misconduct and promote public debate about racial tensions or the use of force by police.[74] However, making video of the police readily accessible to the general public might also implicate privacy interests. This can more obviously be the case if police are off-duty. Police officers, like school teachers and arguably school principals, are not public figures even though they serve a public function.

---

70   See, e.g., *Smith v. City of Cumming*, 212 F.3d 1332 (2000): while rejecting plaintiff's claim that his First Amendment rights were violated when the police prevented him from video-taping them, the court acknowledged that the right of ordinary citizens to gather information of public interest on public property is no less protected by the First Amendment than the right of the press.

71   *Commonwealth v. Hyde*, 434 Mass. 594 (2001), referred to in Chapter 1; see also *Commonwealth v. Manzelli*, 864 N.E.2d 566 (2007); and *Gouin v. Gouin*, 429 F.Supp.2d 62 (2003).

72   *State v. Graber*, 12-K-10-647 (Maryland, 2010); cf. *Johnson v. Hawe*, 388 F.3d 676 (2004); *Commonwealth of Massachusetts v. Glick*, No. 0701 CR 6687 (2008); *Jean v. Massachusetts State Police*, 492 F.3d 24 (2007); *People v. Beardsley*, 503 N.E.2d 346 (1986); *Robinson v. Fetterman*, 378 F.Supp.2d 534 (2005). For further discussion see Jory Canfield, *Don't Shoot: Police Privacy and Accountability in the Digital Age*, Senior Honors Thesis, Florida Atlantic University Wilkes Honors College (2011); Kreimer, "Pervasive Image Capturing"; and Dina Mishra, "Undermining Excessive Privacy for Police: Citizen Tape Recording," *Yale Law Journal* 117:1549–58 (2008).

73   *Hornberger v. ABC*, 799 A.2d 566 (2002).

74   Heidi Anderson, "The Mythical Right to Obscurity," *I/S* 7:544–602 (2012).

But even footage of police when on-duty and in a public place, taken without their consent, might conceivably implicate legitimate privacy interests. An extended close-up of an officer's facial features or tattoos would rarely be helpful in evaluating the officer's ability to perform his duties and therefore something the general public would need to see. But so long as attention is focused solely on a police officer's actions in their official capacities, documenting traffic stops or arrests in public places is unlikely to implicate legitimate privacy interests that would outweigh the public's interest in having a check on police misconduct.

In contrast, those who are arrested, even in a public place, may well have a legitimate interest in keeping information about the arrest private. Consider the following hypothetical. Principal Skinner is happily married with three children, well-liked in the community, and has no prior criminal record. One evening he was in a bad part of town visiting the parent of a student at his school to discuss the student's academic record. As he headed back to his car, a woman known by the police to be a prostitute approached him, pulled out a cigarette and said, "Hey, honey, I'll turn a trick for you, alright?" Skinner, who is hard of hearing, and seeing her cigarette, thought she said "Hey, honey, can I have a flick of your light?" Reckoning that she did not have a match, he replied in his typically exuberant voice, "Yes, by all means!," and searched his pocket for one. At that moment, a police officer who was hiding nearby and recording the scene with his digital camera pounced on Skinner and arrested him for solicitation. Skinner protested to no avail and was placed in handcuffs as the arresting officer, Sergeant Roughshod, who resented Skinner because of an incident when he was a student at Skinner's school, put him in the backseat of the cruiser.

Roughshod phoned a reporter at the local Fox News station to let her know of the arrest and provide his estimated time of arrival at the precinct. A half an hour later, the reporter, accompanied by a cameraman, saw Roughshod drive up with Skinner. It was nearly 11pm and the streets were empty. The cameraman began filming as Skinner was taken out of the car, escorted half a block from the parking lot to the front of the building, and led up the stairs and inside the precinct house. Skinner tried to hide his face from the camera but the handcuffs made that difficult to do. The next morning, the Fox TV station aired video of the "perp walk" with a caption: "School principal arrested for soliciting a prostitute." The segment also included a short snippet from Roughshod's video in which a woman was heard saying "Hey, honey (etc.)" and Skinner was heard responding "Yes, by all means!"[75] The same day that the video aired, Skinner was released after he convinced the assistant district attorney that he was not seeking the services of a prostitute. But the damage was done. Word spread quickly

---

75 Jeffrey Rosen defends privacy as a means of avoiding judgments based on "snippets," in *The Unwanted Gaze* (New York: Random House, 2000).

among the teachers and students at his school, and among family, neighbors, members of his religious congregation, and friends; even when he tried to explain, many people had lingering doubts. Why was he in that part of town so late at night? Did he really misunderstand the prostitute's words? The video appeared on the Fox News station's website and soon appeared on YouTube.

What happened to Skinner is not *entirely* fanciful. While in some European countries such perp walks are found to be shocking, in the U.S., television stations do broadcast perp walks, sometimes even staging them;[76] and it is common for individuals who are arrested to have their mug shots and information about their charge posted on websites or published in newspapers. Nor are perpwalks restricted to the U.S.: there are equivalents in Canada, Colombia, and Mexico;[77] and in Israel it is reported to be a common practice to lead arrested suspects in handcuffs and leg restraints through city streets on the way to the courthouse, though there are laws forbidding the practice.[78] The shaming punishment and humiliation people are exposed to from such unwanted attention may be excessive punishment for a misdemeanor, and is completely undeserved if someone turns out to be innocent. Courts in the U.S. have typically rejected privacy claims of those who have been arrested, on the ground that reports of a person's arrest are a public fact in which one cannot have a legitimate privacy interest; consequently they make no effort to balance the public's interest in knowing about the arrest against a privacy interest.

For example, an Ohio court of appeals ruled unanimously that an innocent bystander with the misfortune of being in a bar when the police made a drug raid did not have his privacy violated when a TV news crew filmed him being frisked and handcuffed by officers. The police mistook him for the suspect, and the station broadcast the footage of the arrest multiple times.[79] The court held that the arrest was a matter of legitimate public concern and that in any case one could not reasonably expect privacy in a public place such as a bar, and so it did not reach the further question of whether showing the arrest would be highly offensive to a reasonable person, a threshold for providing tort relief.[80] In *Paul v. Davis*, the U.S. Supreme Court also refused to recognize the privacy interests of those who have been arrested. A chief of police alerted local merchants to possible shoplifters in the Louisville area by distributing flyers that included a mug

---

76 In France, shock was expressed when former IMF Chief Dominique Strauss-Kahn was filmed in handcuffs after his arrest in New York City, see Andrew Cohen, "Hey France, You are Right about the Perpwalk," *The Atlantic*, May 20, 2011.

77 Sandrine Boudana, "Shaming Rituals in the Age of Global Media," *European Journal of Communication* 29(1):50–67 (2014), p. 52.

78 Nir Hasson, "Israeli Public Defenders Protest Handcuffed Perp Walks," *Haaretz*, December 10, 2012.

79 *Penwell v. Taft Broadcasting*, 469 N.E.2d 1025 (1984).

80 469 N.E.2d 1025, 1028–1029.

shot; Davis appeared in one of these flyers though the charges against him were eventually dismissed after the flyer was distributed. The Court held that disclosing the fact that one was arrested for shoplifting does not violate a right of privacy because arrests are a matter of public record.[81] Another court rejected a claim that broadcasting a "perp walk" violated privacy rights, reasoning that while they may be entertaining to see, they also serve to deter crime and educate the public about law enforcement efforts, both of which are legitimate government interests which the Court believed outweigh any privacy interests.[82]

At least one court, however, has hinted that broadcasting a perp walk may not be appropriate though it did not go so far as to say that doing so violates a right to privacy. In *Lauro v. Charles*, the perp walk at issue was staged. About two hours after Lauro was brought in to the precinct squad room by a detective, the detective received a call from a local Fox News producer requesting footage of the arrest. The police agreed to escort Lauro outside, put him in a car, drive around the block, and then permit the television crew to film him being removed from the car and escorted back into the station.[83] In an earlier case, *Ayeni v. Mottola*, a court ruled that the filming of the police searching a private home was an impermissible "seizure" that violates the Fourth Amendment's prohibition against "unreasonable searches and seizures."[84] In *Lauro*, the Court similarly held that there was an unreasonable seizure in violation of the Fourth Amendment.[85] But the Court did not consider whether publicizing the arrest constituted a tortious intrusion upon privacy. The Court did say that casting images in a humiliating situation implicates dignity interests;[86] and it noted that there was no legitimate government interest to justify this intrusion. The legitimate interest in accurate reporting of police activity is not well served "by an inherently fictional dramatization of an event that transpired hours earlier."[87] According to this reasoning, however, there would be no objection to filming the original arrest.

---

81   424 U.S. 693 (1976). Davis sought damages and injunctive relief under the federal statute 42 U.S.C. 1983, which provides relief when a state actor violates someone's constitutional rights. In this case, Davis claimed that he was denied his 14th Amendment liberties "without due process of law." Another basis for the court's decision was that it did not think Congress intended to make all torts of state officials federal crimes.

82   *Caldarola v. County of Westchester*, 343 F.3d 570 (2nd Cir. 2003). In this case county officers videotaped a post-arrest perp walk that it choreographed, and distributed the tape to the media.

83   *Lauro v. Charles*, 219 F.3d 202, 213 (2002).

84   35 F.3d 680 (1994).

85   219 F.3d 202, 208. Ultimately the police in *Lauro* were granted immunity because though *Ayeni* does suggest that the police should not allow the press to film searches in homes, that case is sufficiently different that the court was unable to say that existing law clearly should have indicated to the police in *Lauro* that they acted illegally.

86   219 F.3d 202, 211–212.

87   219 F.3d 202, 213.

That someone has been arrested might be a newsworthy public fact if there were a rash of crimes instilling fear in the general public; knowing that an arrest has been made, people could rest easier. But does the public have a legitimate interest in knowing that the person arrested for solicitation was Principal Skinner, or in seeing the video of his exchange with a prostitute? We first must ask if one can have a legitimate privacy interest in not having the fact of one's arrest made readily accessible to the general public. Arrests descriptively are public facts since they are known to the police, reporters, and anyone who knows how to access court dockets, though it is not inevitable that they are readily accessible. Court dockets in Spain, for example, do not as a rule include the names of defendants in criminal cases.[88] Skinner's arrest took place on a public street but it would not have been readily accessible to the general public had the television news reporters not been invited by Officer Roughshod to the scene, something it might have been wrong of him to do. Even if Skinner was arrested in view of other people, and reporters and cameras were already present, he could have a legitimate privacy interest in not having his arrest memorialized, which is associated with an interest in his reputation that could have economic consequences, and the related interest in avoiding undeserved or disproportionate punishment. Unless he can compel YouTube and other websites to remove the damaging videos, he could face unjust punishment for the rest of his life. In contrast, when making arrests, police do not usually have reputation or related interests at stake and if they do, these may be outweighed by the public's interest in monitoring police conduct. On the other side of the balance, is the fact that Skinner was arrested newsworthy? The public has a legitimate interest in knowing the police are making arrests; but that can be conveyed without revealing the identity of those who have been arrested but not yet convicted. Where the state needs additional witnesses or evidence to establish that they arrested the right person, revealing the identity of the person arrested might be important; but this may not be a reason with much force in Skinner's case. Posting video of his arrest serves mainly to humiliate and shame him, and encourages the general public to form judgments based on unproven accusations. Filming the police arresting someone can serve a legitimate public interest by showing that police are being diligent, or by revealing whether they are abusing their authority. But these interests could be served by pixelating the faces of people who are arrested and not identifying them.

---

88 Jacobs and Larrauri, "Are Criminal Convictions a Public Matter?," *Punishment and Society* 14(1):3–28 (2012).

7 Remedies

I have argued that we should sometimes be able to expect privacy even in public places or in public facts, even if this means restricting some speech. The argument is not "I prefer privacy and therefore so should you." It is that failing to respect someone's privacy by giving them unwanted attention can fail to respect them as a person and affront their dignity, diminish their ability to control how they present themselves to the world, and to manage their intimate relationships, subject them to unjust punishment and other reputational injuries, and expose them to psychological and economic harm, and we should be sensitive to the interests people have in not being treated in these ways when doing so does not keep us from adequately pursuing our own aims. I now want to conclude by turning to the question of remedies.

Google Glass with face recognition

Google Glass could change the world but not just for the better. Suppose a complete stranger comes up to you and calls you by your name. He tells you how impressed he is by your $275,000 home on Euclid Avenue and jokingly asks how you can afford it with your job teaching at a public school; he asks about your children, who he names. He then asks about your trip to China last year, and notes that he enjoyed the same dumplings at the specialty shop in Shanghai that you and your family so obviously relished. He knows these things because the face-recognition application that his Google Glass runs could identify you from the self-portrait you submitted for your school district's website, and information about you could then be located through a search engine.[1] I expect that many people

---

1   As I discuss below, Google presently does not authorize the use of facial recognition apps with Glass, but no law currently precludes Google from changing its policy. Such apps currently exist, see James Vincent, "Nametag: Facial Recognition App Scans Faces for Dating Profiles, Criminal Background," *The Independent*, January 9, 2014; online at www.independent.co.uk/life-style/gadgets-and-tech/facial-recognition-app-scans-strangers-faces-for-dating-profiles-criminal-background-9049568.html.

DOI: 10.4324/9781315763132-7

will find this unsettling; some will feel violated or even threatened. A stranger now knows many things about you, and with knowledge comes power and possibly control. This can be threatening even for people with nothing to hide. While none of the information that is available to the stranger, such as your identity, address, names of your children, or place of employment, are secrets, by having it all readily accessible he can assume the position of someone who knows you, usurping a role that should be yours to assign. Individuals with something to hide will have further objections to being exposed by this technology. Suppose the Korean dog owner discussed in Chapter 1 moves to another country hoping to establish new roots. People using Google Glass with face recognition will learn she is "Dog Poop Girl" unless she can defeat it by changing her appearance, and this could make it difficult for her to form new ties.[2]

In previous chapters, I pointed out a number of cases in which the unwanted attention people received had severe consequences, leading to public humiliation and punishment, loss of employment, and in rare cases suicide and murder.[3] What if anything should be done about this? Are we resigned to live in a world where it is increasingly difficult to control who has access to information about us? If we do think something needs to be done, then what? There are of course existing legal remedies for people who stalk, harass, assault, or murder, but these remedies would not help most of the individuals who suffer unwanted attention.[4] Should we ban Google Glass? Face-recognition software? Restrict the use of search engines? Impose penalties for people who put potentially embarrassing content on the Internet? Require providers of interactive computer services to delete such information and constantly monitor their sites to ensure it does not resurface? To those who find it liberating to have ready access to diverse sources of information, some of these proposals will be worrisome, even alarming.

I want to be clear that my purpose is not to assess the relative merits of different schemes to regulate the flow of information. But I do hope to have made a convincing case that we should be amenable to some restrictions on speech in order to give due respect to legitimate privacy interests. The

2   Mark Tunick, "Privacy and Punishment," *Social Theory and Practice* 39(4):643–668 (2013), p. 667.

3   In another extreme case, a young woman, Amy Boyer, was murdered by a man who stalked her; he was able to find her place of employment only with the help of search engines and online "information brokers," see *Remsburg v. Docusearch, Inc.*, 149 N.H. 148 (2003); cf. Herman Tavani, "Search Engines, Personal Information and the Problem of Privacy in Public," *International Review of Information Ethics* 3:39–45 (2005), p. 42.

4   Elsewhere I consider and reject the argument that apart from these existing legal remedies we should create a new legal remedy that targets not the person who puts embarrassing content on the Internet but those who, seeing this content, mete out unjust non-legal punishment: a legal cause of action for unjustly punishing would be unworkable and undesirable—see Tunick, "Privacy and Punishment."

prevalence and popularity of information sharing technologies such as smartphones, search engines, and social networking sites does not force us to conclude that privacy has become a norm of the past; it means that we need to take into account the unprecedented threats posed by this technology and rethink our norms and laws concerning privacy—particularly in the U.S., where the norm has been to treat information about one's past that is in a court record, and one's behavior in a public place, as public facts in which one cannot reasonably expect privacy. This is happening already in Europe, where there is some support for a "right to be forgotten." Proposals have been made for giving some information an expiration date after which it has less value and should be made harder to find;[5] and in 2014, the European Court of Justice ruled that Google could be ordered to stop listing certain private information in its search engine results when a citizen files a legitimate complaint about having their past made readily accessible by a Google search.[6]

Remedies

Identifying the culprit in cases of unwanted attention can be a difficult task, and a remedy that may be effective in some cases may be ineffective in others. Consider the case of the stranger who walks up to you. You would have remained anonymous were it not for Google Glass. Yet Glass itself might not be the culprit if it is merely a more convenient substitute for a smartphone or tablet. In other cases, it may well be the culprit. What makes Glass more threatening is that it allows someone to uncover information surreptitiously. The man who went into a YMCA in Ohio and used his cellphone to take pictures of other men showering was caught; had he used Glass he might not have been.[7] But the real obstacle to your remaining anonymous to the stranger is not Google Glass, but the face-recognition application it ran. Without that technology, he could not have acquired information about your house, family, job, and last year's vacation merely by looking at you.

Consider also the case of Marvin Briscoe that was discussed in earlier chapters. In 1968, *Reader's Digest* published an article on hijacking that included this sentence: "Typical of many beginners, Marvin Briscoe and

5   See Siry and Schmitz, "A Right to be Forgotten," *European Journal of Law and Technology* 3(1)(2012), on the German High Court's ruling regarding the Sedlmayr murder, discussed in ch. 3; Viktor Mayer-Schönberger, *Delete: The Virtue of Forgetting in the Digital Age* (Princeton: Princeton University Press, 2009), pp. 171–173; and the discussion of a "life cycle for information" by Fernando Pérez, publisher of a Spanish government publication, quoted in Suzanne Daley, "On its Own, Europe Backs Web Privacy Fights," *New York Times*, August 10, 2011.

6   *Google Spain SL v. Agencia Española de Protección de Datos (AEPD)* [2014] Case C-131/12. See also Ambrose, Friess, and van Matre, "Seeking Digital Redemption," *Santa Clara Computer and High Technology Law Journal* 29:99–162 (2012–13), p. 158; and Daley.

7   *State v. Dennison*, 92 Ohio App.3d 106 (1994), discussed in Chapter 6.

[article lists the other person's name here] stole a 'valuable-looking' truck in Danville, Ky., and then fought a gun battle with the local police, only to learn that they had hijacked four bowling-pin spotters."[8] Because of this one sentence, Briscoe's daughter and friends found out about his past crime, which he had kept a secret, and abandoned him.[9] Unlike Dog Poop Girl or those who committed crimes more recently and whose mugshots are available online, there may be no photo of Briscoe online or otherwise accessible to Glass; if so, Glass would pose little threat to his anonymity. But suppose he or his accomplice would want to keep their criminal record a secret from those who knew them—their concern would be that someone could type their name into a search engine and learn about the crime. The fact that Briscoe is a former criminal is readily accessible to anyone who enters his name in a search engine only because he filed suit against *Reader's Digest* and became the subject of a well-known, published court opinion that generated significant commentary.[10] But if he had not, or if the courts redacted his name from the court records, then people who entered "Marvin Briscoe criminal record" in a search engine might not easily learn of the crime.

The California courts that ruled on his case did not publish the name of his accomplice, though *Reader's Digest* did, and so the accomplice's situation differs. Neither man's criminal record was readily accessible prior to the appearance of the *Reader's Digest* article. While their names probably were reported in local newspapers in 1956, news archives were not readily accessible to the public in 1968; 1950s Kentucky newspapers are not readily accessible even today. Today the name of Briscoe's accomplice *is* readily accessible, but only because someone published a work on the Internet that mentions it in connection with Briscoe—a fact I learned when I gave my students the assignment of finding it out. Without that work, my students would have had to access a print edition of a 1968 volume of *Reader's Digest*, as that volume was not freely available on the Internet. Without the search engine, Briscoe's accomplice would remain practically anonymous to anyone not very intent on identifying him. Search engines make information readily accessible that is otherwise obscure or hard to find. In some European countries they are seen as the real culprit.[11] But we can also say that Dog Poop Girl and Briscoe's accomplice are subject to unwanted attention only because of the actions of the persons who uploaded information about them to the Internet.

8   Bill Surface, "The Big Business of Hijacking," *The Reader's Digest*, January 1968:115–119, p. 118.

9   *Briscoe v. Reader's Digest Assoc., Inc.*, 4 Cal.3d 529 (1971), discussed in Chapters 1 and 3.

10   The opinion is available for free to anyone (e.g. http://scocal.stanford.edu/opinion/briscoe-v-readers-digest-association-inc-27624), unlike some opinions available only in a legal database such as Westlaw or LexisNexis that cannot be accessed for free.

11   Daley, "On its Own, Europe Backs Web Privacy Fights."

Laws restricting access to face-recognition databases might be an effective way for people to remain anonymous in public places where they are not known. At the time that I write this, Google's policy for those who develop applications for Glass prohibits the use of face-recognition applications: "Don't use the camera or microphone to cross-reference and immediately present personal information identifying anyone other than the user, including use cases such as facial recognition and voice print. Glassware that do this will not be approved at this time."[12] But what if at some time in the future Google decides to approve such applications? Or what if hackers do what Google does not officially approve?[13] Perhaps in part because of its potential to take away our anonymity, signs conveying the message "Ban Google Glass" are now surfacing.[14] That strong opposition is being generated already and even Google recognizes a problem suggests that laws restricting access to face-recognition databases may be politically viable. People may come to realize that whether technology that prevents people from maintaining their anonymity should be widely available is not Google's call to make.

There will be greater reluctance to regulate search engines because they can be so important in enabling individuals with a legitimate need to know information to readily access it; but precisely because search engines can make personal information so readily accessible, the European Court of Justice recently held, in *Google Spain SL v. Agencia Española de Protección de Datos (AEPD)*, that Google can be required to remove such information from results lists produced by its search engine in some cases where the information is "no longer relevant." The Court recognized that the ready access to information that search engines afford may pose "a more significant interference" with rights to privacy than the publication of that information on a web page.[15]

There could be practical difficulties with targeting search engines as opposed to website operators. When one law firm in England noticed that search engine results for anyone entering the firm's name would feature

---

12 https://developers.google.com/glass/policies#c_what_you_cant_do_in_your_application, accessed May 21, 2014.

13 Katie Collins, "Hacker Gives Google Glass Facial Recognition Using his Own OS," *Wired.co.uk*, July 19, 2013; at www.wired.co.uk/news/archive/2013-07/19/google-glass-facial-recognition.

14 http://stopthecyborgs.org/google-glass-ban-signs/ (accessed August 6, 2013). Cf. Casey Newton, "Seattle dive bar becomes first to ban Google Glass," news.cnet.com, March 8, 2013; and Richard Gray, "The places where Google Glass is banned," *The Telegraph*, December 4, 2013 (noting some bans or possible bans in cinemas, strip clubs, restaurants, hospitals, and other places).

15 [2014] Case C-131/12, Pars. 94, 84-5. The Court relied on the privacy protections afforded by Directive 95/46/EC and Article 8 of the Charter of Fundamental Rights of the E.U. For an overview of an emerging law on search engines see Urs Gasser, "Regulating Search Engines: Taking Stock and Looking Ahead," *Yale Journal of Law and Technology* 8(1):202–234 (2006).

links to the "Solicitors from Hell" website and include snippets of defamatory statements about its solicitors, it made several requests to Google to remove the links, and Google agreed; but soon after a new link would appear, and listings also appeared on other search engines.[16] Still, manipulation of search engine algorithms can have an appreciable effect. Following the filing of a lawsuit against a website that posts mugshots and then charges people to take them down, Google was able to adjust its search engine to demote the mugshot websites on results pages, though the mugshots are still available to people willing to make the effort to find them.[17]

One might propose as an alternative to regulating search engines or Glass with face recognition that people who are very concerned about unwanted attention should simply be careful not to post their photographs on the Internet. Perhaps if you had never posted your photo on your school district's website, and face-recognition databases would not otherwise have included your photo, the stranger with Google Glass would not have identified you. But there are two problems with this solution. First, you should be able to share your photograph with students, colleagues, old classmates, and relatives without having it included in a face-recognition database. One of the U.S. Supreme Court's more egregious rulings is that when we knowingly expose the phone number we dial to the phone company so that it can route our call, we thereby waive all claims to privacy in the fact that we dialed that number, and so we have no ground for claiming that the government violates our privacy when it obtains this information without a warrant.[18] This logic was later used by the 5th Circuit Court of Appeals to hold that users of cellphones cannot reasonably expect privacy in their location since they "voluntarily" convey this information to their cellphone company.[19] Just as I should be able to reveal to the phone company what number I wish to dial so they can place the call without this implying that I am revealing to the government who I call or where I go, I should be able to share a photo on the Internet without this meaning that strangers should be able to know what the value of my house is or the names of my children merely by looking at me with Google Glass. Helen Nissenbaum, in discussing the idea of contextual integrity, makes the more general point

16   *The Law Society v. Kordowski* [2011] EWHC 3185 (QB), Par. 43.
17   John Caniglia, "Ohio Lawsuit over Online Mug Shots Reaches Settlement," *The Plain Dealer*, January 7, 2014; and David Segal, "Mugged by a Mug Shot Online," *New York Times*, October 5, 2013.
18   *Smith v. Maryland*, 442 U.S. 735 (1979): "When he used his phone, petitioner voluntarily conveyed numerical information to the telephone company and 'exposed' that information to its equipment ... In so doing, petitioner assumed the risk that the company would reveal to police the numbers he dialed" (744).
19   *In re Application of the United States for Historical Cell Site Data*, 2013 WL 3914484 (July 30, 2013). But see *Commonwealth v. Shabazz Augustine*, 467 Mass. 230 (February 18, 2014) (finding a reasonable expectation of privacy in cellular site location information).

that giving someone access to data for a particular purpose does not mean the data may be legitimately used for other purposes. For example, providing information to your doctor about your medical condition does not mean it may be used by potential employees in deciding whether to hire you.[20]

But another objection is that even if you were careful not to put your photo online, someone else could, and tag you. Perhaps your friend took a photo of you and your family in a Shanghai dumpling shop and posted it on his public Facebook page. Glass with face recognition might then enable anyone who looks at you to learn your name and uncover a good deal more information. The unwanted attention Dog Poop Girl received was not anything she could have avoided by being more restrained in what she posts, since someone else published the picture that made it possible for her to be identified. While people who want privacy have a responsibility to take measures to help ensure it, protecting privacy may sometimes be the burden not just of those who do not want attention but of everyone in society: in Chapter 5, I drew on the work of Jeremy Waldron to defend the position that in a liberal society others may need to be sensitive to our legitimate privacy interests.

New social norms

One measure to protect privacy would be to revise the codes of ethics for professional journalists and the media to acknowledge the need to be more sensitive to privacy interests that are at stake when information that is public in the sense of being accessible to some is made readily and permanently accessible to a much broader audience. But as I noted in Chapter 4, self-regulation by journalists and the media is unlikely to itself result in a fair balancing of interests.[21]

Nor would these codes be binding on non-professional "citizen journalists." Prior to the age of social media, not just anyone could widely publish a photo of Dog Poop Girl, or an article about Briscoe's prior crime, or gossip about an ex-boyfriend. To publish an article in a newspaper or magazine one would normally have to be trained and hired as a journalist; freelance writers would have to submit their story for approval. To share a photo, one would have to take the trouble to reproduce and distribute it, which could require significant resources in time and money. The obstacles to publishing served as a check on those who might otherwise act

20 Helen Nissenbaum, *Privacy in Context* (Stanford University Press, 2010), pp. 53–58; cf. "Protecting Privacy in an Information Age," *Law and Philosophy* 17:559–596 (1998).

21 See Anita Allen, "Why Journalists Can't Protect Privacy," in LeMay, ed., *Journalism and the Debate over Privacy* (Mahwah, NJ: Lawrence Erlbaum, 2003). Some journalists, not surprisingly, have been fervent critics of restrictions on speech; see, for example, Joshua Rozenberg, *Privacy and the Press* (Oxford: Oxford University Press, 2004), pp. 232, 242, 247–248.

impulsively. But today technology makes it possible for anyone to share information widely with a click of a button, with little incentive to think about the consequences of what one is doing. New social norms could provide one check on the much broader population of individuals who make use of the Internet and social media. Social norms, reinforced through education and exhortation, could preempt behavior that needlessly intrudes upon privacy, behavior such as taking a photo of Dog Poop Girl or writing an article that gratuitously includes the name of Briscoe's accomplice and putting it online. These norms could encourage those with legitimate interests in free speech to find avenues of expression that are more sensitive to privacy interests. For example, to point to the need for people to be more courteous to others one might describe Dog Poop Girl's inconsiderate behavior without identifying her.[22] Identifying her and sharing her photo through social media only serves to shame and punish her; and while it is not inherently unethical to shame or impose other non-legal punishment on those who deserve it, because the Internet makes this information available so readily to so many for so long a time, this punishment is likely to be grossly disproportionate and unjust. In situations in which you have information about someone who breaks the law, you can promote the legitimate interest in facilitating just legal punishment by sharing that information with the authorities rather than taking it upon yourself to mete out shaming punishment.

Legal remedies and their limits

It may be difficult for new norms to emerge without the background threat that laws can provide. In the United States for the most part, one may post images of an event that takes place in a public place or share information that is a matter of public record without facing legal consequences. Some people may stubbornly point to the fact that the law permits such behavior as an indication that there is nothing wrong with it. Their reasoning is flawed: the purpose of laws is not to prohibit all inappropriate behavior. Not all unethical behavior should be illegal, and the fact that behavior is legal does not imply it is ethical. But nevertheless, it may be harder to promote compliance with norms if those norms are not supported by the force of law. To establish a legal right to privacy would be to "show how seriously we take that right."[23]

If we did decide to use the law to restrict what information can be shared through social media, we would have to confront some difficult questions. Should the law target those who create and upload intrusive images or text, perhaps by lowering the bar to succeed in privacy tort actions? Should it

---

22   Tunick, "Privacy and Punishment," p. 666.
23   Fried, "Privacy," in Schoeman, ed. *Philosophical Dimensions of Privacy* (New York: Cambridge University Press, 1984), p. 219.

target interactive computer service providers that refuse to remove offending material? Or search engines that make this material easy to find?

Lawsuits have been brought against Google when results its search engine produced gave unwanted attention to an individual, with conflicting results. In one U.K. case, a large European provider of adult distance-learning courses sued both Google and an Oregon-based company that provided a digital forum for reviews and comments. The forum included highly derogatory statements about the distance-learning company including claims that its programs were a "scam." Google was sued because when someone typed the name of one of the company's programs into a Google search box, the result would include a snippet from the derogatory statements and a link to the full comments. Justice Eady ruled that Google was not liable as a publisher for the results of its automated search engine; as the process was automated, Google could not have intended to defame. He suggested as an alternative that the owner of the website on which defamatory posts appear might be directed to remove the material or arrange for it to be coded so that it would not be searchable.[24] For example, a robots.txt file could be inserted into a webpage to tell Google to cease indexing the tagged material after a certain period of time.[25]

In contrast, the Supreme Court of Victoria in Australia did find Google liable for defamatory search engine results.[26] In this case, when the plaintiff was googled, a user would be taken to a results page showing the plaintiff's image alongside images of gangster figures in Melbourne and an article suggesting that he is a prominent figure in the criminal underworld. The plaintiff had his solicitor at the time contact Google and demand that the material be removed from the search results. Google decided not to take action, and directed the plaintiff to contact the webmaster of the page that provided the defamatory matter. The Court rejected the reasoning of Eady that because Google merely programmed a search engine to function automatically, its role was passive and it lacked the requisite intention of a publisher. The computer programs used to generate search results were written by human beings and did exactly what Google intended, and Google had more than a "merely passive role."[27] While Google could deny fault for defamatory imputations it was not aware of, the Court ruled that Google lost the defense of innocent dissemination once it was made aware of the material its search engine brought up.[28] The plaintiff, who already

---

24 *Metropolitan International Schools Ltd v. Designtechnica Corp and others* [2009] EWHC 1765 (QB), Par. 63. Justice Tugendhat later assessed damages of £50,000 against the website company, see [2010] EWHC 2411 (QB).

25 See Anthony House, Oxford Privacy Information Conference: "The 'Right to be Forgotten' and Beyond," June 12, 2012; online at www.csls.ox.ac.uk/conferences/oxpilsconference2012; and www.robotstxt.org/robotstxt.html.

26 *Trkulja v. Google Inc.* [2012] VSC 533.

27 [2012] VSC 533, Par. 28.

28 [2012] VSC 533, Pars. 16–21.

was awarded $225,000 in a related action against Yahoo, was awarded $200,000. Similar reasoning was used in a case decided by the German Federal Court of Justice in which the plaintiff sued Google because it claimed an "auto-complete" result damaged its reputation. When someone began typing "R.S." into a Google search box, Google's auto-complete program would predict that the user wanted to find results for "R.S. Scientology" or "R.S. Fraud," based on data about what this and other users have searched for in the past. A lower court found that Google was not responsible for auto-complete search results, which merely report the most popular phrases that are entered into its search engine. But the appellate court ruled otherwise, on the ground that auto-complete results are not arbitrary but are due to the work of Google programmers. While it would be impractical to require Google to monitor all possible auto-complete results and filter out any that could infringe on someone's privacy or reputation interests, it does have a duty to prevent recurring instances of an infringement once it is made aware of the infringement.[29]

Google has taken the position that it is inappropriate to restrict search engines because doing so infringes on the right to access information, and even if search engine results were manipulated, the objectionable material would still be online. One Google representative argues that if you deal with the problem of unwanted attention given by online content solely by restricting search engines, the publisher of the information may not know they have been censored and this makes it harder for them to defend their rights.[30] A problem with that argument is that the information is not quite being censored—it is just being made less accessible—and there is no right that the information one wants to share must be readily accessible—a position implicitly taken by the European Court of Justice in *Google Spain SL v. AEPD.* I have argued in earlier chapters that whether information is readily accessible or whether it requires some nontrivial effort to obtain can make all the difference to someone's legitimate privacy interests. Even if consumers (as opposed to publishers) of information had a right to access publicly available information they had a need to know, we should not assume that any member of the general public has a right *readily* to access such information. That would be to assume interests in free speech are always more important than legitimate privacy interests. That Google search algorithms or face-recognition databases have powerful and beneficial uses does not mean we must permit their indiscriminate use. Technology that permitted one to see through walls would also have tremendous benefits but that would not mean it should be available to everyone for any use. However, the Google representative also notes that Google gets requests

29   Case VI ZR 269/12 (May 14, 2013); reported in "Liability of Search Engine Operator for Autocomplete Suggestions that Infringe rights of Privacy," *Journal of Intellectual Property Law and Practices* 8(10):797–802 (2013).
30   Anthony House, "Oxford Privacy Information Conference" (2012).

from public officials in Spain to remove search results so as to alter the public record.[31] This points to the need for some mechanism to fairly balance legitimate privacy and free speech interests.[32]

A more direct approach to the problem of unwanted attention would target the publisher of the damaging material—not the search engine, but the website that hosts it, or the person or persons who created and uploaded it. Courts currently are grappling with the legal question of whether interactive computer service providers can be held legally liable for facilitating unwanted attention. In the United States, §230 of Congress's Communications Decency Act (CDA) has been interpreted to provide immunity for providers of interactive computer services, including website operators; they are treated not as the publisher of the intrusive material but merely as a conduit of information created and developed by third parties.[33] Even if a service provider makes an editorial decision such as deciding whether or not to publish a comment, or makes minor changes to the spelling or grammar of third-party content, they can still retain §230 immunity.[34] However, a website operator can be both a service and content provider, and can be subject to liability for content that it does provide, such as comments at the end of posts by third parties.[35] Some courts have also held that a website operator may be held responsible if it "specifically encourages *development*" of offending content.[36]

While interactive computer service providers generally cannot be held liable in the U.S. for hurtful information posted within its domain by a third party, courts are presently developing standards for determining when they might at least be required to identify pseudonymous posters of offensive material so that plaintiffs can seek tort remedies against them. In *Pilchesky v. Gatelli*, several John Does posted comments concerning local politicians on an Internet message board hosted by Pilchesky. The plaintiff served on

---

31 Ibid.
32 The need for a "fair balance" was recognized by the European Court of Justice in *Google Spain SL v. AEPD*, [2014] Case C-131/12. The Court held that Google can be ordered to remove data that is personal and no longer relevant from its search engine results. Whether information must be removed depends on its sensitivity as well as on the "legitimate interest of internet users potentially interested in having access to that information" (Par. 81).
33 See *Barnes v. Yahoo!*, 570 F.3d. 1096 (2009); *Parker v. Google, Inc.*, 422 F.Supp. 2d 492, 500–1 (2006); and *Nemet Chevrolet v. Consumeraffairs.com, Inc.*, 591 F.3d 250, 254 (4th Cir. 2009).
34 *Fair Housing Council of San Fernando Valley v. Roommates.com, LLC*, 521 F.3d 1157, 1170 (9th Cir. 2008).
35 *Hare v. Richie, et al.*, 2012 WL 3773116 (2012) (denying immunity to the operator of the website "thedirty.com," which provides a forum for users to "submit dirt" on individuals, including video and text, insofar as Mr. Richie, the founder and editor-in-chief of the site, includes his own comments at the end of each post).
36 *Hare v. Richie*, 2012 WL 3773116, p. 18, my emphasis; citing *FTC v. Accusearch, Inc.*, 570 F.3d 1187, 1199 (10th Cir. 2009).

the city council, and various messages called her a "bitch," "whore," the "world's biggest asshole," and "crony-ridden." The Court held that Pilchesky could be required to identify these posters if there is sufficient evidence for a prima facie case of defamation, if the request for identification is made in good faith and is necessary for relief, if the John Does are notified so they can contest the petition, and if the Court conducts a balancing test that takes into account First Amendment interests.[37]

Courts in England, in contrast to those in the U.S., have held an Internet Service Provider (ISP) liable for defamation if it had knowledge of and did not subsequently remove a defamatory posting. In *Godfrey v. Demon Internet Ltd*, Mr. Justice Morland held that while the Defamation Act 1996 provided a defense to defamation if the person was not the author or publisher of defamatory material, and while the defendant in this case, an ISP, was not the publisher, that defense does not protect those who knew that the material they were handling was defamatory. The ISP was liable, but the Court added that any award of damages is "likely to be very small" in this case, since the defamatory material expired of its own accord about ten days after the ISP was made aware of the request to remove it.[38] In a more recent case, a court similarly decided that Google could be liable for defamatory comments published by a user to its Blogger.com site, and is obligated to take reasonable measures to remove the material once it is notified. The case involved a Conservative Party candidate in a local election in Thanet who resigned after it was reported in a newspaper that he made inappropriate remarks, calling girls "sluts." A blog soon appeared that accused him of making other disparaging remarks, of being a drug dealer, and alleging that his mother was convicted for theft. Google had argued that it has no control over blog content and that it did pass on the complaint to the blogger, who took the material down voluntarily. But over five weeks elapsed between the time Google was notified and the time when the blogger removed the material. The Court ruled that while Google is not the primary publisher and was under no obligation to know of the defamatory comments prior to being notified, once it is notified it could be regarded as a publisher.[39] However, the Court noted that the defamatory comments had moved their way down on the website and it is highly improbable that a significant number of readers had ready access to them prior to their removal, so any damage to the claimant's reputation would be trivial; therefore the claimant must lose the appeal.[40] Parliament has since

37 *Pilchesky v. Gatelli*, 12 A.3d 430 (2011); see also *Ghanam v. John Does*, 2014 WL 26075 (Court of Appeals of Michigan 2014).
38 [1999] EWHC QB 244, Pars. 22, 50, 52.
39 *Payam Tamiz v. Google, Inc.* [2013] EWCA Civ 68, Pars. 27, 35, 46; modifying [2012] EWHC 449 (QB) in which Justice Eady did not regard Google as a publisher because its role is purely passive but noted that even if Google could be regarded as a publisher the damages would be trivial and the "game would not be worth the candle" (Par. 50).
40 [2013] EWCA Civ 68, Par. 50.

enacted the Defamation Act 2013 that may provide protection to operators of websites that host user-generated content, provided they comply with procedures to resolve disputes between a complainant and an author.[41]

In the 2013 case of *Delfi AS v. Estonia*, the European Court of Human Rights also held the operator of an Internet news portal liable for defamatory comments posted by users. The users objected to a company's decision to destroy a planned ice road to make way for its ferry transport service. The website operator did eventually remove the posts when asked. But because the request for removal was sent by mail, the postings were accessible to the public for six weeks.[42] The company that was the recipient of the threatening comments sought damages for the loss to its reputation. The Strasbourg Court noted that the website operator had a history of allowing critical comments, and should have anticipated potential harms to reputation. Its policy of allowing anonymous postings and of not allowing posters to modify or delete their comments once they were posted meant that the company exercised a substantial degree of control over the comments even if it did not author them. The Court added that special caution is due in the age of social media, where information "once made public will remain public and circulate forever." Putting the onus on the media company by imposing an award of EUR 320, it ruled, was not a disproportionate interference with the Article 10 right to free expression, in light of the insulting and threatening nature of the comments that were posted.[43]

How to arrive at the right balance between privacy and free speech interests when considering regulations of interactive computer service providers or search engines is a complex question. But without needing to agree with the specific determinations of the European courts, I do think the approach they take of balancing competing interests is preferable to the policy of blanket immunity currently in force in the U.S. As I argued in Chapters 4 and 5, the slippery slope argument on which that policy rests—that if we restrict some information sharing on the Internet we threaten its very foundation as a forum for free speech—ignores the importance of other interests besides free speech.

Conceivably the law in the U.S. could be reformed to compel companies like YouTube or Facebook to remove offensive material when they are made aware of it, though that would create the problem of how one determines if a request is reasonable. Daniel Solove recommends modifying the Communications Decency Act (CDA) so that website operators would be granted immunity only before they are alerted but would have a legal

---

41 www.legislation.gov.uk/ukpga/2013/26/section/5/enacted. Eric Goldman suggests that this may create a disincentive to allow anonymous user-generated-content, see www.forbes.com/sites/ericgoldman/2013/05/09/uks-new-defamation-law-may-accelerate-the-death-of-anonymous-user-generated-content-internationally/.

42 [2013] ECHR 941, Par. 88.

43 [2013] ECHR 941, Pars. 86, 89, 94.

incentive to remove offensive material once they are notified.[44] It might be preferable to rely on self-regulation rather than coercion. The CDA does not prevent companies like Facebook from voluntarily removing material that an individual finds objectionable. But presently Facebook is reluctant to do so. Facebook's policy is to appeal to community standards in judging whether material someone finds disturbing should be taken down, and in the U.S., where free speech is valued so highly, a typical response it has given is that "since you're an adult writing in from the U.S. we won't be able to remove this content for violating your privacy."[45] Facebook's language implies that social norms prohibit it from removing the content. Its language is similar to that used by NBC's reporter Chris Hansen to explain his response to the request a rabbi made to obscure the rabbi's face and not mention his occupation when exposing his sexual perversities to a national television audience on the program "To Catch a Predator": Hansen writes that "these were obviously conditions we couldn't comply with."[46] Despite what they say, neither Hansen (and NBC) nor Facebook are prevented from complying with requests for privacy. In NBC's case, at least, doing so was simply not in its economic interest, because publicly shaming a rabbi would increase the show's ratings. If the social norms Facebook points to are reevaluated to acknowledge the importance of privacy interests, Facebook's stated reason for not removing objectionable content would no longer apply; and if §230 of the CDA continued to provide immunity, removing some content would not expose Facebook to liability even though it takes on the editorial functions of a publisher.

Instead of removing offending content, Facebook presently helps users in the U.S. send tailored messages to the offending poster such as "Hey, there's something about this photo that bothers me. Would you mind taking it down? It's a little embarrassing to me."[47] If we are successful in developing societal norms that encourage sensitivity to legitimate privacy interests, this approach may be all that we need in many cases. But it will not help when it is difficult to identify the individual who creates unwanted attention. Nor will this approach work if the poster remains insensitive.

One possible reform of law in the U.S. that might be suggested by the framework I have proposed would be to lower the currently high bar for plaintiffs to succeed in privacy tort actions.[48] Legislators might require that

---

44 Daniel Solove, *The Future of Reputation* (New Haven, CT: Yale University Press, 2007), pp. 149–160.

45 Kelly Broderick, "My Picture was Stolen and Turned into a Fat-Shaming Anti-Feminist Meme on Facebook," www.xojane.com, August 21, 2013.

46 Chris Hansen, *To Catch a Predator* (New York: Penguin, 2008), p. 27 n.4; discussed in Chapter 5, 'Feasibility Problems'.

47 See Yasmin Anwar, "UC Berkeley Psychologists Tackle Spats over Disliked Facebook Posts," *U.C. Berkeley News Center*, January 21, 2014.

48 Presently, plaintiffs seldom prevail, see David Ardia, "Reputation in a Networked World," *Harvard Civil Rights-Civil Liberties Law Review* 45(2):261–328 (2010), p. 312; and Solove, *Future of Reputation*, p. 122 (noting that only 13% of plaintiffs in defamation suits win).

for the defendant to prevail in a case where substantial privacy interests were implicated, it must be shown that the speech was newsworthy to the specific audience it reaches, or that the defendant could not have used some substitute or omitted details without diminishing the value of the speech. Or judges might take it upon themselves to take such considerations into account when they balance privacy and free speech interests. In light of the unprecedented ease with which anyone can now make information readily and permanently accessible to a wide audience, judges might also modify their understanding of the plain view doctrine and of the circumstances in which one can have a legitimate privacy interest by considering the ways, discussed in Chapter 3, in which one might reasonably expect privacy even in a public place or in public facts.

There are important limitations to using the law as a remedy even if the law were reformed. Among the most significant limitations of tort law are the cost and jurisdictional barriers, which may be insurmountable for many people; and plaintiffs have to relive the humiliation—although this could be addressed to some extent if they could remain anonymous, as Solove proposes.[49] The young woman from Canada who objected when her photograph was published in a magazine without her consent probably gave more attention to the photograph by suing. Fewer than 800 issues of the magazine were sold originally; but after she won her case in Canada's Supreme Court, the photograph became part of the public domain and can be found on the Internet.[50] But the mere availability of a tort action that would in theory protect legitimate privacy interests—even if an individual would not want to pursue a claim in court—might in itself promote the development of social norms. People would be less likely to assume they are entitled to give me unwanted attention by sharing images of me through social media without my consent, or believe that there is nothing wrong in doing so. The background threat of legal action might motivate them to give pause before clicking "upload."

Other alternatives

My emphasis throughout the book has been on the ethics of giving someone unwanted attention. While I have engaged extensively with arguments of judges and legal scholars, my primary goal has been to argue that individuals can have legitimate privacy interests in remaining anonymous in public places, in facts about their past misdeeds, and in not having undue attention given to their activities. To focus attention on someone by capturing their image or uncovering information about their past and then

---

49 Jacqueline Lipton, "We the Paparazzi," *Iowa Law Review* 95:919–984 (2010), p. 961; Solove, *Future of Reputation*, pp. 120–122. For other suggested legal reforms see Murchison, "Revisiting the American Public Disclosure Action," in Kenyon and Richardson, eds., *New Dimensions in Privacy Law* (Cambridge: Cambridge University Press, 2006).

50 Referring to *Aubry v. Editions Vice-Versa* [1998] S.C.J. No. 30.

sharing it with the general public may be to act badly, unless there is a compelling reason to share this information. My main target is those who believe that in the age of YouTube and Google Glass one can no longer expect privacy. One might argue against them, and for new social norms appropriate for new times, without committing to a particular legal remedy. Norms may need to be backed by law and so legal remedies cannot be ignored. Nor are norms the only way to protect people against unwanted attention: technological developments and market solutions are options as well.[51]

Technology and architecture

Technology can be employed to deal with the problem of unwanted attention. For example, "stealth clothing" is being developed that activates a beam of light when someone is taking unwanted pictures, blurring the resulting photo.[52] One can envision the development of an app that with the click of a button blurs identifying features of individuals appearing in photos or videos before the images are shared, enabling one to convey information without implicating legitimate privacy interests. It is also possible to restrict access to information on the Internet by affecting its architecture. For example, the entertainment industry used to pursue those who shared unauthorized copies of music and films on the Internet by filing law suits against them. A newer strategy relies on the cooperation of ISPs: anyone suspected of piracy would be sent an email warning, and after several repeat warnings and an opportunity to defend themselves against the accusations, the ISP would slow or shut down the person's Internet connection so they can no longer access the web. Of course there are limits to this strategy: people can find other access points to the web; and it requires the cooperation of ISPs.[53] Another approach is that images or comments posted to websites could be given an expiration date after which they would be automatically deleted or expunged.[54] One messaging service, Snapchat, allows users to send photographs that self-destruct, and once the photo is viewed by all the intended recipients it is deleted from the

---

51 See Lawrence Lessig, *Code* (New York: Basic Books, 1999) (identifying technology—such as speed bumps, or computer code that controls who has access to certain webpages—as an example of an architectural constraint on behavior, to be distinguished from the constraints that can be imposed by laws, norms, or markets).

52 See Jenna Wortham, "Stealth Wear Aims to Make a Tech Statement," *New York Times*, June 30, 2013; and Nick Bilton, "Shields for Privacy in a Smartphone World," *New York Times*, June 25, 2012.

53 See Ben Sisario, "Net Providers Plan Penalties to Slow Piracy," *New York Times*, July 8, 2011, p. A1.

54 Mayer-Schönberger notes this possibility regarding information one posts oneself, in *Delete*, pp. 171–173.

server.[55] The use of robots.txt files could also limit accessibility of some information by not making it searchable—but this, too, would require the cooperation of those who control the offending webpage. This approach would not have helped those who received unwanted attention on the "Solicitors from Hell" website.

Market solutions and their limits

Those who think there is value in preserving a record of all information ever available on the Internet may object to efforts to limit access to or expunge any information. My argument has been that they need to show how the value of having ready access to that information outweighs potential privacy interests. The real problem we face is how to make information that implicates legitimate privacy interests accessible to those with a need for it without making it readily accessible to just anyone. The "preservationists" would be rightly concerned if we expunged useful information, or made it too difficult to acquire by those with a need for it.

One way to address this problem is through market solutions. Rather than resort to lawsuits to require the removal of information about oneself that you do not want to be readily accessible to the general public, one might pay to have it removed. One can now pay reputation management firms to monitor one's online reputation, remove some data, and manipulate search engine results. One such firm, reputation.com, explains that its services are "designed for any individual or business whose reputation has been tarnished online through blogs, articles, and review sites by disgruntled clients, enraged friends, or former employees." The company contacts other companies who list private information and asks them to remove it; but also manipulates search engine results through techniques that it claims to have perfected. Their strategy is based on the assumption that "[e]ssentially anyone that Google's you or your business won't look past the first couple pages of search engine results."[56]

This approach has been criticized as amounting to "censorship by the market."[57] Implicit in that criticism is an assumption that there is a natural way search engines should function such that it might be wrong to manipulate that function, and that this natural function is to satisfy the preferences of users for ready access to information in which they might be interested. But that assumption needs to be challenged. Providing ready access to

---

55 There are potential loopholes, such as taking screenshots of the photos; and it was reported that Snapchat handed over unopened photos to federal authorities at their request, see www.theguardian.com/world/2013/oct/15/snapchat-hands-snaps-pictures-to-federal-law-enforcement.

56 www.reputation.com/reputationwatch/articles/remove-negative-reviews-from-google, accessed August 9, 2013.

57 Ambrose *et al.*, p. 122.

information is an important goal, but a liberal society has other goals, among which are to ensure that its members are shown respect and treated with dignity and have some control over how they present themselves to others. We might consider the natural function of artifices constructed to serve human needs to be to promote these other goals as well. A greater concern if we relied solely on this market solution is that there would be an incentive to exploit people with strong privacy preferences by repeatedly publishing embarrassing information about them and making them pay to remove it.[58]

Another example of a market solution would be for individuals to use the Internet and other avenues of communication to counteract hurtful speech with more speech that might restore their reputation. Of course if the concern is that you do not want the attention, responding in this way may be self-defeating by casting more attention on yourself.[59] Nor does everyone have the resources and skills to successfully counteract such speech. In many cases the speech is true and so there is nothing to refute. The concern is that one does not want to be forever defined by this speech.

The market is a potential solution not just for people whose reputation is threatened by the wide dissemination of embarrassing information, by providing them the means for deleting or limiting the ready access to that information or counteracting it with more speech. In a society that limits access to information that implicates legitimate privacy interests, the market could be a means to assure that people with an interest in acquiring that information get access to it without it being readily available to everyone, by enabling them to pay for the information. For example, if Mr. Briscoe's neighbors are deciding whether to ask him to babysit their children, they could pay to find out whether he has a criminal record by hiring a private detective; or today, in the U.S., they could pay around $20 for a month of unlimited online criminal background checks, though it is unclear how thorough these reports are as the companies providing this service may have to negotiate with each state for access to states' arrest records.[60] One such site promises that the person being checked will not know.[61] One problem with this market solution is that it is not clear that results of criminal background checks should be so readily available to just anyone who is willing to pay for them, or that they should be provided to individuals outside of law enforcement without the knowledge of the person being investigated. Outside the U.S., data on criminal records is not so accessible.

58 See Chapter 2, "Avoiding unjust punishment."

59 This has been called the "Streisand effect," see Evgeny Morozov, *The Net Delusion* (New York: Public Affairs, 2012), pp. 120–123.

60 For one discussion of the use of such background checks by individuals and employers, see Eric Dunn and Marina Grabchuk, "Background Checks and Social Effects: Contemporary Residential Tenant-Screening Problems in Washington State, *Seattle Journal for Social Justice* 9:319–371 (2010).

61 www.instantcheckmate.com; see also www.intelius.com; accessed January 12, 2014.

In European countries there are "neither private vendors nor direct access to a criminal conviction register" that would, for example, enable private sector companies to conduct a background check to screen prospective employees; and Article 8 of Directive 95/46/EC considers criminal convictions sensitive personal data and requires such data to be kept under the control of the state authority.[62] Nor is it clear that just anyone should be able to purchase other information that may soon become available, such as access to live satellite images that in the past were available only to government intelligence officers.[63] Face-recognition data, records of prior arrests or convictions, or location or phone data is information in which an individual can have a legitimate privacy interest. Private detectives are licensed and presumably adhere to professional standards guiding the responsible use of sensitive information. But there is no such check on potential abuses if anyone can purchase such information.

Underlying the market solution is the idea that was developed in earlier chapters that it can be important for certain circles to have information that it is not important for the general public to have. In Northern Ireland care is taken to ensure that sex registry information is accessible only to police, prison officials, and criminal justice social workers and is not posted, as it often is in the U.S., on publicly accessible websites. Third parties with a need to know are also provided information but only if the offender presents a risk of serious harm to the third party, there are no less intrusive means to protect the individual, and only after considering whether disclosure would endanger the rights of the offender, such as their right to life. Disclosure must be only to the "right person"—a person "who needs to know"; and the person receiving the information must be made to understand its confidential and sensitive nature.[64] The problem with an unregulated market solution is that it would use willingness to pay as a proxy for "need to know"—but the fact that one is willing or able to pay for information does not mean one has a legitimate need for it.

There is yet another way in which one might understand the market to provide a possible solution to the problem of unwanted attention. If websites post mugshots or images of people acting badly along with harsh comments, or television stations broadcast humiliating perp walks, or sports announcers make fun of colorful baseball fans, and people regard this as unethical and offensive, the websites might get fewer visits, and the television network's ratings might decline, costing them advertising revenue, and this could serve as a deterrent to giving someone unwanted attention. The problem with this market solution is that a majority of people are interested

62   Elena Larrauri Pijoan, "Legal Protections against Criminal Background Checks in Europe," *Punishment and Society* 16(1):50–73 (2014), p. 54, and note 30.
63   See Anne Eisenberg, "Microsatellites: What Big Eyes They Have," *New York Times*, August 11, 2013; see also http://planet-labs.com/.
64   *Re NJ* [2011] NIQB 122, Par. 9.

in this information. As I noted earlier, "To Catch a Predator" was one of Dateline NBC's most popular programs; and after British newspapers reported the salacious details of Max Mosley's sex orgies, sales increased. The market solution makes no distinction between information that society has a legitimate interest in accessing and information that is merely entertaining. I have argued that even in a society in which a majority of people do not have a strong preference for privacy, the majority should be sensitive to the interests and aims of those who do. The market measures the value of privacy by what people willingly pay for it, and is likely to undervalue the privacy interests of those who suffer from unwanted attention who would be willing to pay for privacy but are unable to because they lack the economic resources. Unless a cost is imposed on sharing sensitive information, either through the pressure to respect people's privacy that social norms might create, or through legal remedies or changes to the architecture of gathering and sharing information, the greater value as measured by what people pay may be on the side of free speech rather than privacy. But using an unregulated market might not be the best way to measure the value of either.

Conclusion

The technology of gathering and sharing information has changed so rapidly in recent years that we barely have had time to reflect on appropriate social norms to govern its use. Should it be acceptable for people to wear Google Glass when they enter a bar or gym or visit a public beach where nude sunbathing is permitted? Is it wrong to share gossip you learn about from someone in your Google + circle with someone who is not in that circle? Is it appropriate to use one's smartphone to film a mother who spanks her child in a grocery store and share this through social media as a means of expressing your disapproval of corporal punishment? Is it really acceptable for newspapers or websites to post online mugshots of people who have been arrested for a non-notorious crime but not yet convicted?

One of my goals is to contribute to public debate about these questions, debate that is a first step in developing new social norms for the age of social media. My hope is that we will recognize the importance of privacy interests in not receiving unwanted attention, and question the presumption that free speech should necessarily prevail over these competing interests. Some people who act badly in public may deserve to be blamed but do not deserve the disproportionate and perpetual punishment that they would face if their misdeeds are broadcast to the world and made readily accessible to anyone who enters their name in a search engine. They should be able to choose which information to share with their friends and loved ones, or be able to reinvent themselves and forge new ties without a past mistake hanging over them forever.

I am not arguing that we should ban Google Glass—though I do think there are compelling arguments for restricting access to face-recognition databases. Nor am I concluding that restrictions should be imposed on search engines—though I do think that we should explore ways to regulate search engines that would appropriately balance privacy and free speech interests. What I do conclude is that one can have a legitimate privacy interest in behavior in public places or in public facts. While one cannot expect not to be seen or heard by others who are in plain view or earshot, one can nevertheless retain a legitimate privacy interest in not having one's behavior memorialized by an audio or video recording that is then shared without one's consent to a potentially wide audience. More generally, one can have a legitimate interest in not having information that may be readily accessible to a particular circle of people made readily and permanently accessible to the general public. While that interest may at times be less important than the interest people have in keeping informed about what goes on in their world, and while not everyone values privacy, a liberal society should be sensitive to the needs of those who do.

Bibliography

Acquisti, Alessandro and J. Grossklags. "Privacy and Rationality in Individual Decision-Making," *IEEE Security and Privacy* 3(2): 26–33 (2005).

Alexander, Larry. "The Doomsday Machine: Proportionality, Prevention and Punishment," *The Monist* 63(2): 199–227 (1980).

Allen, Anita. "Why Journalists Can't Protect Privacy," in Craig LaMay, ed., *Journalism and the Debate over Privacy* (Mahwah, NJ: Lawrence Erlbaum, 2003).

Allen, Anita. *Unpopular Privacy* (New York: Oxford University Press, 2011).

Altman, Andrew. "Liberalism and Campus Hate Speech: A Philosophical Examination," *Ethics* 103: 302–317 (1993).

Altman, Irwin. *The Environment and Social Behavior* (Monterey, CA: Brooks/Cole, 1975).

Ambrose, Meg, Nicole Friess, and Jill van Matre. "Seeking Digital Redemption: The Future of Forgiveness in the Internet Age," *Santa Clara Computer and High Technology Law Journal* 29: 99–162 (2012–2013).

Amsterdam, Anthony. "Perspectives on the Fourth Amendment," *Minnesota Law Review* 58: 349–477 (1974).

Anderson, David. "The Failure of American Privacy Law," in Markesinis, ed. (1999).

Anderson, Heidi Reamer. "The Mythical Right to Obscurity: A Pragmatic Defense of No Privacy in Public," *I/S: A Journal of Law and Policy for the Information Society* 7: 544–602 (2012).

Andrejevic, Mark. "The Kinder, Gentler Gaze of Big Brother: Reality TV in the Era of Digital Capitalism," *New Media Society* 4: 251–270 (2002).

Anwar, Yasmin. "UC Berkeley Psychologists Tackle Spats over Disliked Facebook Posts," *U.C. Berkeley News Center*, January 21, 2014.

Ardia, David S. "Reputation in a Networked World: Revisiting the Social Foundations of Defamation Law," *Harvard Civil Rights Civil Liberties Law Review* 45(2): 261–328 (2010).

Barendt, Eric. "Privacy and Freedom of Speech," in Kenyon and Richardson, eds. (2006), 11–31.

Becker, Gary. "A Theory of Marriage: Part I," *Journal of Political Economy* 81(4): 813–846 (1973).

Benn, Stanley. "Privacy, Freedom and Respect for Persons," in Schoeman, ed. (1984), 223–244.

Bennett, Christopher. "The Varieties of Retributive Experience," *Philosophical Quarterly* 62(207): 145–63 (2002).

Bentham, Jeremy. "Anarchical Fallacies," in *The Works of Jeremy Bentham*, vol. 2, ed. Bowring (Edinburgh: William Tait, 1843).

Bentham, Jeremy. *Principles of Morals and Legislation* (New York: Prometheus Books, 1988) (orig. 1781).

Berlin, Isaiah. *Four Essays on Liberty* (London: Oxford University Press, 1969).

Bezanson, Randall. "The Right to Privacy Revisited," *California Law Review* 80: 1133–1175 (1990).

Biba, Steven. "A Contractual Approach to Data Privacy," *Harvard Journal of Law and Public Policy* 17: 591–611 (1994).

Bloustein, Edward. "Privacy as an Aspect of Human Dignity: An Answer to Dean Prosser," in Schoeman, ed. (1984), 156–202.

Böll, Heinrich. *The Lost Honor of Katharina Blum or: How Violence Develops and Where It Can Lead*, tr. Leila Vennewitz (New York: McGraw Hill, 1975).

Boudana, Sandrine. "Shaming Rituals in the Age of Global Media: How DSK's Perp Walk Generated Estrangement," *European Journal of Communication* 29(1): 50–67 (2014).

Brin, David. *The Transparent Society* (Reading, MA: Addison-Wesley, 1998).

Broderick, Kelly. "My Picture was Stolen and Turned into a Fat-Shaming Anti-Feminist Meme on Facebook," *www.xojane.com*, August 21, 2013.

Bygrave, Lee. "Balancing Data Protection and Freedom of Expression in the Context of Website publishing—Recent Swedish Case Law," *Privacy Law and Policy Reporter* 8: 83–85 (2001).

Canfield, Jory. "Don't Shoot: Police Privacy and Accountability in the Digital Age," Senior Honors Thesis, Florida Atlantic University Wilkes Honors College, 2011.

Cavell, Stanley. *Must We Mean What We Say?* (New York: Charles Scribner's Sons, 1969).

Clissold, Bradley. "Candid Camera and the Origins of Reality TV," in Holmes and Jeryn, eds. *Understanding Reality Television* (London: Routledge, 2004), 33–53.

Cohen, Andrew. "Hey France, You are right about the Perpwalk," *The Atlantic*, May 20, 2011.

Cooter, Robert. *The Strategic Constitution* (Princeton, NJ: Princeton University Press, 2002).

Dawes, Simon. "Privacy and the Freedom of the Press: A False Dichotomy," in Petley, ed. (2013a), 43–58.

De Bruin, Boudewijn. "The Liberal Value of Privacy," *Law and Philosophy* 29: 505–534 (2010).

Dostoevsky, Feodor. *Crime and Punishment* (New York: Norton, 1989).

Dunn, Eric and Marina Grabchuk. "Background Checks and Social Effects: Contemporary Residential Tenant-Screening Problems in Washington State," *Seattle Journal for Social Justice* 9: 319–371 (2010).

Eltis, Karen. "Breaking through the 'Tower of Babel': A 'Right to be Forgotten'," *Fordham Intellectual Property, Media and Entertainment Law Journal* 22: 69–95 (2011).

Engelmann, Bernt. *In Hitler's Germany* (New York: Schocken Books, 1986).

Etzioni, Amitai, ed. *Rights and the Common Good: The Communitarian Perspective* (New York: St. Martin's Press, 1995).

Etzioni, Amitai. *The Limits of Privacy* (New York: Basic Books, 1999).

Fagundes, David. "State Actors as First Amendment Speakers," *Northwestern University Law Review* 100: 1637–1688 (2006).

Feinberg, Joel. *Harm to Others* (New York: Oxford University Press, 1984).

Fiss, Owen. *The Irony of Free Speech* (Cambridge, MA: Harvard University Press, 1991).

Flaherty, David. *Privacy in Colonial New England* (Charlottesville: University of Virginia Press, 1972).

Foot, Philippa. "The Problem of Abortion and the Doctrine of the Double Effect," in *Virtue and Vices and Other Essays in Moral Philosophy* (Berkeley: University of California Press, 1978).

Fried, Charles. "Privacy," *Yale Law Journal* 77: 475–493 (1968); in Schoeman, ed. (1984), 203–222.

Gajda, Amy. "Judging Journalism: The Turn Toward Privacy and Judicial Regulation of the Press." *California Law Review* 97: 1039–1104 (2009).

Gasser, Urs. "Regulating Search Engines: Taking Stock and Looking Ahead," *Yale Journal of Law and Technology* 8(1): 202–234 (2006).

Gavison, Ruth. "Privacy and the Limits of Law," *Yale Law Journal* 89: 421–471 (1980); in Schoeman, ed. (1984), 346–402.

Gilmore, Jonathan. "Expression as Realization: Speakers' Interests in Freedom of Speech," *Law and Philosophy* 30: 517–539 (2011).

Glaeser, Edward and Bruce Sacerdote. "Sentencing in Homicide Cases and the Role of Vengeance." *Journal of Legal Studies* 32: 363–381 (2003).

Goffman, Erving. *Behavior in Public Places* (New York: Free Press, 1963).

Gregor, Thomas. "Exposure and Seclusion: Study of Institutional Isolation among Mehinaku Indians of Brazil," in Tefft, ed. (1980).

Hansen, Chris. *To Catch a Predator* (New York: Penguin, 2008).

Hegel, G.W.F. *Elements of the Philosophy of Right*, ed. Allen Wood (Cambridge: Cambridge University Press, 1991).

Heyd, David. "Education to Toleration: Some Philosophical Obstacles and Their Resolution," in McKinnon and Castiglione, eds., 196–207 (2003).

Hill, Thomas. *Dignity and Practical Reason in Kant's Moral Theory* (Ithaca, NY: Cornell University Press, 1992).

Jacobs, James B. and Elena Larrauri. "Are Criminal Convictions a Public Matter? The USA and Spain," *Punishment and Society* 14(1): 3–28 (2012).

Jay, Rosemary. *Data Protection Law and Practice*, 4th ed. (London: Sweet and Maxwell, 2012).

Kagan, Jerome, J. Reznick, and N. Snidman. "Biological Basis of Childhood Shyness," *Science* 240: 167–171 (1988).

Kant, Immanuel. *Groundwork of the Metaphysic of Morals*, tr. H.J. Paton (New York: Harper Torchbooks, 1964).

Kant, Immanuel. *Metaphysics of Morals*, tr. Mary Gregor (Cambridge: Cambridge University Press, 1991).

Kaplow, Louis, and Steven Shavell. *Fairness versus Welfare* (Cambridge, MA: Harvard University Press, 2002).

Kenyon, Andrew T. and Megan Richardson, eds. *New Dimensions in Privacy Law* (Cambridge: Cambridge University Press, 2006).

Kirkpatrick, David. *The Facebook Effect: The Inside Story of the Company That Is Connecting the World* (New York: Simon and Schuster, 2011).

Kosa, Tracy Ann and Khalil El-Khatib. "Measuring Privacy," *Journal of Internet Services and Information Security* 1(4): 60–73 (2011).

Kravets, David. "Mug-Shot Industry Will Dig Up Your Past, Charge you to Bury It

Again," Wired.com, August 2, 2011; http://www.wired.com/threatlevel/2011/08/mugshots/.

Kreimer, Seth. "Pervasive Image Capture and the First Amendment: Memory, Discourse, and the Right to Record," *University of Pennsylvania Law Review* 159(2): 335–409 (2011).

Larrauri Pijoan, Elena. "Legal Protections against Criminal Background Checks in Europe," *Punishment and Society* 16(1): 50–73 (2014).

Larson, Robert G. "Forgetting the First Amendment: How Obscurity-Based Privacy and a Right to be Forgotten are Incompatible with Free Speech," *Communications and Law Policy* 18: 91–120 (2013).

Lessig, Lawrence. *Code and other Laws of Cyberspace* (New York: Basic Books, 1999).

Lever, Annabelle. "Mill and the Secret Ballot," *Utilitas* 19(3): 354–378 (2007).

Lever, Annabelle. *On Privacy* (New York: Routledge, 2012).

Lipton, Jacqueline D. "'We the Paparazzi': Developing a Privacy Paradigm for Digital Video," *Iowa Law Review* 95: 919–984 (2010).

Loewy, Arnold. "The Fourth Amendment as a Device for Protecting the Innocent," *Michigan Law Review* 81: 1229–1272 (1983).

Machiavelli, Niccolò. *The Prince*, tr. Donno (New York: Bantam Books, 1981).

Markesinis, Basil S., ed. *Protecting Privacy* (Oxford: Oxford University Press, 1999).

Mayer-Schoenberger, Viktor. *Delete: The Virtue of Forgetting in the Digital Age* (Princeton, NJ: Princeton University Press, 2009).

McClurg, Andrew. "Kiss and Tell: Protecting Intimate Relationship Privacy through Implied Contracts of Confidentiality," *University of Cincinnati Law Review* 74: 887–939 (2006).

McDonald, Barry. "The First Amendment and the Free Flow of Information," *Ohio State Law Journal* 65: 249–356 (2004).

McKinnon, Catriona, and Dario Castiglione, eds., *Culture of Toleration in Diverse Societies* (Manchester: Manchester University Press, 2003).

Meiklejohn, Alexander. *Political Freedom: The Constitutional Powers of the People* (New York: Harper, 1960).

Menninger, Karl. *The Crime of Punishment* (New York: Viking Press, 1966).

Mill, John Stuart. *Collected Works of John Stuart Mill*, ed. John M. Robson *et al.* (Toronto: University of Toronto Press, 1963).

Mindle, Grant. "Liberalism, Privacy, and Autonomy," *Journal of Politics*, 51(3): 575–598 (1989).

Mishra, Dana. "Undermining Excessive Privacy for Police: Citizen Tape Recording," *Yale Law Journal* 117: 1549–1558 (2008).

Moore, Adam. *Privacy Rights: Moral and Legal Foundations* (University Park, Pennsylvania: Pennsylvania State University Press, 2010).

Morozov, Evgeny. *The Net Delusion: The Dark Side of Internet Freedom* (New York: Public Affairs, 2012).

Murchison, Brian C. "Revisiting the American Public Disclosure Action." In Kenyon and Richardson, eds. (2006), 32–59.

Murphy, Richard. "Property Rights in Personal Information: An Economic Defense of Privacy," *Georgia Law Journal* 84: 2381–2417 (1995).

Nelson, Samuel. *Beyond the First Amendment: The Politics of Free Speech and Pluralism* (Baltimore, MD: Johns Hopkins University Press, 2005).

Nissenbaum, Helen. "Protecting Privacy in an Information Age: The Problem of Privacy in Public," *Law and Philosophy* 17(5/6): 559–596 (1998).

Nissenbaum, Helen. "Privacy as Contextual Integrity," *Washington Law Review* 79: 119–158 (2004).

Nissenbaum, Helen. *Privacy in Context* (Stanford: Stanford University Press, 2010).

Nussbaum, Martha. "Perfectionist Liberalism and Political Liberalism," *Philosophy and Public Affairs* 39(1): 3–45 (2011).

Nunziato, Dawn. *Virtual Freedom: Net Neutrality and Free Speech in the Internet Age* (Stanford: Stanford University Press, 2009).

O'Neill, Michael and Pascale Carayon. "The Relationship between Privacy, Control, and Stress Responses in Office Workers," *Human Factors and Ergonomics Society Annual Meeting Proceedings* (1993): 479–483.

Oxford Privacy Information Law and Society Conference: "The 'Right to be Forgotten' and Beyond," June 12, 2012. Online at www.csls.ox.ac.uk/conferences/oxpilsconference2012.

Pager, Devah. *Marked: Race, Crime, and Finding Work in an Era of Mass Incarceration* (Chicago: University of Chicago Press, 2007).

Parker, Emily. *Now I Know Who My Comrades Are: Voices from the Internet Underground* (New York: Farrar, Straus and Giroux, 2014).

Paton-Simpson, Elizabeth. "Private Circles and Public Squares: Invasion of Privacy by the Publication of 'Private Facts'," *Modern Law Review* 61(3): 318–340 (1998).

Peikoff, Amy. "The Right to Privacy: Contemporary Reductionists and their Critics," *Virginia Journal of Social Policy and Law* 13: 474–551 (2006).

Penney, Steve. "Reasonable Expectations of Privacy and Novel Search Technologies: An Economic Approach," *Journal of Criminal Law and Criminology* 97(2): 477–529 (2007).

Petley, Julian, ed. *Media and Public Shaming: Drawing the Boundaries of Disclosure* (London: I.B. Tauris & Co., 2013).

Petley, Julian. "On Privacy: From Mill to Mosley," in Petley, ed. (2013a), 59–76.

Petley, Julian. "Public Interest or Public Shaming?" in Petley, ed. (2013a), 19–42.

Picus, Todd. "Demystifying the Least Understood Branch: Opening the Supreme Court to Broadcast Media," *Texas Law Review* 71: 1053–1098 (1992–1993).

Pitkin, Hanna. *Wittgenstein and Justice* (Berkeley: University of California Press, 1972).

Pitkin, Hanna. "Slippery Bentham," *Political Theory* 18(1): 104–131 (1990).

Plato. *Republic*, in *Collected Dialogues*, ed. Hamilton and Cairn (Princeton, NJ: Princeton University Press, 1961).

Posner, Richard. "Economic Theory of Privacy," *Regulation* 1978: 19–26 (1978).

Posner, Richard. "The Economics of Privacy," *American Economic Review* 71(2): 405–409 (1981).

Power, Robert C. "Technology and the Fourth Amendment: A Proposed Formulation for Visual Searches," *Journal of Criminal Law* 1: 1–113 (1989).

Prosser, William L. "Privacy: A Legal Analysis," in Schoeman, ed. (1984), 104–155.

Quinn, Adrian. "John Leslie: The Naming and Shaming of an Innocent Man," in Petley, ed. (2013a), 201–216.

Rachels, James. "Why Privacy is Important," *Philosophy and Public Affairs* 4(4): 323–333 (1975); in Schoeman, ed. (1984), 290–299.

Rawls, John. "Two Concepts of Rules," *Philosophical Review* 64(1): 3–32 (1955).

Rawls, John. *A Theory of Justice* (Cambridge: Harvard University Press, 1971).

Rawls, John. "The Idea of an Overlapping Consensus," *Oxford Journal of Legal Studies* 7(1): 1–25 (1987).

Rawls, John. *Political Liberalism* (New York: Columbia University Press, 1993).

Réaume, Denise. "Indignities: Making a Place for Dignity in Modern Legal Thought," *Queen's Law Journal* 28: 61–94 (2002).

Regan, Priscilla. *Legislating Privacy* (Chapel Hill: University of North Carolina Press, 1995).

Regan, Priscilla. "Privacy as a Common Good in the Digital World," *Information, Communication and Society* 5(3): 382–405 (2002).

Reiman, Jeffrey. "Privacy, Intimacy, and Personhood," *Philosophy and Public Affairs* 6(1): 26–44 (1976); in Schoeman, ed. (1984), 300–316.

Reiman, Jeffrey. "Driving to the Panopticon," *Santa Clara Computer and High Technology Law Journal* 11(1): 27–44 (1995).

Richards, David A.J. "Public and Private in the Discourse of the First Amendment," *Cardozo Studies in Law and Literature* 12(1): 61–101 (2000).

Robson, Peter, and Jessica Silbey, eds. *Law and Justice on the Small Screen* (Oxford: Hart Publishing Ltd., 2012).

Rosen, Jeffrey. *The Unwanted Gaze* (New York: Random House, 2000).

Rosen, Jeffrey. "The Right to be Forgotten," *Stanford Law Review Online* 64: 88 (February 13, 2012).

Rössler, Beate, ed. *Privacies: Philosophical Evaluations* (Stanford, CA: Stanford University Press, 2004).

Rössler, Beate. *The Value of Privacy*, tr. R.D.V. Glasgow (Malden, MA: Polity Press, 2005).

Rowbottom, Jacob. "To Punish, Inform, and Criticise: The Goals of Naming and Shaming," in Petley, ed. (2013a), 1–18.

Rozenberg, Joshua. *Privacy and the Press* (Oxford: Oxford University Press, 2004).

Sanders, Karen. *Ethics and Journalism* (London: Sage, 2003).

Schauer, Frederick. *Free Speech: A Philosophical Enquiry* (Cambridge: Cambridge University Press, 1982).

Schneider, Carl. *Shame, Exposure and Privacy* (New York: W.W. Norton, 1992).

Schoeman, Ferdinand, ed. *Philosophical Dimensions of Privacy* (New York: Cambridge University Press, 1984).

Schoeman, Ferdinand. *Privacy and Social Freedom* (New York: Cambridge University Press, 1992).

Siprut, Joseph. "Privacy through Anonymity: An Economic Argument for Expanding Privacy in Public Places," *Pepperdine Law Review* 33: 311–334 (2006).

Siry, Lawrence and Sandra Schmitz. "A Right to be Forgotten? How Recent Developments in Germany May Affect the Internet Publishers in the U.S.," *European Journal of Law and Technology* 3(1) (2012).

Smith, H. Jeff, Sandra Milberg, and Sandra Burke. "Information Privacy: Measuring Individuals' Concerns about Organizational Practices," *MIS Quarterly* 20(2): 167–196 (1996).

Smolla, Rodney. *Free Speech in an Open Society* (New York: Alfred Knopf, 1992).

Smolla, Rodney. "Accounting for the Slow Growth of American Privacy Law," *Nova Law Review* 27: 289–323 (2002).

Solove, Daniel. "Conceptualizing Privacy," *California Law Review* 90: 1087–1155 (2002).

Solove, Daniel. "A Taxonomy of Privacy," *University of Pennsylvania Law Review* 154: 477–564 (2006).

Solove, Daniel. "'I've Got Nothing to Hide' and Other Misunderstandings of Privacy," *San Diego Law Review* 44: 745–772 (2007).

Solove, Daniel. *The Future of Reputation: Gossip, Rumor, and Privacy on the Internet* (New Haven, CT: Yale University Press, 2007).

Solove, Daniel, and Paul Schwartz. *Privacy and the Media* (New York: Aspen Pub., 2008).

Stewart, Potter. "Or of the Press," *The Hastings Law Journal* 26: 631–627 (1975).

Sundby, Scott. "Everyman's 4th Amendment: Privacy as Mutual Trust Between Government and Citizen," *Colorado Law Review* 94: 1751–1812 (1994).

Sundstrom, Eric, Robert Burt, and Douglas Kamp. "Privacy at Work: Architectural Correlates of Job Satisfaction and Job Performance," *Academy of Management Journal* 23(1): 101–117 (1980).

Sunstein, Cass. *Democracy and the Problem of Free Speech* (New York: The Free Press, 1993).

Tavani, Herman. "Search Engines, Personal Information and the Problem of Privacy in Public," *International Review of Information Ethics* 3: 39–45 (2005).

Tefft, Stanton, ed. *Secrecy: Cross-Cultural Perspectives* (New York: Human Science Press, 1980).

Thomson, Judith Jarvis. "The Right to Privacy," *Philosophy and Public Affairs* 4(4): 295–314 (1975).

Thomson, Judith Jarvis. "The Trolley Problem," *Yale Law Journal* 94: 1395–1415 (1985).

Tufekci, Zeynep. "Can you See Me Now? Audience and Disclosure Regulation in Online Social Network Sites," *Bulletin of Science, Technology and Society* 28(1): 20–36 (2008).

Tunick, Mark. *Hegel's Political Philosophy* (Princeton, NJ: Princeton University Press, 1992).

Tunick, Mark. *Practices and Principles: Approaches to Ethical and Legal Judgment* (Princeton, NJ: Princeton University Press, 1998).

Tunick, Mark. "Does Privacy Undermine Community?" *Journal of Value Inquiry* 35: 517–534 (2001).

Tunick, Mark. "Privacy in the Face of New Technologies of Surveillance," *Public Affairs Quarterly* 14: 259–277 (2000).

Tunick, Mark. "Ethics, Morality, and Law," in Kermit Hall, ed., *Oxford Companion to American Law* (New York: Oxford University Press, 2002), 275–277.

Tunick, Mark. "Privacy in Public Places: Do GPS and Video Surveillance Provide Plain Views?", *Social Theory and Practice* 35(4): 597–622 (2009).

Tunick, Mark. "Efficiency, Practices, and the Moral Point of View: Limits of Economic Interpretations of Law," in Mark White, ed., *Theoretical Foundations of Law and Economics* (New York: Cambridge University Press, 2009), 77–95.

Tunick, Mark. "Review of Adam Moore, *Privacy Rights*," *Social Theory and Practice* 37(3): 510–517 (2011).

Tunick, Mark. "Reality TV and the Entrapment of Predators," in Robson and Silbey, eds. (2012), 289–307.

Tunick, Mark. "Privacy and Punishment," *Social Theory and Practice* 39(4): 643–668 (2013).

Van den Hoven, M.J. "Privacy and the Varieties of Moral Wrong-Doing in an Information Age," *Computers and Society* September 1997: 33–37.

Van den Hoven, M.J. and Pieter Vermaas. "Nano-Technology and Privacy," *Journal of Medicine and Philosophy* 32: 283–297 (2007).

Vlastos, Gregory. "The Socratic Elenchus," *Oxford Studies in Ancient Philosophy* 1: 27–58 (1983).

Volokh, Eugene. "Freedom of Speech and Informational Privacy: The Troubling Implications of a Right to Stop People from Speaking about You," *Stanford Law Review* 52(5): 1049–1124 (2000).

Wacks, Raymond. *Privacy and Media Freedom* (Oxford: Oxford University Press, 2013).

Waldron, Jeremy. "Toleration and Reasonableness," in McKinnon and Castiglione, ed. (2003), 13–37.

Walzer, Michael. *On Toleration* (New Haven: Yale University Press, 1997).

Warren, Samuel, and Louis Brandeis. "The Right to Privacy," *Harvard Law Review* 4: 193–220 (1890); in Schoeman, ed. (1984), 75–103.

Webb, Stephen. "Privacy and Psychosomatic Stress: An Empirical Analysis," *Social Behavior and Personality* 6(2): 227–234 (1978).

Westin, Alan. *Privacy and Freedom* (New York: Atheneum, 1967).

Wilson, Georjeanna and Mark Baldassare. "Overall 'Sense of Community' in a Suburban Region," *Environment and Behavior* 28(1): 27–43 (1996).

Wolfe, Gregory N. "Smile for the Camera, The World is Going to See that Mug: The Dilemma of Privacy Interests in Mug Shots," *Columbia Law Review* 113: 2227–2275 (2013).

Wolff, Jonathan. "Fairness, Respect, and the Egalitarian Ethos," *Philosophy and Public Affairs* 27(2): 97–122 (1998).

Zaibert, Leo. *Punishment and Retribution* (Aldershot, UK: Ashgate, 2006).

Zittrain, Jonathan. *The Future of the Internet—and How to Stop It* (New Haven, CT: Yale University Press, 2009).

Index

For Product Safety Concerns and Information please contact our EU
representative GPSR@taylorandfrancis.com
Taylor & Francis Verlag GmbH, Kaufingerstraße 24, 80331 München, Germany